Nort... ...gam

Normal Again

✦

Redefining Life with Brain Injury

Dennis P. Swiercinsky, Ph.D.

Writer's Showcase

San Jose New York Lincoln Shanghai

Normal Again
Redefining Life with Brain Injury

All Rights Reserved © 2002 by Dennis P. Swiercinsky

No part of this book may be reproduced or transmitted in any form or by any means, graphic, electronic, or mechanical, including photocopying, recording, taping, or by any information storage retrieval system, without the permission in writing from the publisher.

Writer's Showcase
an imprint of iUniverse, Inc.

For information address:
iUniverse, Inc.
5220 S. 16th St., Suite 200
Lincoln, NE 68512
www.iuniverse.com

The contents of this publication are not intended to render medical advice. While the contents are founded on accepted practices in the field of neuropsychological rehabilitation, patients and families should consult appropriate health professionals for direct advice concerning the unique and individual issues resulting from physical injury or illness.

Illustrations are courtesy of The Diagram Group and Shawn Brannan.

ISBN: 0-595-23716-9

Printed in the United States of America

In Memory

This book is dedicated to the memory of Evelyn R. "Lyn" Powers, the first editor of this book. Lyn was a dear personal friend who shared a passion for writing, for learning, and for wanting to make the world a better place for as many people as she could.

Lyn was completing education and writing projects and preparing to serve in the Peace Corps when she was killed in a traffic accident. She had completed work and was headed home about one o'clock in the morning, Wednesday, March 7, 2001, when her car was hit head-on by a drunk driver. Her dog, Molly, survived with numerous injuries.

Lyn was a significant inspiration for this book. She died as the book was in final editing and in preparation for publication.

Lyn touched many lives with her constant warmth, simple living, and honesty. Her selfless mission in life was to care for others—her son, her granddaughter, her family, the special people she worked with in a group home in Kansas City. Many more people will be touched by Lyn by virtue of her influence in many content areas of this book.

Thank you Lyn.

Contents

Acknowledgements

Acknowledgement is due and deepest appreciation felt for the assistance of those who helped turn an idea into this finished book. Lyn Powers, a writer, teacher, and mother diligently read each chapter as the first draft was completed and offered insights and suggestions for clarity. Kathleen Zeno, a nurse and rehabilitation professional, read a revised manuscript cover to cover, offering suggestions for continuity and balance. Lesley O'Dwyer, sister to a brain injured young man, provided extensive final editing and major suggestions for clarification.

I am indebted also to neuropsychologist, George Prigatano, Ph.D., who read a revised draft and offered further comments. Dr. Prigatano was one of my first teachers when I visited his treatment program at Presbyterian Hospital in Oklahoma City in 1981. His eloquence in teaching and sensitivity in clinical manner provided a model for my own clinical practice and the initiation of Brain Training, the treatment program for persons with brain injury I initiated in Kansas City.

Steven Simon, M.D., contributed information about common medications contained in the appendix. A colleague and mentor at Mid-America Rehabilitation Hospital in the greater Kansas City area, Dr. Simon has been an inspiration to families, patients, and therapists in his comprehensive approach to treating brain injury.

Heartfelt respect is due the participants of the Brain Training program for persons with brain injury whose autobiographical stories are presented herein as "real person" vignettes. Only a few of the many stories could be used but each reflects a struggle and depth of courage that few people accomplish. The names of the writers have been changed for confidentiality but each story is used with the writer's permission. Each "real person" story reflects the reality of thousands of persons who each year in this country are challenged by the life-changing event that we call brain injury.

Chapter nine was written collaboratively with Terrie Price, Ph.D., a long-time friend and neuropsychologist colleague. Her years of daily work in helping return people with brain injury to home, work, and community add the experience necessary to offer practical guidance.

Terrie was also instrumental in the implementation of the Brain Training program in Kansas City. Dr. Price, Dr. Leif Leaf, and social worker Sheila Vadovicky played prominent roles in developing and implementing the Brain Training program. Their assistance and collaboration added immensely to the formulations set forth in this book, for which I am extremely grateful.

Finally, "thank you" to the hundreds of responses from readers of *Traumatic Head Injury: Cause, Consequence, and Challenge*, the little "red book" that Dr. Price and I, along with Dr. Leif Leaf, put together in 1987 for the Brain Injury Association of Kansas and Greater Kansas City. The value of a book that melds science, practical rehabilitation, and inspiration is obviously of benefit to the nearly 100,000 readers that have requested that book over the past fourteen years. The present work is an expansion of the "red book" and incorporates requests for more depth in understanding the personal experience of brain injury, more practical day-to-day suggestions for recovering or coping with losses, and greater depth of information on the blending of attitude and factual knowledge in managing the life change that is brain injury.

Introduction

You are entering a new era of experience, learning, emotions, and change—not by choice, but by necessity. When your brain or the brain of a loved one has been injured, life changes. Sometimes the change is subtle, sometimes dramatic, but always confronting the comfort and security of once "normal" living.

This book is about the causes of brain injury; its physical, psychological, and emotional consequences; the challenge to recover as much function as possible; and the courage to live with change. It is about the acceptance of loss and the acquisition of strength to live, again, contentedly and with self-respect. The goal in writing this book has been to educate and to take some of the mystery out of an oftentimes overwhelming situation. As the first few chapters suggest, the normally-functioning human brain is exceedingly complex. Making sense out of an *injured* brain can be an even more taxing feat.

This book is about empathy as well as about knowledge. Knowledge about the brain provides the technology to make it work as well as possible. Empathy for life with brain injury provides the peace that comes from knowing you aren't in this alone. So, along with the technical and clinical details about brain injury offered in these pages you will find true stories about real people that provide enlightenment and connection with the experience of brain injury.

Terrible things can happen to anyone. Our test as humans comes in turning what is terrible into something at least neutral, if not positive. New beginnings can arise from any change in our lives. Good things can arise from bad events. Sometimes we have to look hard and suffer grief and discouragement, but eventually we can reach the balance point. While brain injury is, indeed, a medical condition—a very serious one at that—it is also a whole-life event that needs to be put into perspective.

Successfully dealing with brain injury demands knowing what to do to minimize losses. Rehabilitation means transforming the disruption of day-to-day living into a different—but productive and satisfying—way of life. Getting on with life means preserving positive personal identity and family unity, and accepting a growth-oriented challenge that eclipses adversity.

While writing, I often had to stop and ask, "Who is going to read this book?" First and foremost, every word herein is directed both to the individual who has experienced a brain injury, recently or a long time ago, and to his or her family. In this case, "family" means all those who love and care about the person whose experience has brought about this excursion into uncharted life territory. Second, this book is for nurses, therapists, doctors, teachers, and virtually anyone who might work, broadly or narrowly, in the field of brain injury rehabilitation. To all, I invite you to listen in, with hearts as well as minds, to the feelings that explode and the perpetual thirst for information that follows traumatic brain injury.

For twenty-five years, I have worked with persons who have had brain injury, their families, therapists, teachers, employers, friends, and the myriad assortment of agencies and persons who provide help. I hope the pages of this book impart the essentials of what I have learned in those years—essentials that are critical for helping meet the challenge and conquering brain injury.

The "real person" stories scattered throughout the book are edited short autobiographies written by persons who participated in the Brain Training group treatment programs offered in Kansas City from 1985 through 1997. The names and key identifying details have been changed for the sake of confidentiality but the stories are otherwise as told by persons who have experienced mild to severe brain injury. They are included to provide personal accounts of the experience and growth with brain injury. The Prologue—The Story of Jett is also a real person account, illustrating the tumultuous but eventually loving nature that can emerge from brain injury, sometimes years after its occurrence.

Insidious, haunting, unrelenting, frustrating, eternally challenging—these are some of the feelings expressed by persons with brain injury and their families. Brain injury can be an emotionally draining experience for everyone involved. Without acquiring essential knowledge about the brain and without accepting and practicing the mental adjustments necessary to cope, brain injury will wreak more havoc on a family than necessary. Words from science and experience comprise this book. Both sources of knowledge are about rising above catastrophe and achieving a measure of contentment, perhaps even the feeling of normal, again.

DPS

Prologue

❖

The Story of Jett

I first saw seventeen-year-old Jett Davis about nine months after his car accident. I was haunted by his still prominently scarred face, his manner of aloof loneliness, his childlike security in holding on to his mother, his silent and vacant presence. I was sitting alone one evening in a large classroom waiting to be introduced as the guest speaker at a support group for persons with head injury. The awkward symphony of voices—some raspy because of laryngeal damage and silent ones whose gestures were as piercing as screams—provided a rich and emotion-flooded background to my thoughts. The reason for the lump in my throat was not out of pity but empathy for the struggle.

Jett sat quietly, and far from attentively through the lecture, resting his head on his mother's weary shoulder the entire evening. He moved very little. He never looked at anyone. He never talked. His posture was cautious when he stood up as it was time to go home. His chiseled body, his sandy hair brushed back over his ears—he could have been a lightweight wrestler, or the pitcher on his high school baseball team. But now, inside this handsome youth seemed utter aloneness.

Jett's mother, in contrast to her son's distance, was attentive to my lecture. She responded to my occasional humor and her eyes looked at times as if we had had a meeting of the minds. She cared for her son by letting him be there, not insisting he act his age or sit up straight. This was no casual evening out where mother and dependent son with brain injury were trying to make the most of seemingly endless vacant time. Jett's mother was there looking for understanding and for answers, stoic, holding in and sorting out the endless stream of emotions she

1

had been experiencing for nine months. The first time I saw tears in her eyes was a few weeks later when she asked me, "What will ever happen to Jett?"

Jett incurred a head and brain injury in a roll-over accident, joyriding with friends after school on a country road. He was thrown from the car, his body landing some fifty feet away. (Do you appreciate what force is behind throwing a 140 pound athletic teenager fifty feet?) His head struck a rock that just happened to be right there like a bull's-eye for his brain. His hard-headedness, literally and figuratively, prevented a skull fracture but his brain was so violently thrashed around inside his skull that he ended up in a coma for two weeks. He was on life-support. He was given last rites, but his stubborn body wouldn't let him die. Jett was to spend the next year in rehabilitation and the rest of his life learning how to be Jett all over again.

For more than twenty years I have sought to understand the mysteries of the brain that produce a changed mind following severe trauma to the head. The hundreds of persons I have evaluated and treated typically have survived car accidents, severe sports injuries, assaults, industrial accidents, slips on the ice, and other split-second misfortunes that change a person's mind and thinking forever.

Typically, a severe blow to the head results in immediate unconsciousness (sometimes quite brief, sometimes lasting weeks or months) and occasionally life-threatening complications such as blood clots on the brain, severe brain swelling, or interruption of breathing. Depending on the extent of damage to important areas of the brain that control consciousness, the person with a brain injury usually and gradually comes around—with marked confusion at first—to more or less normal lucidity. Erratic and sometimes unpredictable periods of confusion and alertness alternate as the brain attempts to heal. Eventually, the person regains a sense of who he or she is, who others are, and walks away from such an injury, sometimes months or years later, to resume a sometimes satisfying but usually not quite "normal" life once known.

The road to recovery with a brain injury is inevitably chaotic and fraught with challenging ups and downs. At some point, usually early on following the accident, the person who experienced the brain injury might feel quite normal. Paradoxically, family, friends, doctors, coworkers, and schoolmates know only too obviously that their compatriot is anything but his or her former normal self. It is this journey to making life normal again that besets every individual with a brain injury and also everyone else whose lives are touched by that person's misfortune.

Even the most rebellious persons with whom I have worked are really exhibiting confused and misdirected rebellion, without the self-confidence to make it work. They want to be their individualist selves again yet cling almost dependently to their anchors—parent, spouse, or friends. It is a rare individual who wants a clinging dependent who cannot be controlled or taught easily and who is emotionally and personally groundless. This limbo between the familiarity of life before the injury and the reaction to insecurity afterwards can either dissolve or, eventually, fortify a family.

My mother once shared with me that she sought to provide my brother and me with the two most important gifts a parent can bestow: roots and wings. I have come to understand that roots are a foothold, first in the warm and secure bosom of mother's love, then emerging and transforming into faith in yourself. Wings provide the faith to be who and what you are without judgment or rebuff. Being a whole person means having faith in yourself, having the freedom to be yourself honestly, and accepting who you are with respect and dignity. Of course, taking root and growing wings is a constantly evolving process. It is a process that some of us eventually reach tenuously, and some of us achieve at best fleetingly.

For years, I have had a bumper sticker on my office desk that reads, "WHY BE NORMAL." Some who see it inquire about the missing question mark while others nod in agreement with its quintessential statement. After I bought it in a local novelty shop, I placed it upright in a brass holder on my desk instead of putting it on my car. Although I have usually been opposed to bumper stickers or otherwise pithy signs, I acquiesced in this case because the phrase seemed to simplify so eloquently a message (or question) I've attempted to convey to my rehabilitation patients for years.

At most, the sign received occasional, nondescript commentary, until one day when one of my young adult patients who had a brain injury came into the office, studied the sign for a few moments, looked at me and said with a wry smile, "Your sign is upside down." I was instantly humbled by his insight and made no objection to his spontaneous 180 degree repositioning of it in its holder, so that to the uninitiated viewer it now would be upside down.

I had, from then on, renewed faith that insight, confident wisdom, and bold honesty were the hallmarks of persons who had grown from brain injury. To my disappointment, however, I have had to reorient the sign myself many times after having had a visit from other patients (some brain injured, others not) who were amazed at my stupidity of having a sign on my desk that is upside down.

I have seen many of these bumper stickers since I purchased mine, on car bumpers (where else?), on attaché cases and student backpacks, and on other sundry places where signs do not belong, always smug that mine, so far as I am aware, is the only one to be oriented in its proper—an apparently arguable point—upside-down position.

Jett, who was eventually brought to me by his mother, is the only patient I ever had who would hide my "Why Be Normal" sign. He would sometimes sneak into my office before his appointment while I was out getting another cup of coffee, remove the sign, and stash it behind some books on a shelf. This was not a frivolous game he played with me. It was not until I eventually noticed the sign gone, and sometimes well after Jett had left the office, that I had to search for it. If I would sometimes discover during our session that the sign had been removed, then find and replace it, he would curse me and wish our session to be ended. He hated that damn sign but he could never tell me why. He could only feel and express a confused embarrassment at his childish prank, and a semi-controlled anger toward what that sign must have meant to him, whether upside down or upside up. I'm sure he always interpreted the sign with a question mark and read it as "Why *Can't* I Be Normal?"

To a teenager, being normal is everything. When that quest is severely thwarted by brain injury—and having to face an unfamiliar and hostile world—life is not very pleasant.

Jett only wanted to be normal more than anything else. He asked me again and again to make him that way. He asked sometimes with anger, sometimes with tears. I grew to love and respect Jett, for the loneliness and turmoil that beset him. Months of therapy and he didn't turn out exactly as we all would have liked him to. After years of family turmoil and even some rejection, numerous job failures, meeting a woman who would become his kindred spirit, buying a home of his own, raising a lovable little dog, and experiencing periods of lonely contentment, Jett is, indeed, developing his own brand of roots and wings. And, after years of struggles and setbacks—and gains—he's really a likeable guy again.

Jett had to become seventeen all over again. He never regained full use of his left arm and can't gracefully kick a football anymore because his agile balance never fully recovered. Jett finally (more or less) accepted the fact that he would always talk with a raspy voice because of damage to the speech center in his brain. Damage to his brain's memory areas makes him incessantly forgetful and this still irritates him. He completed high school a year later than he would have had the accident not occurred.

From his tenuous walk up the three steps to his front door when he came home from the hospital to today, seventeen years later, Jett is still reconciling the losses with the incomplete gains. He is sometimes happy, sometimes angry, sometimes about to give up, sometimes quietly grateful that he is alive, and sometimes setting and attaining important new goals. Soon after he came home from rehabilitation,

Jett's mother sought psychological counseling for him that he might learn to be content with life again.

Jett has forged a new definition of who he is. Now, he mostly likes himself. It shows in his gentle caring for and trust in his dog. He's learned not to get angry anymore. (Well, not *so* angry and not *so* often, anyway.) He has started to work part-time and has grown to know and accept his personal liabilities and assets. Jett visits his parents again after years of alienating them. He and Leena have lived together now for seven years—happily, most of the time. Jett cuts wood and clears brush from behind his home with plans to put up a fence some day. He regularly goes through packs of post-it notes and carries his daily calendar like a Bible, tools he learned to rely on to compensate for his unreliable memory. He has become a warmer person who has replaced snarls with smiles. Jett isn't what he or anyone else thought he would be, and yet he is contented—much of the time.

It is difficult for most people to appreciate the topsy-turvy world brain injury creates. Imagine yourself at seventeen, nearing the end of a tumultuous adolescence, having had to build a tough exterior against the cold and cruel world into which your parents are about to boot you. You have endured many warm summer nights when you couldn't get a date and fleetingly entertained thoughts of self-annihilation. Awareness of the overwhelming and awesome immensity of life became inescapable. You conquered such times adding yet another insulating layer to the toughness that protects you from pain, suffering, loss, uncertainty, insecurity, and more dateless Saturday nights.

Countless experiences mold the moment of being seventeen, the metamorphosis into almost-adulthood. The umpteen number of experiences that pave the way to adulthood is staggering: walking, talking, playing, learning everything you know, cultivating intellectual skills, courting, forming unique personality traits, learning when to be appropriate and when you can "let your hair down," developing athletic prowess, becoming comfortable with your body, and drafting and revising personal values and beliefs. All, and much more, are molded into the emerging uniqueness and complexity of you.

Now, imagine that every experience that formed those seventeen years is lost and must be recapitulated in just a few months. Imagine that you are awakened into the world within the body of a seventeen-year-old, and you have to learn everything that makes you that special person all over again: learning to walk, handle a knife and fork, talk and make sense out of what you say, read and learn, do arithmetic, follow social and etiquette rules, set goals consistent with who you are and what your unique skills are. Now, to add insult to injury, imagine you have to do all of this with dozens of people—known as therapists, parents, siblings, and doctors—pressuring you to do it faster and faster. You have to put seventeen years, start to finish, back together again in just a few months.

If you can imagine this scenario, you will have some sense of understanding of what it is like to wake up from a coma and to recover your old self and personality. You strive to become your normal self again after a severe brain injury, and to do it quickly before insurance money for rehabilitation runs out and before your mother loses her patience from having to care for your every need (always confused whether she should or shouldn't do something for you or let you struggle on your own). Imagine also that this compressed growing up is fraught with setbacks, failures, endless frustrations, agonizing doubts, physical and emotional pains, and often seemingly incomplete successes. When there is little to rejoice about, there is abundant sorrow.

To Jett and his family, the accident of seventeen years ago can never really be put behind them. It is still the marker for a new life: one of stronger and more contemplated values, of a continued search for individualism, and where the losses of the past continue to be replaced by the gains of today. Jett has learned that *different* is now normal.

This book is my testament to Jett. His antics in my office taught me lessons I didn't know I yet had to learn. This book is as much about the heart and soul of surviving and growing as it is about brain and behavior. While my right livelihood is to teach, I am ever so grateful for the lessons my patients and my friends have taught me.

Note: A short version of this true story appeared in the *Kansas City Star and Times*, September 24, 1989. The current story is updated and follows Jett an additional eleven years from the date of his accident.

1

The Head and Brain Injury Experience

The brain, the master organ of the body that directs everything from rhythmic breathing to the depths of thought, sits in a vulnerable position inside the skull. A forceful blow to the head, violent shaking of the head, or a penetrating object such as a bullet, can shatter delicate connections among the billions of nerve cells that make up the brain. Vessels may be broken and leak life-giving blood into tissues, essentially starving nerve cells, or choking them due to the increased pressures from leaking blood and swelling tissues. Chemicals essential for the brain to direct the body, to think, and to allow the person to communicate with the outside world can suddenly be released in lethal amounts. Communication among brain cells (neurons) requires detours and may reach deadends. At the moment of injury, the once smooth, well-oiled operations of the intact brain become confused, if they don't shut down completely.

Over half a million Americans experience head injury every year. These injuries range from relatively mild bumps on the head, but sufficient to cause at least a dazed experience, to blows so severe that the person becomes unconscious or comatose, where coma can last from hours to months. Automobile and motorcycle accidents account for most of the injuries, followed by falls, industrial and work-related injuries, sports accidents, and assaults. If you are reading this book, chances are you are one of those injured persons or have been personally affected by the head injury of a loved one.

A blow to the head may result in laceration of the scalp, surface bruising, or even skull fracture. When the force of the blow to the head is sufficient, serious injury can occur to the brain beneath the skull. When that occurs, we refer to the head injury as a "traumatic *brain* injury."

Everyone has experienced some minor or temporary brain injury, from too much alcohol to too many continuous rides on a wild roller coaster. The dizzy, lightheaded, and confused feeling we've all experienced for one reason or another offers a hint of the greatly magnified version of that experience caused by serious brain trauma. Various estimates count about one hundred thousand Americans who suffer sufficiently severe brain injury every year to cause permanent and usually disabling changes in their lives. Another several hundred thousand may suffer the consequences of a milder brain injury lasting weeks, months, or even years. Even a brain injury of seemingly minimal magnitude can result in lifelong challenges.

An Altered State of Consciousness

Any injury to the head sufficient to cause brain damage results almost immediately in an altered state of consciousness. Banging your head on a door or hitting the ground after a slip on the ice may cause a headache and a sense that thinking is really an effort. Feeling dazed and confused is common for a short time after a relatively mild event. A moderate blow to the head may result in unconsciousness where the individual has no awareness at all of what is going on. The individual may be in a semi-conscious state, still moving about, albeit aimlessly, and perhaps still talking but usually so confused that others cannot understand him or her. If the injury to the brain is severe enough, unconsciousness can be prolonged and so profound that even aimless movement or meaningless gibberish is not produced. This is coma. If the individual does not die from the severe injury to vital brain structures, recovery from coma is often very gradual and prolonged, mirroring the slow healing of brain tissue.

It is the occurrence of some level of altered consciousness that primarily defines a brain injury. Sometimes people who have sustained a relatively mild injury appear never to lose consciousness, perhaps only feeling a bit confused for a while. But later, the individual is virtually unable to recall anything about the injury or events that occurred at the time of the injury, or for some time following it. Sometimes this memory loss, or amnesia, may extend for hours or even days. In severe brain injury, amnesia can extend for weeks, months, or a lifetime.

The brain requires alertness to attend to internal (mental) and external (environmental) happenings. It must maintain cellular connections within its communication systems in order to process thought clearly and meaningfully, to recognize cause and effect, and to understand and generate language. Millions of organized brain cell networks are involved in sustaining this attention and consciousness. The more neural systems that are damaged, the deeper and longer-lasting the unconsciousness. Sometimes, injury to the brain is so severe it threatens the life-sustaining functions of breathing, blood circulation, heart rate, and other vital functions, all of which are controlled by specific areas of brain cells. Over 50,000 Americans die each year from brain injury so severe that one or more of these functions cannot survive. In moderate to severe cases of brain injury, it is the fast acquisition of emergency medical care that may save an individual from such fate.

While consciousness eventually recovers in most cases of brain injury, many people who sustain even mild injuries are often left with altered memory, language, behaviors, or emotions. These changes range from subtle annoyances to life-altering disabilities. Physical pain, seizures, muscle incoordination, and visual and hearing changes may also remain following recovery from the acute stages of brain injury.

While the length of time an individual is unconscious is a reliable gauge of the severity of injury, other indicators are observed as well. The boxed text—Severity of Brain Trauma Injury—summarizes the key characteristics of mild, moderate, and severe injury. It is important to note that any degree of brain injury, even "mild," can result in significant impairment.

BOX 1-1—Severity of Brain Trauma Injury

Traumatic brain injury (TBI) is usually described as mild, moderate, or severe. Criteria for such rating is not standardized but the following guidelines are generally accepted by most health care practitioners.

Mild
(Accounts for about 70-80 percent of TBI hospital admissions)
Loss of consciousness thirty minutes or less, or no loss of consciousness
Glasgow Coma Scale score of 13-15 (about thirty minutes after injury)
Total memory loss post-trauma less than twenty-four hours
Usually normal brain scans and traditional neurological tests
Postconcussion syndrome emerges with many symptoms

Moderate
(Accounts for about 10-30 percent of TBI hospital admissions)
Loss of consciousness greater than thirty minutes
Glasgow Coma Scale score 9-12 (about thirty minutes after injury)
Total memory loss post-trauma lasts 1-7 days
Usually brain injury is demonstrated on brain scan
Focal neurological abnormality
Postconcussion syndrome usually is mild

Severe
(Accounts for about 10 percent of TBI hospital admissions)
Loss of consciousness usually several hours, at least
Glasgow Coma Scale score 3-8 and persists low for some time
Total memory loss post-trauma greater than seven days
Almost always brain damage demonstrated on brain scan
Focal neurological abnormalities
Postconcussion syndrome usually minimal

Collision and Catastrophe

In an instant, brain injury can change the course of a life forever. A roll-over car accident or a head-on collision occurs in a split-second. A bullet enters the skull and brain with such violent force that flesh, bone, and brain cells are intermingled in a mass of indistinguishable tissue. While a thin layer of fluid cushions the brain inside the skull, it is grossly insufficient to protect it from potential injurious forces. An excursion into traffic, a walk down a stairway or icy path, operation of heavy and dangerous equipment, or venturing out into a society where millions of people possess guns pose risks we face on a daily basis.

Brain injury occurs when the skull slams against a windshield, the ground, or some other stationary object. The compression, twisting, and distortion of the brain inside the skull associated with this impact causes localized as well as widespread damage throughout the brain. Approximately the consistency of two-day-old Jell-O, the brain, blood vessels, and multitudes of miniscule sacs of neurotransmitter chemicals can be so violently bounced around that it is a wonder at all that an individual would survive anything but the most mild physical force trauma.

Immediately after a head trauma event, typically, the injured individual may not know he or she was injured. Even if there is only a partial loss of consciousness there is usually complete amnesia for the injury event. If there is total loss of consciousness, there is likely a prolonged period of amnesia extending back in time before the injury. Recovery from trauma does not start immediately after the injury. In fact, there is a cascade of further injury to the brain that can occur for hours or days after the event. Gradual brain swelling may occur from bruised tissue or bleeding into the cranial vault where the pressure has no outlet. Chemical changes within brain cells may cause many of them to die within hours. Random and erratic brain signals may cause severe agitation and thrashing, causing further injury. Injury to other body organs and systems may compound the whole situation.

Once stabilized with medical care, oxygen provided if necessary, drugs administered to prevent swelling, and conditions arranged to calm the individual, recovery from brain injury can eventually begin. The complexity and critical functioning of the brain is profound. Brain tissue doesn't grow back like tissues in many other body systems and the configuration of billions of brain cells cannot reconnect to their precise pre-injury patterns. Brain injury recovery takes on a complex course different from other types of bodily injury. Recovery means gradually regaining a relatively normal level of consciousness, recovering day-to-day memory, and often learning how to walk, talk, and reestablish basic bodily functions again. The brain may have to learn to control bowel and bladder functions all over again. It may need to learn how to recognize sounds and differentiate visual objects again. The mental, emotional, behavioral, and physical changes that brain injury produces may require months to years for recovery, rarely, if ever, completely attaining familiar pre-injury functionality.

In addition to physical trauma, brain injury can occur from other reasons as well. Oxygen deprivation from near drowning or other asphyxiating events can cause scattered brain cell death or dysfunction. Fully twenty-five percent of the oxygen we breath in goes to the brain, yet the brain constitutes only about two percent of the total body mass. Brain tissues depend on an abundance of oxygen.

Carbon monoxide poisoning and other toxic exposures can cause asphyxiation as well, but also may contribute poisonous substances that further damage brain cell membranes or interfere with cells' ability to use oxygen or nutritive substances. Electrocution or lightning strikes may cause interference with the cellular membrane's ability to regulate the inflow or outflow of chemical ions that create neural signals. Other sudden events such as heart attack and stroke can cause severe oxygen deprivation to the brain. Insidious causes of brain injury can be chronic lung disease, hypercholesterolemia (too much fat accumulating in the blood vessels), and infections such as those caused by AIDS or syphilis.

Brain injury is a major life event, often changing the individual and his or her family forever. Experiencing a potentially life-threatening situation, followed by intensive medical care and long-term rehabilitation is usually quite an unsettling experience. The loneliness and fear that

BOX 1-2—Glasgow Coma Scale

A patient is rated on degree of capability in three areas: eye opening, best motor response to stimulus, and verbal response. The scale is used during the initial assessment of depth of coma after an injury, and by repeated ratings to monitor coma recovery. A score of 3 indicates deep coma; a score of 15 indicates no coma.

Eye Opening (E)

Opens eyes spontaneously	4
Opens eyes when asked loudly	3
Opens eyes to pain (pinch)	2
Does not open eyes at all	1

Best Motor Response (M)

Obeys simple commands	6
Localizes motor response	5
Withdraws body part to pain (pinch)	4
Flexes body inappropriately to pain (decorticate posturing)	3
body becomes extended in response to pain (decerebrate posturing)	2
no motor response at all	1

Verbal Response (V)

Normal orientation and conversation	5
Confused and disoriented in conversation	4
Articulates but uses inappropriate words that make no sense	3

| Incomprehensible sounds only, no conversation | 2 |
| Makes no sounds at all | 1 |

Total Glasgow Coma Score is the sum of the E, M, and V ratings. Minimum score is 3; maximum is 15.

accompany the unknown future and the weeks and months of waiting for recovery to occur result in a constant reassessment of personal values. The joys and tears of helping and being helped, the challenge of coping with altered life plans, the anxiety of change, and the emerging breakthroughs in mental and cognitive recovery all accompany the brain injury experience. It is a constantly changing and evolving situation lasting years, often a lifetime.

Basic Neuroanatomy

Some basic notions about brain anatomy can lend greater understanding about the magnitude of possible sources of damage when brain injury occurs. Normally, the brain operates as a whole where parts depend on and communicate with other parts to achieve integrated function. Within the well-oiled machine, there are anatomically identifiable structures that have specific functions that account for some of the effects of brain injury. Fundamentally, the brain is divided into three major divisions: the brain stem, the cerebellum, and the cerebrum.

Brain Stem

The brain stem—the long, thick bundle of nerve tracts at the base of the brain—connects the brain with the spinal cord. The brain and spinal cord make up the continuously connected central nervous system. The brain stem also contains structures vital to maintenance of breathing, respiration, and heart rate. The reticular activating system lies within the brain stem and controls consciousness and arousal. All neural information from the body, from the toes to the neck, passes through the spinal cord and brain stem on its way to being processed in higher brain regions. Information from the senses in the head (smell, sight, hearing, taste) go directly to the brain stem and brain through the cranial nerves. All directives from the brain to the body must pass through the brain stem on their way out to the muscles and bodily organs. Unfortunately, the brain stem at the base of the brain is in a vulnerable position. Stretching and injury to the brain stem occurs rather easily during trauma when the head violently moves, as in whiplash. The cranial nerves, entering the brain at the brain stem, and in contact with bony prominences in the base of the skull, are sometimes damaged, causing dysfunction to eye muscles, facial and voice control, and muscles involved in swallowing.

Figure 1. Rapid acceleration/deceleration can cause hyperflexion/ hyperextension of the head, potentially resulting in stretching and trauma to the brain stem. This usually results in unconsciousness and may threaten vital brain function.

Cerebellum

The cerebellum—the paired cerebellar hemispheres—lies in twin cupped areas (known as fossa) of the cranium just behind and slightly above the brain stem. Responsible mostly for coordinating movement and remembering habitual movement patterns, the cerebellum is sometimes damaged but often not severely. It is relatively well protected compared with many other areas of the brain.

Cerebrum

The cerebrum—the paired cerebral hemispheres—is the major part of the brain in which virtually all higher-level brain activity takes place: language, thinking, initiation of activity, emotional control, creativity, learning and remembering, mathematical reasoning, and expression of personality. The cerebrum, as with the cerebellum, consists of two mirror halves (hemispheres): the right and left cerebral hemispheres and the right and left cerebellar hemispheres.

The convoluted and wrinkled surface of the cerebral hemispheres is called the *cortex*. Complex networks of neurons in the cortex represent advanced brain development unique to humans where intellectual processes take place. The nerve cells that lie beneath the cortex consist mostly of longer nerve tracts that provide the rich source of intracerebral communication. Because the cells of the cortex lie at the surface of the brain, they are susceptible to damage when the brain slams into the inside of the skull during trauma. With enough force of trauma, the deeper, underlying nerve tracts may also be damaged.

Some systems of nerve tracts that lie deeper under the cortex (the *limbic system*, for example, which processes memory and emotions) are vulnerable to damage by virtue of their extensive representation throughout the brain and their long interconnecting axons. Some disruption of these widely dispersed systems is inevitable in brain injury.

Ventricles—pools of watery fluid within the brain's cerebral hemispheres—sometimes fill and swell excessively causing pressure damage to the adjacent brain structures. Ventricles, in their normal state, exist to help maintain proper brain metabolism and to aid in cushioning the brain against minor trauma.

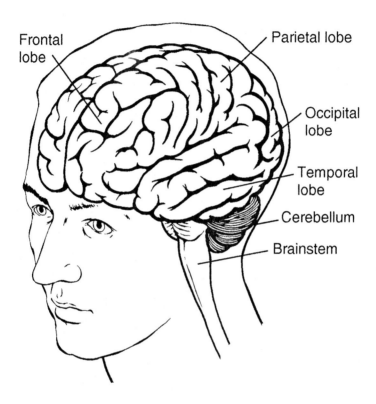

Figure 2. The essential landmarks of the brain are labeled in this lateral view. The anterior portion of the frontal lobes and the anterior tips of the temporal lobes are particularly vulnerable to damage in head trauma.

Both of the cerebral hemispheres are divided into four areas or lobes, each corresponding to a more or less distinct area of the cortex and each representing more or less specific cognitive functions.

The *frontal lobes*, constituting nearly the anterior third to half of the cerebral hemispheres, are the emotional control centers and highest intellectual processing areas of the brain. The frontal lobes may be injured at least somewhat during trauma by virtue of their being situated at the front of the brain and getting slammed into the front of the inside of the cranium. The frontal lobes are involved in a variety of cognitive functions including language, creative thought, problem-solving, initiation of activity, judgment, and impulse control. They are involved with other brain structures in self-awareness and self-monitoring of socially appropriate behaviors.

The *parietal lobes*, lying at the upper midsection of each hemisphere, are involved in sensation, reading, listening, awareness of spatial relationships, mental organization, and memory. The parietal lobes provide the site for most basic intellectual abilities, such as the "3-Rs" of reading, writing, and arithmetic. The parietal lobe of the left hemisphere mostly processes language functions while the parietal lobe of the right hemisphere mostly processes spatial-organizational and non-verbal functions.

Located laterally below the parietal lobes, along both of the hemispheres, above and near the ears, are the *temporal lobes*. These structures, like the frontal lobes, are especially vulnerable to damage as they are hurled against the sides of the bony pockets of the cranium that contain them. Memory, language, thought sequencing, and musical processing are some of the functions of the temporal lobes. They are tightly integrated with the limbic system in processing and controlling emotions and memory.

The *occipital lobes* are located at the very back of the cerebral hemispheres and are the primary sites for visual perception. Of the four lobes in each hemisphere, the occipital is usually least damaged in trauma. However, subtle changes in how efficiently the occipital lobes work in carrying out visual perception is often seen. This is because the visual tracts must pass all the way from the eyes and through the frontal and temporal regions before they get to the occipital lobes. Damage to the tracts anywhere along the way, or injury to the occipital cortex itself, can sometimes cause subtle disruption in seeing, perception, or visual perimetry.

Diffuse Axonal Injury

No injury to the brain, regardless of severity, causes *every* brain cell to die or become dysfunctional. The exception to this might be any event that causes complete brain death. If the individual survives a brain injury, scattered damage to brain tissue in the form of cell membrane injury or changes in the juxtaposition (the combination and relation) of cells one to another typically characterizes the injury. Diffuse injury (scattered about the brain) to the axons (the longer, electrochemical transmission portions of nerve cells) has been observed in microscopic studies of traumatized brain cells. Alteration of the synapses (the tiny space between cells where nerve signals are conveyed) accompanies diffuse axonal injury.

"DAI," as it is called, occurs when the Jell-O like brain substance is contorted during violent movement of the brain within the confines of the cranial vault (skull). Usually, a mechanical process of acceleration-deceleration takes place. The brain is accelerated rapidly forward then suddenly decelerated by impacting against the inside of the skull. The brain may then "bounce" back and forth or sustain additional acceleration-deceleration movement as the skull, attached to a body, is thrown about in a car crash or some other violent event.

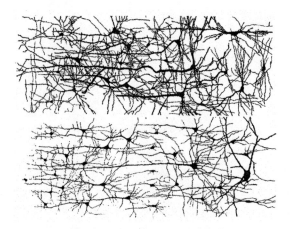

Figure 3. Represented schematically, diffuse axonal injury results in a
gradual reduction in the number of functioning brain cells and
reduced interconnections (lower figure) compared with normally
richly interconnected cell networks (upper figure).

Brain scans taken at the hospital immediately after a brain injury
may be normal. However, the microscopic changes in brain tissue—the diffuse axonal injury—that do not show up on those scans
may account for the altered consciousness, the change in bodily functions, and the change in personal and social behaviors. Sometimes
those changes herald a lifetime of challenges, both for the individual
injured as well as for his or her family and friends.

Brain injury is immediately frightening to the family, while the
injured person is usually oblivious to the event and initially, at least, to
its consequences. It is the days, weeks, and months of recovery that
bring home the substantial and sobering realization of the life-changing event. Maintaining a sensitive and positive outlook, learning how
to take control of one's life again, and cultivating attitudes of conquering rather than succumbing fosters not only survival from a brain
injury but growth, as well.

Complex Neuropathology

The brain's physical structure is changed at the moment of traumatic impact. The precise brain areas damaged or the extent and nature of the damage depend on many factors. The direction of the force of the injury, the degree of acceleration-deceleration force, the angle of brain movement, the number of times the brain "bounces" around inside the skull, and the changes in head and brain angle from bounce to bounce all account for unique injuries to brain areas. Whether the impact is blunt against the head or caused by head movement itself, as in whiplash injury, determines how far destructive energy might permeate into the brain. The vulnerability of certain brain areas intrinsic to the individual or brain damage existing from a prior trauma may make an otherwise milder injury more severe. The presence of compromising factors at the moment of injury such as alcohol or drugs in the blood can also complicate the injury or impede recovery. No two traumatic impacts are precisely the same and the consequences of brain trauma vary and are unique to each individual.

For a few minutes after the impact, the ability or inability of neural tissue to continue receiving oxygen and metabolizing glucose and the degree to which chemical changes may occur will determine whether a sharp deterioration in function occurs. The presence of bleeding into brain tissue, the onset of seizures, and the potential for brain swelling caused by blood changes and inability of tissue to monitor fluid levels may also affect the cascade of potential additional damage.

Primary and Secondary Injury

The boxed text—Primary and Secondary Brain Injury Mechanisms—summarizes some of the potential sources of brain injury from trauma. Possible complicating or secondary injury processes evolve following the immediate, or primary, injury. It is clear that brain injury is a very complex process. Not only can many things go wrong in the brain itself, injury often involves multi-system involvement that com-

---

BOX 1-3—Primary and Secondary Brain Injury Mechanisms

Primary injury usually results from the actual impact and includes:
Skull fracture
Contusion and laceration of brain areas
Diffuse axonal injury
Acute hematoma

A cascade of **secondary injury** may evolve for some time after initial impact and may be the essential cause of long-term problems. These processes include:
Neurotransmitter (chemical) toxicity
Changes in electrolytes (conductors of electrical current in the brain)
Diffuse blood vessel damage
Vasospasm (rapid contraction and dilation of blood vessels)
High blood pressure
Brain swelling
Cell death
Hematomas (pools of noncirculating blood)
Intracranial infections
Seizures
Brain herniation (bulging through skull openings) and mass effect
Systemic (bodily) injury
Degeneration of long neural tracks
Brain atrophy (shrinking due to cell death)
Immune system suppression
Fevers
Anemia

---

promises breathing, blood flow, sodium balance, nutrition, and other metabolic and chemical processes. Spinal cord injury often accompanies head injury as well, affecting the use of arms and legs.

In addition to the primary injury possibilities due to diffuse axonal injury, bruising of brain tissue, and even skull fracture, other injury processes may occur. Blood clots, known as hematomas, can occur if blood vessels break. These can occur outside the brain, between the brain and the skull, or inside the brain itself. In either case, the pocket of blood not only disrupts normal blood circulation in that area, it causes pressure on adjacent tissues, contributing to further damage to that region of the brain. If the hematoma is large enough, brain shifting and distortion can occur (called a "mass effect") as the hematoma presses hard against otherwise undamaged tissue. Mass effect itself can cause widespread brain damage due to the pressure against and contortion of brain cells.

Secondary injury to the brain usually results from the cascade of events that occur for some time after the initial impact or injury. Changes in electrolytes, neurotransmitters, and other biochemical systems may further injure brain tissue or compromise healing. Emergency treatment of brain trauma most critically addresses the potential for secondary injury. Emergency and acute care aims to halt or minimize the cascade of further injury.

Under doctors' care, maintenance of circulation and blood pressure, prevention of infections caused by the breakdown of the blood-brain barrier, prevention of swelling, management of oxygen-free radicals, and prevention of ionic toxicity might continue for hours to days following a traumatic injury. Metabolism gone awry can cause vascular spasms, seizures, high fevers, anemia, and other injurious anomalies, all of which require careful medical monitoring.

Depending on the severity and extent of brain injury, and the availability and aggressiveness of medical treatment, scattered or localized brain cell death may occur as secondary injury evolves. Damaged cell membranes combined with a toxic intraparenchymal (intra-brain) environment can lead to cell death. Medical intervention must be aggressive to prevent as much secondary injury as possible. Medications designed to stabilize physiological processes, or "wake up" the reticular activating system might facilitate the brain's natural homeostatic recovery.

Non-traumatic Brain Injury

While the focus of the previous paragraphs, and of this book in general, is on traumatic brain injury, non-traumatic brain injury can produce very similar effects. Although the primary injury may not be physical force trauma, any compromise to the brain's delicately balanced operations can produce a complex set of secondary processes just as devastating. Depriving the brain of oxygen, as in carbon monoxide poisoning or heart attack, can cause cellular membrane injury, gradual brain swelling, and a host of other metabolic and nutritional changes that can lead to necrosis (cell death).

The temporal lobes and limbic system are as vulnerable to oxygen deprivation as to physical trauma. It is common knowledge that the brain cannot go for more than a few minutes of oxygen deprivation without causing irreversible damage. Those structures deep inside the brain—the limbic system, particularly—and brain stem are especially sensitive to lack of oxygen and are vulnerable to immediate and irreversible damage when oxygen availability drops. Changes in attention, concentration, and memory are just as much the hallmarks of brain damage by non-traumatic causes as by physical trauma.

The Hidden Disability

Often left without scars or other visible evidence of injury, persons who have experienced a brain injury may be shunned because the slower thinking, unreliable memory, difficult communications, and behavioral and emotional effects are not understood. A person who may require more time to formulate a thought and put it into words may be brushed aside as incompetent or mentally retarded. A person who cannot deal emotionally with too much going on at one time or who may seem easily confused, is rejected out of impatience. A person who requires organization and routine rather than flexibility in most activities may be discounted as rigid and unproductive. A person who is easily emotionally overcome may be labeled as mentally ill. These characteristics may be the unavoidable consequences of brain injury and need to be appreciated as such. A person may be doing his or her best in attempting to cope and manage moment-to-moment affairs but can do so only as society provides the patience, understanding, and accommodation to encourage it.

Brain injury heralds a long process of coping and adjusting. Persons with a brain injury and their family members come to learn much more than the average person knows about the brain and the behaviors and mental processes it produces. To seek knowledge and respect for the complex brain is an important first step in reducing the anxiety and frustration of brain injury. Acquiring knowledge of what has happened and what continues to happen inside the brain and about the psychological and emotional processes of recovery helps provide a sense of control over the chaos, making hope seem realistic.

The haunting questions—Will the person who has been injured ever be normal again? Will he or she make a full recovery? Is it reasonable to hope that the survivor of brain injury will get better? Will we ever get used to this new person?—are not easily answered. In fact, coming to terms with these questions is the essence of the psychological aspects of rehabilitation, a significant part of this book. Facing reality with a new sense of values may be necessary. Normality, or the idealized memory of what was once normal, can no longer be idolized. Recovery takes on new meaning including how to do things and how to think in different ways. Hope becomes an attitude of active conquest, not of passive waiting and wishing. The new person that evolves after a brain injury is a mix of the former personality and the courageous accomplishments of facing a challenge without retreat.

Brian—Real Person

In high school I was in the top third of my class, played football in the fall, and ran track in the spring. I worked part time at a service station, drove a terrific '82 Datsun with a T-top, and had a lot of friends. After graduation I worked full time to save for college. I enrolled at Southwestern State as a marketing major.

College was great. I met some great friends and had wonderful times. Studying was more difficult than I thought it would be and my first semester grade point was not too hot. After two years there, I got serious and decided that I wouldn't get any grade lower than a B. I came to realize there is more to life than "happy hour" and late night bar festivities.

Determination paid off. My grades improved. My social life still was great and I pledged a fraternity. I worked two summers painting dorm rooms in an all-girls school. (That was fun!) I turned twenty-one. I moved off campus into a house with two fraternity brothers. My nick-name was T-Bird and theirs were Lunchbox and Hairball. I loved col-lege, working part-time, and…life.

One day, shortly after school started in September of my Junior year, things changed. Fraternity brothers often seem to have to prove some sort of superiority amongst themselves. One brother named Brice thought that since I was quite a bit heavier than he was it would be easy to beat me in a foot race. He challenged me and, of course, I had to accept the challenge. We decided to race on a side street two doors down from my house. Lunchbox went with us to be the official judge. So the race began and I had to win. I went all out and crossed the finish line well before Brice. I had so much momentum built up I couldn't stop quickly. Little did I know, a car was coming up the intersecting street. I woke up from a severe head injury a month later in the Neuro Intensive Care Unit at University Hospital.

It's four years later now. I feel like I'm fifteen again. I have to depend on my parents for transportation and entertainment. I have posttraumatic seizures and short-term memory loss. My friends have now all graduated, moved away or gotten married, or both. I have seen Brice only once since the foot race. I can't get the type of job I want because I'm not educated. I can't go back to college yet because I don't learn very quickly. When I think about all the "can'ts" I get depressed. So, I stop and say, "Brian, you could be dead. Be thankful for the abil-ity to overcome your deficits, and most of all be thankful for your life."

This head injury has confronted me with several challenges, many of which I still have a hard time with. The loss of my short-term memory confronts me every single day. I have had some cognitive therapy but that isn't enough. I have post-trauma seizures for which I have undergone temporal lobectomy brain surgery, extended hyperbaric oxygen therapy, and EEG neurofeedback therapy, and for which I must take several medications. The seizures are less frequent now and happen mostly during sleep. The medications sedate my brain. I really want to drive again—that, especially, is why I feel like I'm fifteen again, instead of twenty-five. I am limited in my physical activities and I get frustrated at my inabilities to be the person I used to be.

Since my injury I depend on a notebook and other people for my memory. I am often frustrated and I get upset more easily. I'm different than I used to be because I occasionally do or say inappropriate things that I don't realize at the time. I sometimes have a hard time dealing with the new Brian, and so do others. I have some hang-ups, like I worry over insignificant things a long time, like when I brush my teeth too hard or cut my nails too short. I guess I'm a little obsessive-compulsive. I don't seem to have the reasoning power I used to have, so figuring things out takes longer. I'm fifty pounds lighter but I don't run anymore.

I now see things differently—things I once took for granted. I am grateful for all the events that I have been able to be a part of. My mother has helped me in any way that was possible. She has devoted so much of her life to helping me become more independent.

I'm a more caring and sensitive person and I like that. So does my family and the two remaining friends I have. I'm more lonely now, but not necessarily depressed. I'm a more religious person. I'm compassionate with people and understand other's handicaps. I think I handle my "cans" and "can'ts" pretty well given my situation. I keep searching for ways to improve my mental and physical functioning. I gradually realize I am involved in life again. But, it's really different now.

[A note from Brian's mom: Is he like he was? No. And I miss him. I'm very grateful for the nice young man who replaced the original nice boy. The eighteen-month window we were told about isn't factual—Brian continues to improve each year. The more we challenge his brain, the more he improves—as long as we don't move too fast. To quote Winston Churchill, "We shall never, never, never give up."]

2

Similarities and Differences in Brain Injury

Whenever a significant characteristic about a person becomes the focus of attention, such as a limb amputation, or having been diagnosed with a severe disease, or having had a brain injury, people often refer to that individual in terms of his or her "condition." We've all heard people referred to as "the wheelchair" (as in, "watch out, wheelchair coming through"), or "the para" (for paraplegic), or "the T-B-I" (for traumatic brain injury, as in "the TBI in room 207").

People are not their conditions, and the shortcut terms we use to refer to them are demeaning. The condition may be a particular focus at a point in time but to allow that focus to deny the person's wholeness and reduce the individual to one particular characteristic or label is disrespectful.

In the case of the individual who has had a brain injury, it is crucial to maintain a balanced view right from the beginning, respecting the wholeness and complex individuality of the person. This is essential because the brain recovering from injury establishes memories and behavior patterns that become the new lifelong traits of the individual. Just as a newborn gradually forms his self-identity largely based on how others treat and regard him, so does a person emerging from brain injury. The individual forms a new concept of who he is, based in part, on how others react to him. The brain recovering from an injury is jumbled and confused. It seeks to reestablish a coherent, integrated sense of self. If all focus is directed to the singular aspect of being "damaged," the brain will recover with a damaged focus. That will be the person's new identity. If, however, the brain receives balanced information, that it is unique and varied, that the person has weaknesses and strengths, the individual will recover within a much healthier context.

The problem of label shortcuts is subtle. It is like becoming acutely aware of a little blemish on your face only after someone has pointed it out to you, despite your having seen it in the mirror and thought little of it. Now it becomes the focus of your every thought. You ask yourself, "What will she think of me with this ugly blotch on my nose?" You constantly pick at it, actually making it worse, and more noticeable to others. You worry if another one will suddenly appear, making you a true pariah. If the minor blemish had been kept in perspective, its importance would be relegated and certainly would not become overwhelming and dominant. While a brain injury is certainly more serious than a minor facial blemish, the principle is the same: keep things in perspective. Relegate brain damage as much as possible and focus on the wholeness and individuality of the person.

While there are many similarities among individuals and the consequences of brain injury—difficulty thinking, memory impairment, distractibility, for example—the effects of brain injury are always expressed against the backdrop of a unique individual. Differences among individuals in the consequences of brain injury are a reminder that the brain and its behavior and personality are richly complex, deserving respect for diversity and wholeness, despite the damage.

It's the Person With a Brain Injury

In the early days of brain injury awareness, the phrase "brain injured person" was used frequently. Persons with brain injury quickly realized their whole identity was being focused on their injury. So, the shortcut term was eliminated and we now refer to the "person who has experienced a brain injury." This subtle wording change puts the *person* first. This is not merely political correctness; it is psychologically powerful.

Respecting Individual Differences Following Brain Injury

Every person who sustains a brain injury enters that experience, some-times a life-threatening and usually a life-changing one, with a preexist-ing, unique personality. Preservation of that uniqueness is crucial for minimizing the disruption and inner turmoil that the individual goes through in gradually reconstituting his or her self-identity. Even though most people observe what appear to be personality changes fol-lowing a brain injury, usually the more the threads of the old personal-ity are retained, the better the recovery.

Some people enter the brain injury experience better equipped with adaptive personality traits than do others. For some individuals, who may have been rigid, angry, and bitter before the injury, threads of a sense of humor, a selfless side to their nature, or an old but repressed trait of affection might emerge during the course of recovery. These positive personality characteristics can be encouraged if not overshad-owed by the tragedy and negativity of brain injury, which would only reinforce the old, negative traits. During recovery, it is important to be sensitive to the positive, adaptive behaviors that might pop up, and to encourage those behaviors.

Brain injury and its functional expression can be very different in each individual. The brain is so exceedingly complex and the effect of injury so unique to each individual's situation that even the label "brain injury" is an oversimplification. The expression, outcome, and resolution of brain injury will be very different depending on the sever-ity and location of the brain injury, possible complications, the age of the person, current and former heath status, and preexisting intellec-tual and mental characteristics.

Even the experience of a change in consciousness can be very differ-ent from individual to individual. Brain injury, if not fatal, ranges from a few minutes of feeling dazed to a longer and gradual arousal from coma. Some people will "wake up" very gradually over the course of days to months; others will seem to have regained normal alertness rather quickly. Sometimes there will be a veil of confusion, of being "not with it," or of a "distance," that will persist and vary for weeks or months.

Despite demonstrating threads of the familiar personality, persons who experience brain injury typically reflect personality changes as well. Quite often a person will exhibit a sense of self-centeredness, a lack of affectionate responsiveness, a lack of depth in relating to others, or a tendency to be "on edge." This may be disturbing to families who may conclude that their loved one is no longer the same person. It is necessary to look for and encourage the preserved positive personality traits that might be overshadowed by the disturbing changes.

The normal consequences of injury that make the individual appear distant and sometimes immature can evoke a response from others that treats the individual in similar manner. This needs to be avoided because such treatment only further reinforces these changes. Continuing, as much as possible, to react to a person in a positive manner and as a unique and whole person, respecting his or her new limitations in brain processing, is essential to foster recovery of a whole person, not a distant and immature person.

It is easy to react negatively to some particularly annoying behaviors produced by a brain that has been injured. It is crucial to remember that those behaviors are not the whole person. A person who is lashing out in anger as he is recovering from brain injury isn't an angry *person*. He's a person who is expressing a part of the emotional and physiological consequences of brain injury. Psychologists call this labeling situation an "attribution error." We react to some specific trait or behavior as if that isolated trait represents the whole person. It is so important to maintain a perspective of the individual as whole and complex, not as "damaged" (or angry, or immature, or distant).

While an adult person who has had a brain injury may talk slower, use simpler words, and even act a bit immaturely, it is important to respond to that person as an adult, not as a child. Talk slower and more deliberately, certainly not condescendingly or with baby talk. Help the person by offering choices instead of making all the decisions for him or her. Let the person tell you what he or she needs or wishes instead of making assumptions. Again, it is the complete, unique person that we want to evolve from the catastrophe. Be aware of attribution error and avoid falling into its trap.

Injury Similarities and Reaction Differences

Almost all persons who sustain a brain injury experience damage to the axis or base of the brain, known as the brain stem. This area of the brain provides neural pathways for heart rate, breathing, blood pressure, body temperature, and other vital functions. Although these functions usually stabilize rather quickly after an injury, another function involving the brain stem seems not to recover so quickly and often never recovers completely: maintaining attention and short-term memory.

While almost everyone who experiences brain injury has trouble with attention and memory, individual reactions to these difficulties depend on how the individual may have reacted to similar but perhaps less severe problems before the injury. Factors such as extent of the injury, preexisting style of coping with frustration, attitudes toward change and challenge, quality of family support, rigidity or flexibility in personal attitudes and adjustment, and attitudes toward and beliefs about life in general affect such reactions.

There are other similarities in brain injury consequences: slower reaction times, slower mental processing, sometimes subtle expressive language hesitations or word-finding difficulties, awkwardness in handling tools and small objects, and oftentimes a sense of disorientation or tendency to get lost. While these changes are common, individual reactions to them determine their impact on the total person and the brain injury experience. This is where an impairment may or may not become a disability. An impairment, or a change in an ability, may or may not be disturbing, depending on how it is viewed or how personal adjustments may minimize its impact. An impairment becomes a disability when it interferes with one's life. The goal of brain injury reha-

BOX 2-1—Typical Cognitive Changes Accompanying Brain Injury

This list describes typical cognitive changes that accompany brain injury. Comprehensive neuropsychological examination is useful to evaluate the extent of cognitive changes and their functional consequences. The cluster of cognitive changes associated with brain injury listed here is fairly similar across individuals but with differing patterns of expression in each person.

Slower responses and thinking: Brain injury almost always causes the electrochemical communications in the brain to become slower by virtue of damaged nerve cells. Even measured in milliseconds of delays, the cumulative effect of thousands of neurons necessary to process thought and responses causes the injured brain to become even slightly "out of step" with others, requiring more time to process thoughts and language.

Inconsistent ability to maintain attention and mental focus: Damage to brain areas responsible for sustaining mental focus shortens one's attention span. Information gets processed in a fragmented manner and memory is affected because only part of the information gets into the brain in the first place. Attention span is short. Mental focus on any task must be aided by repetition, short rest breaks, and organization.

Mental disorganization and difficulty with logical sequencing: "Short circuits" in neural processing following brain injury cause thoughts to become derailed and incomplete. A pervasive sense of disorganization and difficulty correcting that may complicate many cognitive processes. Rehabilitation must focus on strategies to simplify and organize thinking.

Perseverative (inflexible) thinking and problem-solving: Once a brain connection is made, it may just take too much mental effort or produce too much insecurity to let go of that connection in favor of another. Thus, thoughts may become fixed instead of remaining flexible and available to new and potentially modifying information. A person may even seem obsessed with a thought or a conclusion without being open to alternative ideas.

Memory fragmentation and forgetfulness: A combination of incomplete attention, impaired ability to create the neural representations of memories, and difficulty retrieving correct information produces the hallmark characteristic of brain injury—memory problems.

Time sense distortion and inconsistency: Brain injury almost always affects how the individual is able to process the progression of time. Recall of when things occurred in the past or thinking about when they might occur in the future is difficult and often fraught with error. Difficulty sequencing the flow of events in one's life, along with frequent forgetting of bits and pieces of those events, contributes to confusion.

Slowness and inconsistency in learning new information: Because of the slowness in thinking, the normal flow of information may be too fast for the individual with brain injury. Gaps in information awareness and processing, as well as memory dysfunction, make acquisition of new learning difficult, usually requiring considerable repetition and use of multiple learning and memory aids.

Perceptual misunderstanding and confusion: Because of memory problems and subtle changes in how sensory systems (seeing, smelling, tasting, hearing, and touching) pick up new information and compare it to old information, judgments may be fragmented and incomplete. Logic may seem bizarre and quite frustrating to others.

Difficulty integrating and linking information logically: The brain that suffers scattered disconnections among its neurons produces deadends in thinking. When thinking hits a snag, logic becomes incomplete. Unfortunately, persons with brain injury often are not aware that their thinking is illogical and may defend vehemently their conclusions, no matter how illogical or ill-considered they may seem to others.

Slowness and awkwardness finding words and forming language: As with difficulty linking information due to scattered brain disconnections, finding words and formulating language may be quite difficult and frustrating due to weakened memory retrieval and logical processing.

Erratic errors in calculation: Due to a combination of inattention, poor logical thinking, and even perceptual distortion, persons with brain damage are quite prone to making scattered errors in performing both written and mental arithmetic calculations. Usually, they are unaware of their errors. Special techniques for accomplishing accurate calculations must be learned during rehabilitation.

bilitation is to minimize impairments so they do not become disabilities, or at least not such big disabilities.

Personality Changes

Over time, sometimes years, the individual who has had a brain injury develops new personality traits and retains and modifies some preexisting characteristics. The individual also, often with arduous persistence, learns new skills and strategies for coping with lifestyle changes which brain injury has brought about. While addressing recovery of cognitive (i.e., thinking), motor, and various functional changes caused by brain injury is important, it is equally important to encourage the development of adaptive and positive personality and attitudinal characteristics. It is the underlying belief in one's self, the acceptance of challenge, and the attitude of acceptance of differences that enables, rather than disables, one's adaptation to life changes after a brain injury.

Recovery from brain injury, stated more accurately, is actually recovery *with* brain injury. Brain injury is almost never completely eradicated. Some aspects remain permanent and the brain injury needs to be subjugated to make the person whole again. How all this happens is a complex process and depends not only on the physical consequences of the brain injury, but on the individual's commitment to rehabilitation. Important in this process are constant family participation and support, acceptance of new ideas and change, and the willingness to do things differently in order to function more efficiently.

Life Is All in the Perspective

It is essential to keep a perspective about life in a broad sense, and disability in a specific sense, after a brain injury. Actually, everyone is disabled in some respect, but we normally focus on our strengths and

BOX 2-2—Typical Personality and Behavioral Changes Accompanying Brain Injury

Listed here are some of the more typical changes in personality traits following brain injury. There is considerable variability from one person to another who has sustained brain injury in the way personality is affected. All of these characteristics are usually not seen in each individual. The expression of personality and behavioral changes depends not only on the extent and location of brain injury but on preexisting personality and personal adjustment. The essential thing to remember is that these changes have their foundation directly in damage to brain cells.

Illogical or weak judgment: The individual with a brain injury may not always be able to analyze a situation correctly or take into account the probable or multiple consequences of his or her actions. Difficulty imagining (visualizing) and thinking through logical consequences of actions will produce behaviors that reflect incomplete judgment. Drawing logical conclusions with analysis and support of all the facts is difficult, due to fragmented thinking and memory impairment.

Immature social behaviors: Social skills are impaired when the individual lacks sensitivity and emotional concern about his or her surroundings and disregards usual priorities, usually because of impulsivity and disinhibition. As with most personality changes following brain injury, the individual is usually unaware of the problem, which is due directly to the physiological injury to the brain. The individual's unawareness of the problem makes it difficult to point out the problem, often causing conflict between the person with the injury and others.

Irritability and short temper: As with many emotional and personality changes following brain injury, a combination of the injury, emotional reaction to life changes, and preexisting personality characteristics produces these problem behaviors. Irritability stems from difficulty mentally integrating information and sorting it out, resulting in a pervasive sense of befuddlement. Sometimes the "straw that breaks the camel's back" will seem inconsequential to others but be overwhelming to the individual who is already having a tough time making sense of a changed world.

Self-centeredness: An almost incessant focus on one's self and one's problems is sometimes seen following brain injury, especially during the early recovery stages. This may reflect a weak ability to integrate the goings on in the environment and the needs of other people. Self-centeredness may also reflect the individual's psychological effort to come to terms with his or her new experience of the self. Usually self-centeredness resolves somewhat as the individual's cognitive resources and self-concept recover.

Depression and withdrawal: The combined results of physiological changes in the brain, emotional reaction to losses, general sense of inadequacy, and preexisting personality produce the degree to which the individual with a brain injury may become depressed and withdraw from social activities. The cause of depression must be professionally investigated so that proper treatment can be obtained.

Dependency: Associated with weakened self-confidence, the individual with a brain injury may become quite dependent on a spouse, a parent, or a friend. Dependency may arise out of fear that one's thinking is incomplete and cannot be trusted. Dependency may also evolve out of passivity, finding that it is easier to let others make all the decisions.

Domineering presence: Similar to self-centeredness, this characteristic may be associated with an aggressive attempt to overcome a weakened sense of self-confidence, the opposite reaction of dependency. While formerly quite uncharacteristic of the individual, the assertive and domineering behaviors may be quite irritating to others. As with many problematic behavioral changes, rehabilitation must include addressing the complex psychological and interpersonal needs of the person with brain injury.

Suspiciousness: Usually a sense of suspicion that others are potentially harmful or untrustworthy comes from being unable to think through a situation logically. Suspicion that someone else is to blame for something is impulsive, based on inability to think through a situation more completely or rationally. Suspiciousness may also arise from defensiveness growing out of a sense of personal inadequacy and a devastated self-concept.

Hypochondriasis: A focus on physical ailments and complaints may be a manifestation of self-centeredness. It may be easier for the individual who has experienced brain injury to understand the concrete, physical manifestations of the body while remaining confused about, or even unaware of, changes in thinking and mental capabilities. Thus, the person may focus on and exaggerate physical ailments.

Insecurity: This characteristic may underlie many personality changes following brain injury. There may be a pervasive sense that it is just too difficult to understand many things and may result in depression, withdrawal, defensiveness, denial, anger, or a host of other reactions.

Denial: In an effort to appear whole and unimpaired, an individual may deny that anything has changed or minimize any recognition of changes. Some persons are truly unaware that their behaviors have changed and will not realize the existence of problems. This produces unrealistic attitudes and/or weak excuses for their problems. Denial may be due to a combination of brain injury and psychological defense.

Apathy: Actually a form of denial, the person with a brain injury may show little interest in anything. This may stem from damage to specific areas of the frontal lobes. Apathy may also be a psychological reaction to protect against failures and insecurity. (If you are afraid to do something and don't do it, you can't fail.)

Lack of drive or motivation: Difficulty starting activities independent of motivation supplied by others reflects difficulty imagining and planning action steps and sequences in order to accomplish goals. This is almost always due to specific damage in the frontal lobes.

Emotional lability: Inappropriate or exaggerated laughing or crying is due to a loss of emotional control related to a damaged limbic system, frontal lobes, brain stem or other brain structures. Sometimes the individual will switch from high to low emotions unpredictably. Emotions may also be intense and appear suddenly. Chemical changes and injury to brain networks usually account for emotional lability.

Impulsivity and disinhibition: Impulsivity is observed when the individual acts or speaks without considering the consequences of actions, attempts tasks beyond his or her capabilities, and starts tasks before heeding full directions. Disinhibition (impulsive lack of self-restraint) is usually associated with changes in attention span and may be due to frontal lobe injury.

Weak tolerance for frustration: Giving up easily and an unwillingness to stick with tasks because they become extremely frustrating is usually caused by information overload and weakened ability to sort things out mentally, organize them, and take them step-by-step. The individual with a brain injury who finds many tasks frustrating must learn to take things slower and in smaller steps, and to acquire assistance where needed.

Rigid and inflexible thinking: When the individual is unable to understand and integrate the facts of a situation, a resulting lack of insight may appear as blatant and illogical arguing. This characteristic leads to poor decision making in general. Ironically, once a decision is made, even new facts or information acquired may not easily produce insight sufficient to change the original decision and thinking appears quite rigid.

Verbosity: An apparent inability to control the amount of talking one does sometimes results in incessant rambling. This usually reflects an ineffective attempt to gain attention, to make up for a sense of intellectual inferiority, or merely to avoid the fear of feeling left out. Rambling may be due to the person just feeling like he or she is unable to organize thoughts sufficiently to make a point. This, as well as other psychological consequences of brain injury, stems from a loss of sensitivity toward one's own behavior and toward the social situation as a whole. Verbosity may also reflect a physiological loss in the ability to stop a behavior once it is started.

Confabulation: Due to a combination of confusion, forgetfulness, and unwillingness to appear impaired, an individual may fabricate ideas that are partly or completely false. Bits and pieces of real or formerly understood information may be incorporated into a conversation the individual truly believes, being unaware of the inaccuracy. Sometimes confabulation masquerades as a tendency to be overly sure of something that everyone else knows is inaccurate.

Anger: If this is a personality change from preexisting characteristics, it usually reflects injury to limbic system structures and connections with the frontal lobes. It may be a raw emotional characteristic having no psychological basis at all. This type of anger must be treated medically rather than psychologically.

Fatigue: The brain requires a great deal of rest and sleep during healing. Fatigue can exhibit itself in irritability and unreasonableness.

potentials rather than on our "disabilities" or the things we don't do so well. As a lifelong adjustment strategy, we learn to disregard our inabilities. For example, someone might not have 20/20 vision but makes up for it with corrective lenses. Another person might not understand complex systems so avoids pursuing a career in brain surgery. Still, someone else might not understand mechanical stuff so hires work done on his car. Or, one might not feel comfortable relating to people so avoids social gatherings. All these minor disabilities seem small and inconsequential because we have put them in personal perspective and learned how to deal with them. We have merely learned what we are good at and what we aren't so good at. For anyone, brain injured or not, knowing how to manage strengths and weaknesses enables us to feel comfortable with ourselves.

So, too, with brain injury. Recovery means becoming comfortable with our abilities and weaker abilities rather than staying frustrated and irritated with hopelessly diminished abilities, constantly letting them haunt and torment us. The focus in rehabilitation is to sharpen residual skills and learn new ones, always working around the weaknesses. There is a limiting feeling about being disabled, about being something second class. There is a prideful feeling that can accompany being different, unique, something more than just normal. Achieving a perspective of wholeness is the key.

Despite the catastrophic results of traumatic brain injury, learning how to minimize disabling consequences is the real challenge. Doing, thinking, and saying whatever is necessary to see yourself as different, yet unique and self-respecting in the face of loss, disappointment, and permanent change is difficult but not impossible. Life change that comes suddenly can result in a feeling of powerlessness because it is so overwhelming. Building a perspective of pride, of making being different okay, represents healthy growth and positive psychological adjustment.

A fallacy in any illness or injury is to compare present functioning with what existed in the past. Most people experience, from time to time, at least some periods of dissatisfaction with their quality of life. If this becomes a persistent preoccupation, it will lead to loneliness and depression, and possibly even to becoming suicidal. The imbalance created by failing to accept the unchangeable, and to change what one can, defeats wholeness. Quality of life is defined in one's own terms, but help from others is valuable in developing a positive, self-accepting path.

Being Normal Again

The question often asked about a person with a brain injury is, "Will he or she ever be the same again?" The question often asked by persons who are experiencing brain injury is, "Will I ever be *normal* again." These questions reflect sadness and grief brought about by loss of the familiarity in the person. A brain injury produces physical change in brain tissue: some cells are lost, some are disconnected, some are damaged. The physical and emotional experience of the injury, intensive medical care, the process of rehabilitation, and time itself change one forever. There may be at least the threads of the familiar personality, interests, and characteristics, but everyone involved must adapt to a new uniqueness, a personality molded from the past and changed by the present, the physical and emotional effects of trauma, and a new view to the future.

It is defeating to wait for the old, "normal" person to come back after a brain injury. The person who has experienced a brain injury will never again be exactly the same. After the change in the once familiar person is mourned and the dramatic upheaval of changes settles down, the challenge of living begins anew. The new normal cannot be defined in terms of what was in the past.

"Recovery from" brain injury means "growing with" brain injury: restoring cognitive abilities where possible, accepting new ways of doing things, and modifying career or life plans. This change process is potentially lifelong, with periods of accelerated growth and periods of plateau during which little seems to be happening. Recovery with brain injury, in this sense, never stops. As humans, we are always striving for something—better self-acceptance, more learning, greater physical prowess, greater happiness and satisfaction.

The more we learn about brain injury and the functioning of the brain and mind, the more we respect the wonders of individuality. Modern neuroscience and psychology are complex fields of study. Current theories of brain functioning are fashioned after complex models of how billions of neurons work together in systems of neural networks. Even the most formidable of these theories actually includes a large measure of unpredictability and uncertainty. While we would always like to be able to predict with a high degree of certainty the effect and outcome of brain injury, this is just not possible. Instead, we are challenged to discover a new normal as recovery with brain injury progresses.

The similarities among the effects of brain injury are fairly universal: attention and memory changes, thinking changes, and emotional changes. Underlying these similarities are the differences of individual personalities. Uniqueness, not normality, gives us each a sense of importance, a sense of individuality. The common effects of brain injury force upon us the need to confront our new uniqueness. While this is usually unsettling at first, it becomes the enduring challenge. We all come, eventually, to the question, "Why be normal?"

Brain Injury in Children

The psychological concepts presented above apply to children and adults alike. However, there are certain differences in the brain injury and the recovery process in children that deserve special mention. There is both a physiological and a psychological difference in brain injury in a youngster still in the formative years of life.

From birth, the experiences of growing up paint themselves on the brain in the form of new neural connections and networks of related experiences. Basic skills in using the body and exceedingly complex personality and intellectual characteristics evolve on the brain's canvas.

Developmentally, children must learn certain basic things before they can learn advanced activities and ideas. Abstract concepts cannot be understood before basic, concrete ideas are mastered. Complex motor activities cannot be learned before basic, gross motor coordination is achieved. Experience and neural growth occur hand-in-hand. One cannot progress without the other.

From the vantage of brain plasticity (the capability of brain tissue to recover or form new connections), it would seem that children possess the potential to recover from brain injury more quickly and completely than would an adult. A child's brain develops rapidly and richly during the first fifteen years or so. At any age, the brain continues to change wiring to accommodate new learning and new experiences, however its actual growth in overall richness of cellular interconnections begins to slow sometime during adolescence. During the years when neural growth is advancing, damage would seem to be addressed aggressively by a brain that is still in the growth mode. Indeed, in many instances, children who have sustained traumatic brain injury seem to produce relatively minor lasting results as they become adults. Research shows that age, in general, correlates with quality of recovery in a negative relationship: the older you are, the less complete the recovery from brain injury appears to be.

The importance for rehabilitation of brain injury in a child, from the perspective of plasticity, is that recovery of impaired functions can sometimes be accomplished by backing up to an earlier stage of learning and starting over. This allows for the normal course of healing to duplicate what was once already accomplished, yielding fewer residual effects of the damage than might be the case in an adult brain. This neurodevelopmental strategy works well in formal rehabilitation. The brain must relearn fundamental skills before it can resume learning more complex skills.

There is a complement to this line of thinking, however. Because the youthful brain is less rich in its interconnections and less robust in its sheer size, damage to specific neural networks destined to serve a specific function, such as left hand and arm coordination, might be sufficiently and extensively damaged that adjacent nerve tissue cannot take over that function. In other words, while plasticity exists generally in a youthful brain, the availability of recovery of a *specific* function may be less likely if a very specific (and small) cellular network that exclusively serves that function is damaged beyond repair. In an adult brain, the size of the left hand and arm coordination network might be larger and more robust, involving a larger number of neurons and more wide-spread network configurations. Damage to portions of those adult networks might have less impact than very specific damage to the limited network configuration that has so far developed for that specific function in a child. Recovery, then, depends both on the extent of damage to specific brain areas and to the plasticity potential of the damaged cells (roughly reflected in the age of the individual).

There is really no way to know what the situation is initially in any child injured by brain damage. The lesson from the foregoing line of reasoning is that comprehensive assessment of functional changes must be done very early after a brain injury and neurodevelopmental training replicated in an aggressive rehabilitation program to encourage brain plasticity and recovery of functions.

The psychological side to brain injury in children is the disruption in, and vulnerability of, key social developmental stages. The child is in school, learning how to learn, learning who he or she is from a peer relationship standpoint, and learning his or her role within a family. When the child experiences a brain injury, all this development halts temporarily and learning, personal and social role formation, and self-identity formation become quite confused.

As with recovery of physical injury, rehabilitation of personal and cognitive injury from brain damage needs to be orchestrated, with sensitivity to the sometimes subtle effects of the brain injury. Just getting a child back into a normal classroom experience as soon as possible after an injury is usually not the appropriate route. Teachers, if not already trained in the effects of brain injury, must be educated to understand the needs of the child: slower-paced learning, less distractions, potential attentional problems, and greater organizational needs. The chaotic disruption in personal identity and emotional control may overshadow all other behaviors and needs.

Peer and sibling education is also important. Children need to understand that their classmate has experienced an injury that deserves understanding rather than jeers. Children are quite sensitive to their own potential weaknesses and often treat with disdain others who exhibit those dreaded weaknesses. Engaging children in a helping mode within a cooperative rather than competitive learning environment is usually best. Educational opportunity to learn respect and helpfulness, in the face of major individual differences can provide a foundation for acceptance, and respect, rather than prejudice.

Brain Injury in Adolescence

As the child becomes an adult, that dreaded in-between phase of life called "adolescence" can be particularly difficult if brain injury interferes. Adolescents face their own challenges in learning who they are, responding to peer pressures to conform, adapting to rapidly changing bodies and hormones, and figuring out what personality characteristics are appropriate and which result in social rejection. The tumultuous passage of adolescence is usually not very well appreciated by most people anyway, let alone when all this turmoil is further disrupted by brain injury.

As in the case with young children, special educational effort for parents, teachers, peers, and siblings needs focus on helping everyone understand the short-fused temper and the apparent lack of emotional control. Even more egregious and shockingly inappropriate behaviors need to be accepted and gently corrected. Self-loathing that results from suddenly becoming the underdog, and the frustration at having to return to school in special education classes can be humiliating. The gradual social shunning from the dating pool needs to be understood in an empathic way. The challenge is to initiate educational opportunity and sensitivity to the effects of brain injury as early as possible.

Formation of body image is a crucial evolution in adolescence. Its development is brittle in that the slightest deviation from that saintly standard—normality—can result in seemingly catastrophic emotional breakdown. While it may be hard enough for an adult to adjust to changes in how one sees his or her body after its function is tainted by brain injury, it can be devastating for an adolescent. A mild limp, a slight foot drag, an awkward pitching arm, tendency to get off balance easily and almost trip or fall, or failure to participate in normal gym class can draw unsettling attention to oneself.

While the subtle and not-so-subtle physical changes that often accompany brain injury might be dealt with relatively well within the confines of a hospital or rehabilitation ward, or even at home, they mushroom into ominous clouds when the adolescent must meet his or her peers at school, on the athletic field, or in any of those already awkward-enough courting situations.

Just as teachers, parents, coaches, and others provide a role model for the adolescent transition, so must they provide a particularly sensitive model for the adolescent who is also coping with a brain injury. This sensitivity can become quite trying at times because of the seemingly limited payoff. It is particularly important, however, for adults close to the adolescent who has experienced a brain injury to fortify themselves with regular doses of reminders of what the brain injury experience is like. Parental support groups, teacher in-service training, and supportive counseling are usually necessary to learn and sustain a supportive role.

Amidst all the physical and medical changes and concerns going on in a person who has experienced brain injury, the psychological changes have the most lasting and potentially damaging effects. While "brain injury" is a label that implies certain common consequences, it also heralds dramatic individual expression. An empathic acceptance of the person should result through appreciation of the complex interactions of coping resources, family dynamics, educational and work environments, and normal developmental processes.

Marty—Real Person

The best way that I can put it, before my brain injury I did not clown around as much as I do now. I do not get embarrassed as easily as I did before. I will do wild things and not feel bad about it. I am definitely not shy anymore. It is different to think of yourself before and after a head injury. Sometimes my only insight as to difference is what people tell me. My memory isn't so good anymore and I get dizzy real easy.

My injury was caused by getting hit by a car while I was loading up a stranded car on my tow truck. The car hit me going about forty-five, resulting in multiple injuries, including brain trauma. I was hospitalized for a week. I was unconscious for about three days. I don't remember being in the hospital at all. I think I remember coming home. I definitely remember that my whole life is very strange to me now.

The consequences of this injury have been lack of memory and difficulty finding words I want to use. Pressure is hard for me to take, so I have to take things slower in order to understand and make sense of things. I can't be around a lot of people because I start to "act up" and that embarrasses my wife and family.

The challenges that face me are that I need to learn to think again. That's mainly it. I need to learn to control my temper better. I get frustrated when things don't go as planned. I also get on laughing kicks that are hard to break.

Who am I now? Well, I still love my wife, my kids, and my family. It is very difficult to say who I am now. I don't very much know how I used to be before the injury. I'm learning how to be a real person again. I do volunteer work whenever I can find it. I don't drive so I'm learning to use buses and friends. I play golf. I enjoy company and a good laugh. I just wish I could stop laughing when everyone else does.

3

Diagnosis, Treatment, and Prognosis

Traumatic brain injury, particularly in milder form, begins as an inference, not necessarily a demonstrable fact. When someone hits his or her head or is involved in an accident where the head is struck, the *potential* for brain injury is there but is not necessarily sustained in every case. This is why it is crucial to distinguish between "head" and "brain" injury, and to further differentiate the injury into meaningful and treatable diagnoses. It is possible to incur a variety of injuries to structures of the head, the brain, or any combination. Proper understanding of injury begins with differential diagnosis. While diagnostic clarification may seem elementary, it is often overlooked.

When an injury is sustained to the head, contusion can occur as well to the scalp, face, shoulders, back, and neck. In an accident, because of its vulnerable position sitting atop the neck, the head is often violently moved side-to-side or forward-and-backward (referred to as "whiplash"). This extreme stretching movement, along with any contusions (or bruising) to the tissues of the head and upper body, can cause what is known as "soft tissue injury." This includes muscles, connective tissue, skin, and blood vessels. Bruising and stretching of ligaments and muscles can result in significant and often protracted weakness and pain. Such violent movement can also cause subtle but painful injury to vertebral (skeletal) structures in the neck. Headache is a very common occurrence secondary to soft tissue injury of the head, neck, shoulders, and vertebrae. Headache may or may not be a symptom of *brain* injury.

It is when the force of an injury to the head is sufficiently great—a direct blow to the head or severe shaking of the skull even without a direct blow—that potential *brain* injury can occur. Even then, the injury to the brain can range from mild, resulting in a dazed feeling for awhile, all the way to severe, resulting in a lengthy coma. Diagnostic clarity of the severity of actual forces applied to the brain, as well as to soft tissue or vertebral structures, is essential in understanding the consequences of an injury.

Other kinds of injury may result somewhat irrespective of the degree of force injury. Depending on individual vulnerability, a blow to the head, even a mild one, can result in a blood vessel breaking in the brain causing a stroke. A mild injury might cause a focal injury to a specific area of the brain while essentially sparing the rest of the brain. Fractures may occur in vulnerable parts of the skull, sinus bones, and delicate inner ear structures. Damage to the jaw, known as temporomandibular joint injury, can occur and result in or contribute to persistent headaches. Injury to inner ear nerves can contribute to dizziness, balance problems, headache, and nausea. Any number of nerve branches in the face, head, and neck can cause paralysis (weakness) or pain. Any of these symptoms can contribute to fatigue, irritability, weakened concentration, depression, and other problems.

In physical injury, there is always the potential for significant damage to the spinal column and to individual vertebrae. Violent movement of the head can stretch tendons, connective tissue, and intervertebral structures well beyond normal range of motion. Coupled with any of the injuries described above, this can cause pain and discomfort for a long time. Scapular and other shoulder injuries may further contribute to the problems associated with head and brain injury.

To make matters even more complicated, it is somewhat rare that an individual would sustain a head or brain injury without also sustaining injury to other body parts. Anything from cuts and scratches to severe internal organ damage can accompany an accident that also results in head injury. Compromised functioning of the organs of the body can compromise the body's overall healing process. Peripheral nerve damage can occur and must be differentiated from central (brain-specific) nerve damage.

The point is now probably well appreciated: differential diagnosis of head and brain injury is complex and must consider multiple anatomical systems. Differential diagnosis and understanding of the myriad sources of injury must be achieved before adequate treatment and rehabilitation can be undertaken.

As the sources of pain, cognitive problems, and emotional difficulties following a head injury are understood, complex injury becomes more manageable. It has been axiomatic in medicine for decades that 90 percent of the cure lies in the diagnosis. This certainly applies to the challenge of head and brain injury diagnosis where there are so many factors to sort out.

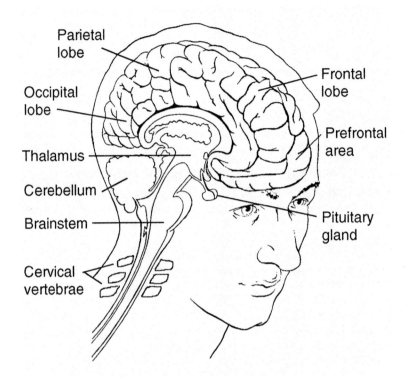

Figure 4. Twisting and hyperflexion of the head and neck during many types of traumatic injury may cause disruption in communication between the brain and the rest of the body. Injury to the atlas (first cervical vertebra) and axis (second cervical vertebra), as well as to the muscles and connecting tissues in the neck may occur in addition to injury to the brain.

Achieving Initial Diagnostic Understanding

Diagnosing brain damage requires astute observation, a myriad of medical tests, and time. Initially, emergency service personnel and emergency room physicians will make rapid assessment of consciousness, vital functions (breathing, heart rate, and temperature), complaints (or history from witnesses), essential health history, and the mechanism of what caused the injury. Physical examination will look for fractures, bleeding, and functioning of essential joints. Basic nervous system integrity will be examined. Ability to communicate with the individual will be assessed. Formal testing will be done of reflexes, muscle tone, pupillary reaction, eye movements, and ability to respond to commands. All this is accomplished in a few minutes by a trained emergency medical specialist. The physician will then observe for progression of symptoms, whether they begin to resolve or whether new symptoms begin to appear within the first minutes to hours after an injury.

Special neurological tests may be administered to help identify life-threatening bleeding or swelling in the brain. Computerized tomography (CT scanning) will usually be taken. If there is any suspicion of skull or vertebrae fractures, x-rays of the neck and back may be done. To assess brain electrical activity when there is compromise in level of consciousness, an electroencephalogram (EEG) may be obtained. Later on, to check for possible increase in intracranial pressure or to look for other brain structural abnormalities, magnetic resonance imaging (MRI) may be performed.

In the case of an individual sustaining potentially multi-system injuries, specialists may be called in to examine the individual. Pulmonary (lung), cardiac (heart), endocrinological or internal medicine (body chemistry and physiology), orthopedic (bones and joints), neurological (nerves), or neuropsychiatric (mental and behavioral) specialists might be asked to examine the injured person. The primary physician takes the responsibility for pulling all the sources of information together to establish the "big picture." It is this big picture of what is going on in the body and in the brain that begins to yield comprehensive diagnostic understanding. More than a label or two, diagnostic understanding is the dynamic appreciation of the interacting injury factors that are producing the clinical picture. It is through comprehensive diagnostic understanding that appropriate treatment priorities can be established and long-range predictions and treatment initiated.

Sometimes, clarification and diagnostic understanding may evolve for some weeks after an injury. The interaction of emergency medications and altered consciousness may mask some injuries that may become apparent only later on. As some symptoms resolve and others persist, clues to the nature and location of injury to bodily structures and to the brain will become more apparent. Sometimes, it may take detailed investigation into the mechanism of injury to understand the persistence of some symptoms.

To aid diagnostic understanding and selection of treatment options at various stages, families might consider keeping a detailed record of events. The boxed text provides suggestions for practical documentation. Although this may seem burdensome at a time when there is already enough going on, maintaining a well-organized, written (and filmed) record can be a very centering thing to do.

Many families of individuals with brain injury find that documenting the details of their experience can be both empowering and beneficial to the recovery of the patient. It helps those family members who are dealing with the situation to feel a sense of their own ability to help at a time when feeling helpless is the norm.

Medical Treatment for Brain Injury

Early on after a possible brain injury, diagnosis and early treatment are interwoven. Responses to treatment can provide diagnostic insights. Evolution of diagnostic hypotheses and clarification will direct further treatment options.

Keeping the Person Alive

The first action in the case of a possible brain injury, or other severe bodily injury for that matter, is to keep the individual alive. Emergency medical intervention is designed to do just that. Maintenance of appropriate body fluids, keeping the airway open, making sure blood pressure is sufficient to achieve proper circulation, and preventing deterioration of any physiological system that might endanger life are all part of the emergency response effort. Of course, many persons who

BOX 3-1—Practical Documentation

Families of an individual with a brain injury should document the accident site, course of the injury, diagnostic studies, treatment, responses, and significant events. This record will prove invaluable, not only as a memory aid during a time when a lot is happening, but as a chronicle documenting the evolution of events. Such documentation may become invaluable in providing a running record of observations, communications, and changes that may be crucial components in diagnostic and prognostic understanding as the individual gradually heals. A chronological record also helps provide order to what may seem like a chaotic situation.

A combination of written journal, copies of crucial documents, and photographs is invaluable. Use of still photos or motion video can provide a whole other perspective to the chronology of injury and healing.

Date and record these entries:

- Descriptions of where the accident occurred, what happened, who was involved

- Detailed observations of the behaviors of the persons injured Symptoms observed and complaints offered as they change over time

- Changes and improvements in behaviors and emotions

- Summaries of medical tests and their outcomes

- Summaries of meetings with doctors and treatment teams

- Advice and explanations communicated by doctors, therapists, nurses, insurance personnel, and other members of the treatment/ rehabilitation team (Always include full names of the people you talk with and write them down.)

- Outcomes from application of advice

- Results of agencies and resources contacted

sustain mild head injuries, which may or may not lead to actual brain injury, may not need all this extensive emergency intervention. If there is any change in consciousness, from confusion to coma, the total body needs to be attended to by emergency personnel. Experienced observation is essential in order to catch the sometimes subtle signs of brain injury as soon as possible.

In the case of a significant accident where the individual is at least confused or likely unconscious, a series of quick interventions is accomplished to sustain life and prevent further damage. A person suspected of having a head injury should be moved only by trained personnel with the right equipment necessary to stabilize the neck and head to prevent further possible damage.

Quick medical management is crucial if brain injury is suspected. Medicines may be used to stop seizures, control bodily fluids that might result in brain swelling, stabilize blood pressure, ease pain, or calm an agitated patient whose semi-conscious restlessness may cause him or her more harm or may even endanger treating personnel.

Minimizing Injury Cascade

Brain injury is not necessarily sustained only at the moment of impact. A cascade, or sequence, of injury processes can occur for hours after an injury, especially in the case of a severe injury. Changes in the body and brain's chemical and electrical neural functioning can result in toxicity and progressively more and more damage to tissues. Seizures may result within hours after a trauma. Chemical damage to nerve cells can occur if abnormal stretching of nerve fibers occurs (known as diffuse axonal injury). Medical intervention aims to prevent, slow, and reverse this cascade.

Many modern medicines are being introduced that retard the cascade of injury to neural tissue in the brain. These drugs block abnormal calcium and other ionic exchange across the neural cell membrane preventing further cellular damage. Certain drugs may neutralize the toxic effect of a sudden and lethal release of neurotransmitters (the brain chemicals that allow normal neural communications). Lowering body temperature very soon after an accident may also have a lifesaving and damage-reducing effect on the brain.

Healing Begins

Recovery needs to start as soon as possible after a brain injury. There is a steady transition between treating the immediate injury, managing the cascade, and facilitating the healing process, all occurring within minutes to hours of an injury. Two kinds of healing processes occur and interact with each other—spontaneous and directed recovery.

Spontaneous recovery refers to the body's own miraculous capability to heal itself. "Homeostasis" refers to normal balance in all body systems—structurally, chemically, and metabolically. Brain structures such as the thalamus and hypothalamus are responsible for maintenance of normal homeostasis in the brain and body. Within limits, these structures attempt to return the injured body and brain to normal functioning following injury. Unfortunately, the system isn't able to recover optimum homeostasis if key structures are damaged. Spontaneous healing may take a very long time and may be quite incomplete. It is said that the brain is the slowest healing organ of the body. Its complexity and the fact that it virtually controls the entire body makes this understandable.

Directed recovery refers to medical and various rehabilitation interventions that facilitate and complement spontaneous recovery where natural healing is insufficient or is impeded by critically damaged brain structures. Initially, directed recovery starts in the emergency room. As time progresses and the injured person's condition is observed, evaluated, and reevaluated, additional directed interventions may be necessary. These can range from surgical interventions to relieve muscle tightness caused by erroneous signals from the brain or damage to the neuromuscular junctures, to implementation of a variety of casting, electrical muscle stimulation, other physical therapy techniques, and medicines. Of course, long-range cognitive remediation and behavioral interventions may also be necessary to address the mental and emotional injuries. This would include teaching techniques to slow down thinking and organize thoughts, using strategies such as writing things down to improve memory, and prompting others to repeat what they say or to say things slower so that comprehension can be improved.

As time progresses after an injury, the effects of spontaneous and directed recovery are constantly evaluated. Although there are considerable individual differences that result from brain injury, as described in the previous chapter, there is a rather general course of recovery from the initial unconsciousness that defines brain injury. One of the scales frequently used to monitor such recovery is the Rancho Los Amigos Scale. (See boxed text.)

A variety of therapies, some considered experimental, may be implemented in individual cases to complement healing. Use of hyperbaric oxygen (saturation of body tissues with oxygen at greater than normal atmospheric pressure) is sometimes used very early on after a brain injury in an attempt to infuse brain tissue with the healing effect of oxygen. "Smart drugs" are being used to help stimulate regrowth of brain interconnections. Stimulant medications that act on the reticular activating system are sometimes administered to help "wake up" a patient who is in a coma. The big picture of the patient's injuries always needs to be preserved in order to choose the appropriate recovery techniques that will complement the natural healing process.

The long-range directed recovery process from brain injury is termed "rehabilitation." After medical stabilization, rehabilitation becomes a multifaceted intervention to help the individual recover damaged functions and to learn new ways for coping with damaged functions that cannot be completely recovered. Rehabilitation is usually intensive at first and then becomes gradually less intensive as time progresses. Rehabilitation can last indefinitely, as long as the individual is willing to learn new strategies for minimizing the disabling consequences of a brain injury.

BOX 3-2—Rancho Los Amigos Scale

The eight-level Rancho Scale is used to judge where a person is in terms of overall recovery from a brain injury. The scale covers a long range of time, from coma to maximum recovery. It is based on the generally observed sequence of recovery characteristics of the typical person with a brain injury. Since no one follows a stereotyped pattern, the scale provides only a general sense of where the individual is in terms of brain healing. The speed of movement of an individual through the stages reflected in the scale provides some sense of prognosis.

Level I, No Response: No response to pain, touch, sound, or sight. The individual is comatose and completely unresponsive.

Level II, Generalized Response: Generalized or gross, inconsistent, delayed, non-specific reflex responses (usually to pain) suggest emergence from coma.

Level III, Localized Response: Specific but inconsistent response to stimuli is seen such as eye blinks to strong light, turning toward or away from sound, responding to physical discomfort. Responses are inconsistent and delayed and usually reflect little awareness of what is actually going on. Some response bias may be demonstrated toward certain persons.

Level IV, Confused-Agitated: Alert, very active, aggressive, inappropriate, confused behaviors are seen within a broader context of poor attention span and only gross awareness of the environment. Motor functions are typically not purposeful. The individual responds mostly to internal confusion and shows poor discrimination of events in the environment.

Level V, Confused, Inappropriate, Non-agitated: Appearing alert but only grossly attentive to the environment, the individual is highly distractible and requires continual redirection and structure. Too much stimulation can bring on agitation. Social conversation may be inappropriate. Learning new tasks is difficult. Self-care behaviors are usually performed relatively well.

Level VI, Confused-Appropriate: Emerging orientation to time and place is inconsistent. New learning is retained only for a short while but the past is recalled somewhat and some learning carryover is observed.

Simple directions can be consistently followed and behavior can be goal-directed when assisted. Some awareness and recognition is evident but selective and still somewhat impaired.

Level VII, Automatic-Appropriate: Daily routines are performed in highly familiar environments in a non-confused but automatic and robot-like manner, often dependent on some external direction. Skills may noticeably deteriorate in unfamiliar environments. The individual lacks realistic planning and judgment, and problem-solving is impaired and unrealistic.

Level VIII, Purposeful-Appropriate: Alert, oriented, able to recall past and recent events, responsive to culture, and independent in routine behaviors that provide foundation for vocational rehabilitation. Some lingering judgment and problem-solving difficulties.

Prognostic Understanding

Constantly evaluating the big picture of all that is going on in a person with a brain injury (physiologically and psychologically), from emergency intervention to acute rehabilitation and long-term recovery, is essential in order to predict and facilitate recovery. Prognosis in the case of brain injury is not a simple matter. Prognostic understanding involves estimating potential recovery based on pre-injury level of functioning across many domains (motor, balance, memory, cognition, etc.). Prediction of physical adaptability is based on assessment of residual strengths necessary to plan physical therapy. Anticipated use of personal and family resources and vocational rehabilitation helps determine the course for cognitive intervention. The complex mix of ongoing diagnosis, prognosis, and treatment is progressively refined as the individual moves through recovery.

Just as simple diagnostic labels are grossly incomplete in understanding the consequences of brain injury, so too are prognostic terms like "good," "guarded," or "poor." It is the maintenance of the complete—and multidimensional—picture that really counts. Many questions must be asked, the answers guiding the appropriate selection of treatment intervention. What are the real sources of tissue damage and how extensive or limited is the damage? What is the expected permanency of the physical damage? What has the recovery picture looked like so far? What community resources are available to work with? What personal resources does the individual possess that will enable him or her to learn to cope and live with permanent injury consequences? The rehabilitation team, including the patient and his or her family, continually strives to obtain clearer and clearer answers to these questions through formal assessment, evaluation of treatment outcome, and frequent and open discussions.

Achieving both diagnostic understanding with prognostic understanding (what are the recovery expectations) requires extensive communications among treaters. The total treatment team is essential in painting the big picture of an individual's injury and consequences and refining the picture regularly. Physicians, psychologists, social workers, physical therapists, neurologists, neurosurgeons, internists, occupational therapists, speech therapists, nurses, case managers, family members, and friends need to get together to share observations and to seek a common ground of understanding. Multiple sources of information—including accident investigation reports, emergency response documentation, and pre-accident medical and educational records—need to be culled by the team and considered in assessing the individual's diagnostic and prognostic status, and to translate that into treatment.

A powerful concept to keep in mind as diagnostic and prognostic assessments are pursued is that the brain is dynamic. It's neural structures, interconnections, and chemistry are always changing. Unlike the more or less static structure and unity of function of other bodily organs, the brain must process unfathomable amounts of information, constantly learn and integrate new information, make decisions, and function both on a conscious and an unconscious level, even working while the body sleeps. The potentials inherent in the dynamic brain provide the foundation for ever-evolving change and growth.

BOX 3-3—Variables that Affect Recovery from Traumatic Brain Injury

The complexity of the brain is reflected in the array of potential variables that must be considered in achieving prognostic understanding of brain injury. Most brain injury health practitioners agree that these variables contribute, in varying ways and degrees, to the outcome from brain injury.

- Coma duration

- Glasgow coma scale score

- Prior brain injury

- Pre-injury physical health

- Pre-injury emotional health

- Alcohol or drug use pre-injury

- Intoxication at time of injury

- Secondary complications from trauma

- Extent of brain injury

- Localized versus generality of lesions

- Rate of recovery

- Pre-injury coping resources and attitudes

- Age at injury

- Intracranial pressure stability

- Blood pressure stability

- Systemic injuries

- Spinal cord injury

- Seizures

- Pain

- Extent of amnesia (memory loss)

- Extent of motor involvement

- Attitude of the patient

- Attitude of friends and family

"Brain reserve potential" is the term used to describe that portion of the brain's potential that lies in reserve for emergencies or unusual situations. Everybody has a reserve potential. Einstein called it the 90 percent of the brain few of us use. While that might be an overestimation, particularly after brain injury, the reserve capacity of the brain to muster extra energy and to do extraordinary thinking, must be tapped to facilitate healing and returning to a comfortable level of mental functioning.

Another term sometimes used to describe certain patients who spend a long time in rehabilitation is the "slow to recover" patient. This refers to the individual who appears to be making functional progress but whose recovery is inordinately slow. Sometimes this is due to the severity of injury, complicating medical factors, complicating personal or family factors, or lack of financial resources to purchase more aggressive rehabilitation. Whether fast or slow, rehabilitation needs to be monitored with ongoing whole-team communications. This would include assessment revisions in diagnostic and prognostic understanding, and treatment success.

Rehabilitation and Recovery

If the primary goal of emergency medical management is to keep the body alive, the primary goal in rehabilitation of the person with a brain injury is to keep the spirit alive. Catastrophic emotional, social, and physical reaction is common in severe brain injury, and sometimes even in mild brain injury. This can lead to profound discouragement. Such a reaction can only weaken spontaneous healing and defeat attempts at directed recovery. In every case of brain injury, mild to severe, directed recovery in the form of rehabilitation needs to be a part of the total diagnosis-treatment-prognosis effort. The foundation of rehabilitation must be hope, realistic appraisal of the situation, and encouragement to achieve a personal best.

In cases of mild brain injury the individual might see only an emergency room doctor for a few minutes. The individual may be discharged with a head injury checklist, receiving little to no education about what brain injury means. This can leave an individual scared, confused, and exceedingly worried about why he or she isn't just jumping back to normal functioning. Many people who receive no follow-up treatment or education regarding a possible mild brain injury create in themselves high anxiety, depression, and diminished self-worth. They feel they have lost control over their lives, their temper, their ability to communicate, and their ability to stay mentally organized. All these may be normal consequences of mild traumatic brain injury but unless someone helps the injured person understand these things, the frustration can increase to a compounded situation. At the very least, an individual who has sustained a mild brain injury should have a visit with a neurologist, neuropsychologist, or other health provider who specializes in treating the comprehensive consequences of brain injury.

Whatever resources one finds to help maintain the big picture throughout the course of treatment and rehabilitation, it is important to clarify expectations and reality. Prognosis is a bit trickier than diagnosis because some aspects are more subjective. Often, our subjective wishes and emotionally-laden expectations get in the way of reality. Of course, we want to (and should) be positive and expect the best. It is psychologically important to have a positive expectation. Knowing at least something of what to expect of one's self down the road reduces anxiety. Within this concept of realistic prediction and expectation there is a companion concept just as important—hope.

Hope is more vague and is not dependent on specific goals or expectations. Hope is the undercurrent of rehabilitation. Hope is reflected in the statement, "What will be, will be; we will adjust." It is not merely an idle wish but a determination that things will improve through active rehabilitation and in whatever way nature takes its course.

Brain injury leaves a person different, in some ways for life. Part of the expectation from rehabilitation is that the person will recover as much as possible, but also recognizing that that means there will be some residual, permanently altered functioning. Despite the changed functioning and the need to think and do things differently than before the injury, it is commitment to a positive, conquering attitude that allows wholeness back into life and for hope to evolve, accepting change and seeking contentment with that change. Commitment to learning about the brain and doing what it takes to make it work at its best despite impairment is a significant key to recovery. If one stays singly focused only on the wish for a full recovery of former functioning, without compromise, disappointment will surely beset the family and the person injured.

Special Problems for Diagnostic Clarification

In addition to the general cognitive and personality changes that typically accompany brain injury presented in the previous chapter, a few special problems are discussed below that require special diagnostic and prognostic clarification. These problems typically need clarification as to their causes and consequences for long-term brain health and rehabilitation.

Sometimes, in persons who have sustained brain injury, a psychiatric-like diagnosis might be given for a special problem or behavior that emerges. This shortcut method for describing behavior is unfortunate. Usually, such a diagnostic label is not meant to imply that the individual is psychiatrically disturbed, something separate and apart from brain injury, but unwittingly it carries that connotation. Any label, particularly a psychiatric label, presents the risk of failing to look deeper—beyond the label, for a neurological or medical explanation. Labels often refer to a behavior, such as "obsessive-compulsive" behavior. The label does not explain underlying factors that might explain the behavior. Thus, one should not settle for a label without, at least, asking, "What would cause such behavior?"

Of course, there are cases where a psychiatric condition coexists with or is modified by brain injury. Sometimes a brain injury can lower the threshold for expression of problematic behaviors that existed at a mild or subclinical level before the injury. As with brain injury itself, special problems deserve careful and complete diagnostic understanding.

Obsessive-compulsive behavior

In the case of obsessive-compulsive behavior, certain acts are performed over and over again, such as hand washing or repeatedly testing a locked door knob. Some people who sustain brain injury incur physical and/or chemical damage to certain frontal lobe areas which cause such behavior. In fact, persons exhibiting obsessive-compulsive behaviors who have not incurred brain injury are now being treated with a medication that helps supply the frontal lobes of the brain with more of a certain neurotransmitter that will prevent such behavior. It is exactly that same neurotransmitter that can become less effective as a consequence of certain kinds of brain injury. Hence, psychiatrists are learning more and more that certain kinds of troubling behaviors may indeed have their roots in brain dysfunction rather than being a purely psychological (i.e., learned) or emotional (i.e., reactionary) problem.

Photosensitivity

Injury to any number of structures in the visual system from the eye to the occipital cortex has the potential to produce an uncomfortable sensitivity to light. Preferring to remain in darkened places and to wear sunglasses, persons with this condition are disadvantaged in their ability to adjust to environments. Usually, photosensitivity is accompanied by other visual symptoms that interfere with reading, recognition of objects, or integrating a lot of visual stimulation at one time. The problem of photosensitivity, and its potential for recovery, needs to be taken into account in understanding, specifically, where brain injury might have occurred and what functional impact this may have.

Over time, as the brain heals, the degree of photosensitivity may decline some. The individual who experiences this condition must learn to use adaptive devices just as a person who has declining visual acuity. Use of tinted lenses and adjustable room lighting may need to be as much a part of everyday adaptation as would be the use of eyeglasses to correct an acuity deficiency.

Hyperacusis

Hyperacusis is an abnormal sensitivity to sounds and the inability to modulate sound reception. As with photosensitivity, the nervous system network responsible for taking in sounds and processing them meaningfully includes a combination of inner ear and brain networks. These can become damaged, making sounds seem much louder and very much more disturbing than they did before the injury. Understanding the cause of hyperacusis and respecting the impact this problem has on restricting environments, travel, interaction with others, and quality of life in general is essential in diagnostics and prognostics. The person with hyperacusis may withdraw and seem irritable and tense much of the time. The impact of this sensory abnormality can have far-reaching emotional and behavioral consequences in the disturbance it causes in everyday functioning.

Depression

For the same reason that obsessive-compulsive behavior might have its foundation in the ineffectiveness of a neurotransmitter in certain brain areas, so too may depression have its roots in abnormal brain chemistry. Some of the same medications that are used to treat obsessive-compulsive behaviors are being found very effective in treating the forms of depression that often accompany frontal brain injury. Neurotransmitter sacs that exist at the ends of neurons can be damaged during trauma. If the chemicals these sacs hold cannot do their job as well as they did before the injury, emotional and behavioral changes occur. One of those changes can be depression.

Of course, depression, the sad mood and flat emotions that can overcome some people quite profoundly, can have many causes, some physiological as in the case of brain injury, and some psychological as in the case of experiencing a loss of a loved one or even the loss of self-esteem. Hence, the cause of depression needs differential diagnosis in order to be treated appropriately. Depression, as well as obsessive-compulsive behavior, anger, or even crying and laughing uncontrollably, is not simply a sign of weakness in the individual character. These problems can be signs of brain damage that need to be understood in terms of their causation just as cognitive problems of memory and thinking need to be understood. Without comprehensive and accurate understanding, appropriate treatment cannot be initiated.

Treatment for depression frequently involves a combination of medical and psychological intervention, depending on the cause of the depression. Medications help change the brain chemistry to lift a mood. Psychotherapy teaches the individual how to change thinking habits that change one's emotional experience.

Crying and Laughing

In some persons with brain injury, the links between the frontal lobes and other, deeper structures of the limbic system and brain stem become broken. This causes what is known as disinhibition. Most people are capable of displaying emotions in a controlled fashion, appropriate to the social environment. However, if the brain cannot inhibit the crying or laughing impulse, these behaviors may become excessive and occur with little provocation and then be difficult to stop. Again, if these behaviors are uncharacteristic for the individual and seem to bother the individual because he or she cannot easily control them, this is a sign of brain dysfunction, not personal weakness. Neuropsychological examination and understanding the brain areas of injury can help identify the nature of these behavioral problems.

Because the cause of disinhibition, laughing, crying, or a number of other behaviors associated with brain injury is complex, treatment is often targeted in more than one direction. Different medications focus on changing the chemistry in specific brain regions. But even the correctly-targeted medication may not compensate for extensively damaged neurons. Broad psychological interventions may help deflect inappropriate thinking, help improve self-awareness and behavioral self-controls, or help the individual and the family accept and manage behaviors that cannot be changed or eliminated entirely.

Anger

As with other emotional inappropriateness, anger can have its roots in brain dysfunction. As with excessive crying and laughing, anger can occur because of the individual's inability to inhibit irritating thoughts or because of chemical irritation in the limbic system. Anger can stem from injury to specific parts of the brain that results in emotional releases that are inappropriate and even potentially dangerous. Reactive anger, on the other hand, is rather easy to understand as daily life can be filled with irritating events when the individual finds he or she doesn't have the motor control that was once familiar, doesn't have the social control others expect, and gets mentally lost easier than ever. Frustration, once usually constrained to a few choice words, might erupt into full blown rage.

To some extent, medical treatment can address anger that is directly precipitated by brain injury. Often, antiseizure medications are used to help maintain an inner calm and to prevent the nervous system from exploding into anger at the slightest provocation.

Seizures

A seizure is an uncontrolled burst of electrochemical activity in a particular area of the brain. A seizure may remain confined to a small area of the brain or may become widespread. Seizures are particularly important in prognostics. The unpredictability of seizures places an individual at great risk of injury for certain work situations, driving, or other activities. Uncontrolled seizures can cause further injury to the brain as errant electrical impulses fire over and over again. Thus, seizures represent another special problem associated with brain injury that deserves thorough diagnostic clarification as to causation, location in the brain, implications for broad neuropsychological functioning, and treatment planning.

In summary, understanding these special behavioral and emotional problems requires sensitivity to the unique nature of brain injury that might account for them. It is crucial to avoid the advice, "If you'd just stop this anger (or crying, or being depressed) you'd feel much better." The homespun advice to "try harder" just doesn't work in these instances. Diagnostic sensitivity is required to understand the behaviors and emotions in terms of their *physiological* and *psychological* causes and to focus on a treatment that will allow the individual to regain a sense of self-control. Without such diagnostic understanding and appropriate treatment, behavioral and emotional dyscontrol only erodes the individual's self-confidence more and more because he or she recognizes it is not simply a matter of not trying hard enough.

Mary—Real Person

After twenty-six years of "institutionalization" in corporate America, I decided to take back my own life. I loved bowling and, low and behold, there it was in the job opportunity ads: Wanted—assistant manager at South Bowl. I had been bowling for 12 years, became a certified youth bowling coach, and was secretary for a league. I got the job! The next two years were spent getting to know the bowlers, working with the children, and patrolling the teenagers in the pool room. My rules were law and the kids followed them! Life was busy, happy, and free.

One night one or more scumbags hid up in the ceiling of the bowling alley restroom. After I had locked the doors and was filling out my nightly reports, they slithered down and attacked me and beat me with a pool cue. My thoughts at the time were that maybe I made someone angry for enforcing my rules. I was beaten unconscious, got three broken ribs, and lots of bruises on my head and face. Of course my broken heart was the worst wound. Somehow, but I don't remember it, I was able to call 911. I spent four days in the hospital and endless weeks at home recuperating.

Since the attack, I've seen dozens of doctors, taken way too many neuropsychological tests, and found out all the problems my new life now has to offer. I am so dizzy I get sick a lot. I take a medication for that but it causes a potassium shortage, so I have to take extra potassium and eat a lot of bananas. No one knows why my lungs fill with fluid but I take a medication for that too, and stay on a low sodium diet. I can't be on my feet long so I can't work and someone has to drive me anywhere I want to go. I just found out I have a thyroid problem, which I probably had before my injury but which is now made worse by the antiseizure drug I have to take.

Like most everyone else, I hear about people being robbed and beaten but I was sure it could never happen to me. I was always so sure of myself that I could handle anything and anyone. My pride is gone now that I realize I'm not a super-person. I am angry about what happened. The memory I was so proud of is less than perfect now, something I still need a lot of help with. The ability to read and understand what I read is at a low ebb, but with practice it is getting better. I'm still working on walking straight without using the wall or my cane.

I used to bowl a 175 average. I want to do that again whenever I can pick up a ball again. I used to take things for granted but I don't do that anymore. Most of all I want to rid my heart and mind of the hatred I feel for those despicable strangers that beat me up.

Who am I? That never used to be a difficult question to answer. I'm now the lady who spends so much time at doctor's offices (who always seem to find one more thing wrong with me). I'm the expert on TV programs. Ask me when a program is on and I can probably tell you. That's one thing I never used to be able to do. (wry grin) I have talents for crafts but I haven't picked up a crochet hook, haven't gone to the quilting frame, and haven't picked up a paint brush since my injury. Some days I believe I've lost the will to live until I remember how hard I fought to stay alive lying, bleeding behind the counter on the bowling alley floor. I fought to stay alive when my lungs filled with fluids and I nearly had congestive heart failure.

Well, I don't know for sure who I am right now. I know I'm still a fighter. I know what I want. Ask me again next year; I'm still working on the answer.

[Two years later: Mary returned to the bowling alley and runs the counter again. On busy nights she needs extra help that she didn't need before. She never works alone after the doors are locked. She drives short distances now without difficulty. She's still happy that she left her corporate job and can work where she's really free. She finally was able to go back to bowling and just recently bowled her first-ever 200 game.]

4

Suddenly a New Brain

The brain is a dynamic, ever-changing organ. Every time we think about something, learn something, listen to a new piece of music, write or draw something, or encounter anything new, our brain's wiring changes. That is why and how we remember things, dream up new and creative ideas, and do things we haven't done before. Connections among nerve cells constantly grow and change their activation potential (sensitivity) to fire a signal. Some connections become more inhibited as newer ones fire more frequently. This is all very complex, involving billions of nerve connections, but change is the nature and purpose of the brain.

Despite constant change, each individual's brain functions with a measure of underlying regularity or predictability. This, essentially, is what we refer to as one's personality—that relatively stable set of ways of thinking and behaving that is unique to each of us. Each of us reacts to things, does things, accepts or rejects ideas, and has attitudes and beliefs which are generally consistent over time. This is what gives us our character. People with whom we interact become comfortable, or at least familiar, with our unique character and come to know us by these more or less predictable qualities.

When the brain is damaged it disrupts the familiar way in which the individual's brain functions. If damage causes a change in consciousness, which it almost always does, the degree of change in consciousness reflects the severity and extent of brain cell disruption. As consciousness returns to the damaged brain, residual effects of damaged cells remain—essentially forever.

Once the brain sustains more than trivial damage, it never recovers its wiring configuration exactly as it was just prior to the damage. There are essentially two reasons for this. First, the period of physiological repair (recovery) usually takes months. During that time, the individual continues to experience and think new things that would configure the wiring differently anyway. Hence, a combination of new experiences and normal biological healing produces changes in wiring. Second, dead or severely injured brain cells cannot rejuvenate. Therefore, the course of healing must find ways around nonfunctional cells, producing a wiring configuration different from before, much different in injuries with major and widespread damage.

Actually, there is a third reason for permanent change after injury that exists in some cases. If a focal area of the brain sustains a significant concentration of damaged cells, the function of that specific brain area is now permanently and often radically changed. For example, the language area of the brain exists in certain portions of the left hemisphere. If there is a concentration of damage in that particular area, the individual will always have difficulty with language, possibly even permanently losing language skills. No amount of healing or learning compensation strategies will return the language capabilities that existed prior to the injury.

The change in brain structure due to damage creates what amounts to a new brain, with residuals of the old brain present, but often with some pretty disturbing functional changes that challenge the patience and adaptation of any injured person. Brain damage results in a new personality that has threads of the old and some unique qualities added in.

The Magnificent Brain

The brain consists of an estimated 100 billion nerve cells. Nerve cells are not connected one-on-one with each other in a chain but are arrayed in networks with multiple interconnections and loop back connections, resulting in an estimated 60 trillion (that's 60 with 12 zeros) possible connections at any one point in time. That means that when the brain processes any thought, nerve signals can traverse vast spaces of brain tissue. Just imagine what happens when you hear a train whistle. The memories of sights, images of places and experiences, smells, emotions, and more are aroused from a simple auditory input to the brain. This is because of the richness of the brain's interconnections. One single sound of a train whistle might activate tens of thousands of brain cells—all in an organized and meaningful manner to produce rich memories and emotions.

So that the brain can maintain some sense of organization and order, the billions of nerve cells are clustered into network-like structures so that nerve signals remain primarily within and linkup with specific networks. If a brain activity involves moving part of the body, then gradually only the networks that linkup with signals going to body muscles get activated, and strengthened. That is why when you play tennis you usually don't think about algebra, what you did last night, or the movie you saw a week ago. Your brain maintains a focus on what you have learned about tennis and sends signals to the right places to activate the right muscles, achieve coordination and timing, maintain visual focus, concentrate, and so forth in order to play tennis. If you are a highly competitive personality, your whole game and reaction to it may be different than if you're not highly competitive, again depending on your unique wiring.

Conscious brain activity requires attention. Structures deep in the base of the brain maintain the alertness of the rest of the brain and sustain focused activation of selected areas depending on circumstances. Other structures in the center of the brain relay incoming signals from the senses to appropriate interpretation areas of the cortex of the brain where meaning is achieved. Cortical integration areas connect with other brain structures to activate old memories and lay down new ones. Related ideas are recognized by brain areas and strengthen those connections while weakening those that don't matter. There's a lot going on simultaneously in the brain, most of it without our conscious awareness.

While we often speak of the "normal" brain, there really is no such thing. True, people think along similar lines and interact relatively smoothly because we learn *common* things like rules, conventions, and so forth. However, each of us has a personality (a basic brain wiring pattern) that is just as unique as our fingerprint, albeit infinitely more complex than a fingerprint. There's no denying that we recognize people more by their personalities than we do by any other characteristic. Personality is the configuration of neural networks that brands each of us unique.

The unique wiring of the brain, the personal pattern of memories, the individual ways of dealing with situations, the way one thinks about himself or herself, all interacting with physique, voice quality, gestures, posture, and physical characteristics make each person different. The neurological basis for this complexity becomes overwhelming when all these elements are considered to produce the one-in-three-billion individual. Like a well tuned engine, the brain sustains balanced and predictable functions consistent with the personality that it reflects. When something in the engine breaks, its functions are no longer smooth or predictable.

Magnificence Gone Awry

When the brain is damaged, it takes on a different quality of magnificence in its gallant effort to keep working. Despite its damage, it still tries to do what it knows best. It still wants to think and produce language, although it may do so in strange and peculiar ways that others don't understand very well. It attempts to move muscles to accomplish tasks but may do so with awkward coordination, strength, or rhythm. It communicates and interacts with people but in incomplete ways that appear childish or confusing to others. It works hard to maintain a sense of moment-to-moment continuity but has a difficult time doing so because it isn't laying down continuous memories like it used to, or the memories are fragmented, poorly retained, or confused. All this produces behavior that is strange and no longer familiar, both to the person with the brain injury and to those around him.

"Brain injury" is about as broad a concept as is "normality." Each concept, brain injury or normality, is unique to the individual. While we have a good idea of what is normal in the sense of usual, it is a bit more difficult to conceptualize what we understand as brain injury. The injury starts with the physical aspects but is manifest in the psychological or behavioral consequences. We usually can't see brain injury the same way we can see a broken arm or a laceration or some other injury condition. The effects of brain injury are in the behavior and personality of the individual.

Once the wiring of the brain is suddenly changed, as in traumatic brain injury, automatic healing and compensation mechanisms kick into gear. The body, including the brain, functions on the basis of homeostasis. The concept refers to the drive or tendency to maintain internal balance by adjusting whatever physiological processes are necessary in order to return the system to equilibrium. Thus, once damage occurs to brain tissue, biological systems react to that injury. Sometimes the reaction is really not desirable, as in tissue swelling or sudden ionic changes that occur across neural cell membranes. On a larger scale, the brain attempts to recover doing what it is supposed to do in ways that are familiar to it. Over the long run—days to months—it attempts to regrow connections (but not necessarily new cells) in order to function as close to the way which it used to function. This homeostatic tendency is akin to spontaneous healing that was discussed in the previous chapter.

The "3-A's" of Brain Injury

Aside from motor and coordination problems, known as *apraxia*, the more obvious challenges that face the individual who has sustained brain injury are in cognitive functioning—thinking and using what we usually refer to as "intellectual resources." The term *agnosia* refers to injury to systems of sensory recognition and perceptual meaning. *Aphasia* refers to impairment in communication systems.

Agnosia occurs when the sensory signals to the brain (from the eyes, ears, and skin) are not connected correctly with the brain networks that provide accuracy and precision in recognizing things and how they are used. Agnosia is the brain's error in perception.

Agnosia can manifests itself in difficulty with sensitivity to fine sensory discrimination. Signals sent from the body to the brain are incomplete or erratic. A person with agnosia might not recognize common objects by touch alone. Handed a pencil, without looking at it, the individual might describe it vaguely as a rod or a stick. When told to look at the object, the individual instantly recognizes it as a pencil. Agnosia manifests itself in subtle to obvious difficulty recognizing things by touch as well as by sight. Even familiar objects might not be recognized or may be confused with other objects.

Trouble precisely identifying a pencil by touch alone may seem insignificant. However, using a pencil requires that the brain know what the object is. If a person has trouble recognizing an object without looking at it, it is fairly certain that the brain is going to go through some confusion in coordinating the proper use of the object unless the object is held constantly in sight. Again, this may seem trivial or insignificant but several little incidents of lack of recognition of objects, or reliance on looking at objects constantly while using them (which was unnecessary prior to the injury), indicate the fragile and suboptimum functioning of the brain.

Agnosia can run the gamut of subtle to obvious. If obvious, such as virtual inability to recognize common objects by sight or touch or sound, the impact on communication and ability to function in a once-familiar environment is devastating. If subtle, such as confused ability to recognize objects unless one is looking directly at them, agnosia by itself may have a relatively less severe impact on adjustment to brain damage. However, even subtle agnosia would rarely exist as the sole consequence of brain injury. Combined with many other relatively minor consequences of brain injury and significant impact on overall mental functioning can loom large.

A special form of agnosia exists when an individual is virtually unable to perceive that his or her bodily or mental functions have changed as a result of brain injury. *Anosagnosia* suggests that with certain kinds of brain injury, there occurs loss of awareness of injury itself.

Agnosia, in its various manifestations, is usually best dealt with through adaptation. If spontaneous recovery does not occur, the individual will need to learn ways to work around the agnosia. Some individuals learn to rely on a different sense (as described above). Some use labels profusely to help identify objects. An individual who acquires *prosopagnosia*, difficulty recognizing faces, must learn consciously to associate awareness of other characteristics to identify a person, such as hair length, height, sound of voice, and so forth.

Apraxia is caused by the brain's inability to communicate among those neural structures necessary to achieve meaningful and coordinated motor activity. Inability to draw a clock face and place the numbers and hands in the correct place depicting 6:42, by an individual who otherwise can tell time, suggests apraxia. Difficulty tying ones shoes, not because of injury to joints or peripheral nerves, but because of the brain's inability to access motor sequence patterns smoothly and accurately, suggests apraxia.

As with agnosia, apraxia can result from brain damage in subtle ways or obviously disabling ways. The ability to carry out a simple task of screwing a light bulb into a socket might present a challenge to an individual exhibiting subtle apraxia. While the intention is there, the actual motor process is quite complex—aligning the threads correctly, twisting the bulb counterclockwise to seat the threads properly, then twisting clockwise (and knowing what direction clockwise is), and remembering to hold the bulb until the threads are sufficiently meshed or else the bulb will fall out when the hand is removed to prepare for another twist. Feeling for the snugness of fit is necessary or else the bulb will remain too loose or become tightly jammed into the socket.

Until we pause and consider the myriad mental (that is, brain-controlled) nuances involved in this task, it is easy to fail to recognize how frustrating it could be if the brain's ability to handle all these subtleties is amiss.

Many forms of dysfunction acquired following brain injury, including apraxia, require adaptation through cognitive compensation. Somehow we learn how to screw in a light bulb essentially without thinking. When the brain mechanisms are insufficiently able to do it successfully, such as after a brain injury, the individual still may be able to accomplish the task by consciously thinking through each step of the task. The success of being able to do this depends on the degree of injury.

After brain injury, some individuals must learn to walk only with patiently guided physical therapy. Learning, consciously, to recoordinate putting one foot down in front of the other in careful succession may restore walking. However, learning to coordinate running again may be considerably more difficult or even impossible. Running requires coordinated movements much more complex and executed much more rapidly than walking. Thinking fast enough to send the neural signals necessary for running may be too demanding for a damaged brain.

Rehabilitation of apraxia involves a combination of learning to do things again through conscious awareness, practice, and learning to adapt to life without performing some activities one was used to. This is the typical mix of rehabilitation: relearning and compensation.

Aphasia is the difficulty producing (expressing) and/or understanding (receiving) speech or language. Language is a complex brain process linking speech with vocal-motor actions, interpreting and producing the intonation and emotional content of speech, and maintaining a continuous flow of language that has grammatical structure. As with agnosia and apraxia, aphasia problems can be subtle, as in simple word-finding hesitations, to major, as in virtual inability to formulate speech or understand language.

As always, recognizing the subtle problems in speech and language requires sensitivity and awareness. Difficulty finding the word that describes a pencil may seem like a minor inconvenience. But, if this difficulty is experienced several times in the course of a conversation, frustration mounts rapidly, the pace of conversation slows, speech becomes halting and jagged, self-confidence wanes, and overall communication is compromised. Magnify this many times over when the individual has difficulty formulating a simple expression and you get the picture of expressive aphasia.

Receptive aphasia can be even more frustrating than expressive aphasia because the individual appears locked out when others attempt to communicate. Again, the receptive aphasia may be virtually complete or may be subtle and scattered throughout conversation. Often, persons with receptive aphasia cannot link the sound of a word and the meaning of it stored in the brain. If the brain does finally make a delayed link, there may be almost a startle response, as if the brain suddenly jumped into gear for a moment.

A speech and cognitive therapist is extremely helpful in diagnosing the kinds of brain problems that cause aphasia. The therapist can offer exercises that help the brain form new connections, at least as much as possible. Learning again to produce speech or understand language requires patience, practice, and professional guidance.

While these explanations and examples of agnosia, apraxia, and aphasia are brief, the intention here is to illustrate the complexities and sometimes subtleties of brain dysfunction. Even apparently mild changes in how the brain processes information can have a devastating impact on behavior. The simple task of using a pencil requires vast brain processes. Even one weak link in the chain of brain communications can cause noticeable impairment. If sensory signals are impaired, the individual may inappropriately grip the pencil too hard causing the lead to break easily. Impaired motor signals may cause the pencil to drop from the hand unexpectedly. Inability to think of the right words to write with a pencil renders it functionally useless. Impaired brain signals affect our usual functions in many ways. Awareness of these changes is the first step toward regaining control over them.

As emphasized in Chapter Three, comprehensive diagnosis of the functional effects of brain injury, from the obvious to the subtle, is necessary in order to initiate appropriate treatment. Many individuals, both those with mild as well as more severe brain injury, often become extremely frustrated, angry, and depressed because neither they nor anyone else recognized a problem directly related to the injury. When problems go unrecognized and undiagnosed, the individual may deteriorate in job functioning, may find that interpersonal and family relationships suffer, and may eventually feel like he or she is going crazy.

If a brain-related functional problem is recognized and understood, a combination of therapy to improve the situation and adapt to the problem can be accomplished.

Everything Changes

Traumatic brain injury produces change in almost every aspect of life. For the individual who experiences a relatively mild injury, the experience of change may be very personal and an agonizingly lonely experience. Family and friends may minimize or even trivialize the injury as it seems to produce little, if any, noticeable effect on consciousness and the person seems essentially normal. For the individual who experiences a more severe injury, with a period of obvious unconsciousness and a period of recovery, perhaps having sustained other bodily injuries as well, change is more obviously noticed. Paradoxically, persons who are more severely injured may be the ones failing to sense anything wrong initially (anosagnosia; see above), while family and friends see obvious impairment all too easily. In any event, recovery from traumatic brain injury involves a process of adapting to change.

As has been discussed already, healing involves both the body's physical repair of brain tissue and the psychological process of adjusting to changed brain wiring. Two cognitive processes are almost universally observed in persons who have sustained brain injury: memory impairment and slower mental processing speed. Sometimes subtle, sometimes quite obvious, these functional changes in how the brain works underlie and impact virtually all other consequences of brain injury.

Memory Change

The memory system of the brain is not exclusively localized in a specific brain structure. While there are areas that are crucial to the initiation of memory storage and for retrieving old memories, it is believed that memories are actually stored throughout the brain's cortex. Thus, it is understandable that scattered injury throughout the brain, as in diffuse axonal injury, can impact the availability and accessibility of memory. Laying down new memories is a complex process, partly dependent on the interconnectedness of memories already in the brain. If the old memory networks are damaged, even a little bit, laying down new memories will be affected.

Closely tied to the memory system is the attentional system. The brain's ability to maintain attention and mental focus on one thing, and to shift among thoughts that demand our attention, is located within a relatively specific area deep inside and at the base of the brain. This area of the brain is particularly vulnerable to injury whenever the brain moves rapidly inside the skull. Stretched and damaged networks inside the reticular activating system in the brain stem can impair the ability to pay attention.

Thinking Speed Change

The other hallmark of brain injury is in changed mental processing speed. This change is also easy to understand in light of scattered, diffuse injury. It is simply going to take the brain more time to circumvent damaged cells in order to think. Everyone has experienced memory lapses or blocked recall of some memory. This is magnified in persons who have sustained brain damage and accounts for pervasively slower thinking. The time it takes to get mentally organized, to figure out how to do something, even something once very familiar, is longer.

It is easy to see how slower thinking, even just a little slower compared with before the injury, can create frustration. Difficulty learning and recalling information may make one feel ignorant. Forgetfulness and absentmindedness can occur due to poor functioning of the attentional system. Anger and frustration among family members and coworkers can put pressure on the individual to try to do better but who really can't do better because of the limitations imposed by the brain damage. This can escalate to significant frustration and emotional turmoil.

A Host of Changes

Behaviorally and socially, change becomes obvious, usually more so the greater the amount of damage to the brain. Memory and mental processing systems are closely tied to the emotional control centers of the brain. Damage to the limbic system, which includes the temporal lobes (which are quite vulnerable to traumatic damage), often produces a quality of immaturity or insensitive social behavior. The individual appears to be self-focused. There is a psychological distance that didn't used to be there.

Other characteristics directly due to brain injury add to the impact of adjusting to wide spread changes. Sleep patterns may be affected due to injury to the hypothalamus. Persons with brain injury often experience difficulty sleeping, or find that they can sleep only a few hours a day. Sleep-wake cycles may change and the individual may find that he or she cannot sleep at night at all. Appetite may change with resulting significant weight gains or losses. Even severe acne or other skin problems can appear because of the changes in how the brain and body react to detection of chemical composition of the blood.

Injury to certain areas in the front of the brain, another vulnerable spot, can contribute to changes in social behaviors, motivation, emotionality, and even body image. The individual may see himself or her-

BOX 4-1—A Dozen Typical Life Changes Following Brain Injury

While everyone is different, there are some generalities that characterize many persons who have experienced brain injury. These are offered to reassure families that they are not alone in their experience. The life changes listed here come from the insights of persons who have had a brain injury.

- Slower thinking and problem-solving means the pace of day-to-day living must slow down.

- Shorter attention span means doing one thing at a time.

- Interests become narrower because the brain feels overloaded more easily.

- Vocational plans usually change.

- Life requires more simplicity, which leads to more self-satisfaction.

- Emotional changes persist and may become more variable and unpredictable.

- Family and friendship circles become smaller.

- There is always a sense of "unfinished business."

- Self-confidence is fragile and needs lots of positive reinforcement.

- The threat of forgetfulness seems to loom over everything.

- There is some level of dependency that persists for managing the affairs of living.

- The potential for stress and reactions to stress are unsettling and seem never to go away.

self differently now compared with before the accident. Personal appearance may take on drastic changes, ranging from an obsessive concern about minute details to a virtual lack of concern about hygiene and appearance. While these may not bother the person with the brain injury, the family can be thrust into utter despair and consternation at these unwelcome and even embarrassing changes.

The boxed material in this chapter lists some of the more commonly observed changes in cognitive and emotional functioning following brain injury. The expression of these changes is different for each person, due to the uniqueness of the person and personality onto which brain injury has been inflicted. Appreciating the physiological basis for these changes and the need to integrate the changes into the new daily life routine is the foundation of brain injury rehabilitation. Some changes need to be tackled with the aim to revert back to former ways of thinking and behaving, if possible. Other changes demand acceptance and learning strategies to cope, minimizing their negative impact and adjusting to maximize positive qualities.

Neuropsychological Diagnosis and Treatment

Once the medical crisis of brain injury is stable, orthopedic injuries are treated, neurological issues such as balance problems or dizziness are attended to, attention to the whole person evolves. Getting back to life—to more or less usual activities with family and friends, to work or school, to just being yourself—becomes the priority. This is when the neuropsychological perspective of brain injury becomes everyone's focus.

Neuropsychology is the bridge between neurology and psychology. It is the discipline where behavioral consequences of neurological function and dysfunction are the concern. It is the discipline that studies the integration of personality, cognitive, emotional, vocational, family, and social aspects of living from the vantage point of the brain.

Understanding this complex matrix of psychological and neurological interactions begins with a neuropsychological examination. This is a clinical assessment that provides a comprehensive and detailed description of the unique behavioral, cognitive, and psychological consequences of brain injury. An assessment of this kind documents the array of functional strengths and weaknesses so that rehabilitation can tap resources to help the individual adjust to or compensate for impairments. The assessment may reveal those functional characteristics that might be recovered through specialized cognitive retraining. The neuropsychologist uses scientific techniques to infer what the premorbid (preexisting) characteristics of the individual were like and to provide an index of the extent and type of changes brought about by the brain injury and the individual's psychological reaction to it.

Clinical neuropsychology grew out of years of scientific research with persons who sustained brain injury, with the expectation that better understanding of the physiology and psychology of brain-behavior relationships could greatly assist treatment in many disciplines. Nurses, physicians, occupational and speech therapists, other health care professionals, families, and injured persons themselves, use neuropsychological knowledge for understanding the whole person and for guiding rehabilitation.

Through the application of psychological tests and procedures, mental functions sensitive to brain injury can be measured objectively. Based on an analysis of the profile of test scores and observation of the individual's problem-solving processes, evaluation is made regarding (1) nature, location, and extent of structural brain injury; (2) deficiencies caused by brain damage versus preexisting cognitive characteristics; (3) strengths in an array of cognitive and psychosocial skills; (4) comprehensive diagnostic understanding of the impact of the injury on biological, personal, family, and social aspects of the individual's life; (5) prognostic estimations for recovery and adjustment; (6) the specific course of action needed for best therapy planning; and (7) predictions and practical recommendations for possible return to independence in work, school, driving, home, and other areas of life.

Figure 5. Neuropsychological testing is the only formal diagnostic procedure for understanding the practical, functional consequences of brain injury.

Underlying these specific applications of neuropsychological status is a core body of knowledge available to the individual and his or her family. This knowledge is available on a continuous basis to bolster understanding the consequences of brain injury and how to react to it in adaptive ways. Most people never give brain-behavior relationships much thought, until the impact of a brain injury drastically changes behavior. Neuropsychological knowledge, interpreted in light of an individual's unique injury and preexisting characteristics, can help everyone understand, improve, and accept changes.

Neuropsychological assessment and intervention usually starts fairly early during a person's rehabilitation. Even though a full neuropsychological examination might not be appropriate or necessary until some weeks or even months after the injury, the neuropsychologist may perform periodic testing of specific functions such as attention and memory. This information is useful to help the injured person, his or her family, and rehabilitation therapists gain a growing appreciation for the new challenges. Periodic assessment of basic cognitive areas can also help determine recovery progress and potential.

A full neuropsychological examination involves undergoing several hours of tests, interview, and observation. The case history, including hospital records and laboratory tests, school records (if available), and other historical documentation, is reviewed in detail. Testing, itself, includes in-depth procedures to assess attention span, concentration, orientation, memory, learning, receptive and expressive language, mathematical reasoning and accuracy, spatial perception, abstract and organizational thinking, problem-solving, social judgment, motor abilities, sensory awareness, emotional reactivity, and general psychological adjustment. Tests are used as necessary to clarify diagnostic questions and make accurate predictions.

One of the key concepts in the assessment of neuropsychological abilities is that of "executive functions." This term refers to the individual's ability to think ahead, plan, evaluate, understand consequences, refine plans, and learn from feedback. Brain injury almost always affects executive functions to some extent. The neuropsychologist takes every opportunity to assess these functions and help the person, family, and treatment team know how to improve them or teach compensation for deficiencies.

Every person who has experienced a brain injury, mild or severe, should have a comprehensive, formal neuropsychological assessment as soon as neurological and medical stability has been achieved. The neurologist, neurosurgeon, rehabilitation physician, and other rehabilitation team members can help determine when this stage is reached.

Usually, when spontaneous recovery starts to slow down and directed recovery needs to be intensified it is a good time for a full examination. It is at this time that formal rehabilitative efforts, including occupational, speech, and cognitive therapy, are extremely important. Unfortunately, it is also at this time that lack of motivation may set in as the person believes she or he is back to normal and does not understand the need for additional therapy. A neuropsychological assessment gives the therapists—and the injured person and his or her family—the knowledge and insight necessary to understand the needs and goals for rehabilitation. Hence, the neuropsychological assessment is a key educational tool, as well as diagnostic procedure, and provides the basis and justification for specific rehabilitation treatment.

Periodically repeated neuropsychological examination is useful to monitor progress, to adjust treatment plans and directions, to establish a basis for disability determination, to provide an objective basis for decisions about driving or returning to some form of employment, to identify long-term special needs, for educational or vocational planning, and for ongoing individual and family education and adjustment.

Involving the neuropsychologist long before the first formal assessment is conducted provides an opportunity for interaction with the whole treatment team, the person injured, and the family. Assessing the extent and areas of brain damage thus can begin almost immediately after the injury occurs. By the time the individual is neurologically ready for a full evaluation, the neuropsychologist will have followed the course of recovery and will have made many behavioral observations. This will facilitate both drawing inferences about the future course of recovery and defining therapy and long-term needs.

Neuropsychological treatment usually coexists with physical, occupational, vocational, speech, and other specialized therapies. The role of neuropsychological treatment is to achieve increased self-awareness, to teach behavior change strategies, and to help people and families

BOX 4-2—Guidelines for Relating to a Person Soon after a Brain Injury

To help alleviate uncertainty about how best to communicate with an individual soon after a brain injury, the following suggestions are offered:

- Frequent and brief visits or phone calls (only when in-person visits are impossible) are preferred over longer, infrequent visits. Such short visits do not tax a short attention span, contribute to frustration and agitation, or overload memory.

- Being superficial destroys a relationship quickly. Be yourself and be very careful you don't talk down to the individual. Ask questions as you normally would. Talk about yourself as much as you talk about the other person to maintain a balanced focus.

- Be informed about what has happened to the individual and seek education and understanding about the injury so you can understand the changes you see in his or her behavior.

- Encouragement should focus on how and what the individual is doing now, not in the future.

- Blatant statements to the effect that "everything will be fine," or "you'll be good as new in no time" are meaningless and may even be misleading. Again, focus on something very positive that is happening right now, not some time in the vague and distant future.

- Talk over your feelings with someone if you are confused, or experiencing emotional distress.

- Ask therapists who work with the individual how you can become involved in a helpful way in the evenings or on weekends when the therapist may not be present.

- Gifts, if given at all, should be simple, appropriate, and cheerful.

- Keep conversations simple and without expectations for the individual to remember key things. Do not scold or act surprised if the individual doesn't remember something or someone; just offer a supportive reminder and get on with the conversation.

- Do not ask the individual to make choices (i.e., Would you like this light on so you can see better?). If you ask questions that are designed to be helpful, simply ask in a general manner if there is anything you can do to help out right now and leave it at that.

---

manage the psychological and emotional changes that accompany brain injury.

While the catastrophe of brain injury is certainly not a welcomed life event, the overwhelming initial shock and disdain for the whole ordeal turns into a challenge for discovery. The person injured and his or her family can remain enmeshed in a topsy-turvy world or they can emerge stronger and more resolved than ever to make the new brain a good brain. Change is usually threatening at first. Through increasing one's understanding, taking a hard look at attitudes and values, and experimenting with ways to adapt, change can become a positive challenge. The magnificent brain reveals a fascinating world of discovery. When the magnificence goes awry, mourn the loss and applaud the gains. Change becomes a way of life. Instead of a burden, change becomes a rich path to discovery.

Nate—Real Person

Before the accident my name was Nate Anderson. It still is Nate Anderson. I have two brothers. I am twenty-four years young. I moved out of my parent's house when I turned eighteen. I worked in a hardware store and attended some college. I played softball every summer. I played darts and bowled for fun and enjoyed going to movies. I would pursue college at a later date.

I had recently started a new job with Maple Trucking in June of 1996 delivering agricultural products. It was a hot day. I was finishing up a load for delivery the next day when someone hollered at me. I turned and slipped off the loading dock where I was working, landing several feet below. My head hit the ground first. Well, so they tell me anyway. I don't remember any of this.

I was taken to the hospital in an ambulance and I was very combative. During the next hour I slipped into a coma. I had emergency brain surgery and two blood clots were removed to reduce the swelling in my brain. I remained in a coma and attached to a ventilator for three or four weeks. Apparently, my medical course was quite difficult. One time the doctors told my family they might consider being ready to donate my organs. I am very glad they did not. I would hate to be missing some parts. Four weeks after the accident I was transferred to the rehabilitation wing of the hospital.

One day I just seemed to wake up, wondering why my family and friends were around me while I was in bed. I then realized I was in a hospital. My family told me I had had an accident and was in a hospital. I could not remember falling off the loading dock. It was amazing what I had been through. I was surprised I had no broken bones. I still don't even remember working for the trucking company, let alone slipping off the loading dock.

A couple days after I woke up I could not see as well as I had the day I saw my family. All I saw was black and white from a small lower section of my right eye. I remember trying to walk and it was very hard. Several people worked with me and walking got easier and now I can walk okay without any help. Therapists worked with my vision also and it began to improve a little.

After about five months of therapy, I joined a bowling team with my brother. I have been living at home and I don't know when I will return to live on my own again. Every day I discover new things I need to learn. I'm pretty mellow most of the time. I help my mom as much as I can because my vision still isn't like it used to be. My brothers take me places with them because I don't drive. I will be starting a class at the community college next month and I am looking forward to that. Maybe I'll get a degree after all.

I am Nate Anderson, the same Nate I've been all my life, but also different now. I have become very active in my church and feel my faith is stronger than ever. I stay positive and let my recovery take its course, wherever it will lead. I have started seeing some old friends again but it isn't the same as it used to be. Their lives are very busy and mine is pretty simple. That is okay. I don't know what lies ahead but I am learning how to make each day a good one. I am kind of looking forward to college. I practice remembering things and my mom drills me on that every chance she gets.

I depend on my family and they are usually there for me. I am learning to be as independent as possible so I don't burden them. There's a girl at my church that I am going to ask out to a movie. I am twenty-four and I'll ask my brother to drive us.

5

Taking Stock: Losses and Gains

The emotional impact of traumatic brain injury cannot be understated. It can be one of the most devastating effects experienced by the person with brain injury. While severely injured persons initially may be virtually unaware of their injury—because the injured brain cannot easily be aware of itself or self-assess its condition—eventually a sense of helplessness overcomes the person as failure experiences are recognized. Brain injury becomes a prison from which no escape seems possible. It is like carrying around in your skull a seemingly useless organ.

While thinking might seem relatively normal at first, after the injury, there evolves a sense that self-control could be lost at the drop of a hat. There may be a subtle, or not-so-subtle, sensation of pressure inside the head that just won't go away. There may be a sense of fear that you can't trust your brain, that thinking will miss something, like suddenly realizing you've been going around all day with your pants unzipped. This leads to a reaction that nothing which was done automatically before can be trusted to be done reliably now, without consciously thinking about every step, every aspect of what you're doing. This makes you feel like you're burning brain energy to excess, like you're stuck in first gear and can't get out. It's like wanting to sit it out and wait for the big, dark cloud to pass. It's like thoughts ramming against a brick wall. It is dark despair when you cannot easily think of something you know you should be able to think of, and this happens over and over and over. It is wanting to crawl in a hole when you realize you can't keep up with conversations that once were stimulating. It's the feeling that your body now has someone else's brain, someone of much lower capability. Soon, the overwhelming fear is met: is this going to be forever?

Much of the information in this book is intended to help contain and manage the effects of brain injury and strengthen the intellect and personality an individual retains after a brain injury. The premise herein emphasizes that a person can adjust to permanent changes and still lead a self-respecting, satisfying life. Despite a positive focus in this book, there is no denying that brain injury represents a serious, sometimes devastating, change in functioning, no matter how mild or severe the injury may be. There is also no denying that one of the most valuable ingredients for making it all seem better is time. It takes time to get used to anything, especially a new you that you may not initially like very much. Maintaining an undercurrent of positive focus, no matter how contrived or fake it may seem at first, is a key ingredient to successful—albeit usually slow and eventual—adjustment to brain injury. Learning coping strategies and staying grounded in reality complements the adjustment process.

For every loss, one can find a gain. Life consists of an undulating flow of loss of balance and return to balance. Traumatic brain injury is a powerful force that tips the scales dramatically. The fight to regain balance in life is often long and arduous. Balance can return after brain injury—not in the sense that life eventually picks up as it was before the injury, but that life takes on a new structure with new challenges to keep it balanced.

Losses and Grief

Eventually, as the brain recovers consciousness sufficiently to provide the individual the capability to realize his or her changes, a soul-searching inventory of losses begins. Both spontaneous recovery and the self-awareness brought about through formal rehabilitation gradually increase consciousness. Changes in virtually every aspect of life seem to have occurred. In the case of milder injuries, these changes may be less noticeable to others but to the person who is becoming aware of them, the changes are devastating. In the case of moderate or more severe injuries, changes in thinking, behavior, emotions, social interactions, language, and habits become quite obvious to everyone. The person with the injury learns to manage these changes, sometimes with despairing results.

When a person who has had a brain injury changes the subject in a conversation suddenly and inappropriately, others may think of this as odd but otherwise may think little of it. The person who has had a brain injury and cannot easily follow the conversation at hand may cope with that experience by introducing a new topic of discussion with the expectation that now he or she can recover some sense of social and communication control. Reasons behind the behaviors that are designed to cope with the frustrations of brain changes may, at first, go unnoticed by others but are acutely intentional by the person who is experiencing the effects of brain injury.

Persons with more severe injuries may feel comfortable only by withdrawing altogether from social contact and conversation. The sense of helplessness is met with a mixture of anger, frustration, depression, resignation, and childlike dependency.

Whatever the multitude of reactions and experiences that follows brain injury, eventually a sense of loneliness and grief may overcome the individual. Realizing that the brain is different and that getting one's old style of thinking back just isn't going to happen leads to a period of mourning, anger, and frustration. In some people, these feelings may give way to guilt with increased depression and sorrow. The guilt may come from totally irrational places in the mind, but may be a way to self-punish for the time-worn myth that bad things happen to people who do bad things.

Denial may be another way to cope with grief. In some people, denial occurs immediately and may not be a psychological process at all but rather the effect of the brain's injury preventing itself from recognizing the many changes it is experiencing. Sometimes brain injury interferes with frontal lobe functioning such that it prevents the individual from assessing his or her behaviors against a backdrop of customary or socially acceptable ways of responding. Such individuals are usually quite uninhibited and may be unable to step back and see their changed behaviors more objectively. Denial actually may be unawareness of changes brought about by the brain injury, not by an emotional defense of not wanting to see the changes.

In others, denial may indeed be more of a psychological than neurological process. Denial is a common defense mechanism used by most people at one time or another to mentally block out a painful or disturbing reality. It is rarely a permanent solution and eventually reality must be dealt with.

Almost every person who has experienced brain injury eventually develops some grief and anxiety over the losses and the uncertainty that life now presents. Effectiveness in day-to-day living is reduced, if not virtually shattered. Return to work or school is frustrating, possibly resulting in failures or demotions. A growing sense of marital and family discord sustains tension. The loneliness of being trapped in a body with a brain that isn't cooperating becomes frightening as well as saddening.

Most people live in a relatively predictable world where catastrophic change is unexpected. They buy health insurance to deal with the expected transient changes in physical health but rarely buy disability insurance to help offset the financial drain caused by a possible long-term or permanent health change. When brain injury occurs, catastrophe extends well beyond the physical injury to the brain. Financial, marital, family, and personal turmoil mounts. The snowball keeps growing and growing. What was dreaded but rarely much thought about—the occurrence of any catastrophe (devastating earthquake, loss of job, divorce, or serious brain injury)—has happened. The oddity is that more lives are drastically changed by brain injury each year than are lives changed by tornadoes, earthquakes, or other natural disasters. Yet, most people have given rarely a solitary thought to such a possibility. Every year in America alone, half a million people experience this very situation.

The loss of status within oneself and among one's peers, the injustice and anger over what has happened, the helplessness of irreversibility, the powerlessness to effect positive change fast enough, the dehumanization of personal identity (now being defined only by your brain injury), and the loneliness all these experiences create often leads to overwhelming grief.

Despite the grief, the brighter side emerges, slowly but surely, for those persons and families who don't give up. With education and knowledge, guidance from the neuropsychologist, a will to get beyond the grief, and some strategies that foster growth, positive change does emerge.

Characteristics of recovery from brain injury are as diverse as the effects of the injury. Families need to be aware that the healing brain produces chaotic behaviors. Professional help and the comfort of support organizations are important resources in getting through the tough times.

Gains and Growth

Eventually, with time and with nudging from family and therapists, as well as perhaps your own fleeting conscious awareness, some realization occurs that you must put grief aside and get on with life. That is the moment when you start to take stock of your strengths instead of only your losses and weaknesses. People often tell the person that despite the brain injury he or she can still have a family to love, can still care about people, can still laugh, can still hope. While these affirming reminders might be necessary to start the healing process, they certainly are recognized as superficial when the individual realizes he or she needs help just to go to the bathroom, can't run and play ball anymore, can't converse eloquently anymore, isn't able to return to work, or has trouble with the essential and fundamental things that defined his or her life.

Unfortunately, many people ascribe to the "there but for the grace of God go I" statement about their brain injury. Resigning to see yourself as better off than some other poor soul who is more severely injured than you are is not a healthy self-acceptance. This thinking is only ranking yourself among the injured, merely perceiving someone else's misfortune as greater than yours.

Getting beyond the grief of brain injury doesn't mean comparing yourself with someone worse off. Instead, taking stock of your unique resources, without comparison, and getting on with life adjustment is a commanding and determined strategy. Comparing yourself with someone else clouds your perception as a unique person.

The sarcastic comment of the late 1990s with all the constant media and entertainment hype over the *Titanic* was, "The boat sank; get over it." The point is, tragedy happened; we grieved in shock and despair; things will never be the same; now let's get on with life. While this attitude may seem harsh—even beyond stoic—it reminds us that we can choose to remain stuck or we can choose to muster the energy to get unstuck.

In the arena of brain injury, the same philosophy applies. At some point it is necessary to hunker down, wipe the tears, and decide to get on with life. One way *not* to do that is by upgrading your injury by comparing yourself with someone else who has had a brain injury and considering yourself better off. That only relegates you to the passive ranks of injured victims and keeps you from seeing the *whole* person. Accepting a personal tragedy and moving on is a much more active, determined, self-responsible, and healthy response.

Some strategies are introduced for initiating and getting beyond the growth process: (1) laying the grounds for financial resources and attitudinal changes enabling rehabilitation to work, (2) learning strategies for identifying and making personal gains, (3) choosing thoughts to reduce anxiety when the going gets rough, and (4) carving out a new personal identity.

BOX 5-1—Serenity Prayer

Origin of the Serenity Prayer may be centuries old. It has been adopted by many groups, most notably Alcoholics Anonymous, as a guide to wisdom. Its essential message is to take life one-day-at-a-time, find peace, accept adversity, and rise to the challenge of change and adaptation. It is entirely appropriate for persons and families where brain injury is the challenge.

God Grant me the Serenity to accept the things I cannot change,
Courage to change the things I can,
And Wisdom to know the Difference.

Laying the Foundations for Realizing Gains

One of the first challenges, almost always overlooked in formal rehabilitation programs, is helping the injured person and his or her family lay the financial foundation so that rehabilitation can progress optimally. Many people do not have the financial reserves that are usually required for brain injury rehabilitation, do not carry disability insurance, and do not want to make an economical and lifestyle change to accommodate their new, and inevitably lower financial status. Luckily, some people do have automobile insurance riders, are covered by a worker's compensation program, or have a financially supportive family that can provide financial reserves.

If worry over how the bills will be paid becomes a central preoccupation with the injured person or his or her spouse, rehabilitation will be pressured and geared only toward getting the person back to work as soon as possible, if that is even possible at all. In all too many cases of brain injury, this is a self-defeating and even destructive situation.

As soon as possible during the initial stages of brain injury rehabilitation, a plan should be made for financial stability for the next year or two, at least. Often, a rehabilitation case manager or social worker can help identify specific strategies and resources. Connecting with professional resources who can help address these concerns is usually essential. It is crucial that rehabilitation focus be as unencumbered as possible by prevailing financial worries.

In addition to financial stability, there needs to be a period of time early in rehabilitation when the individual, the family, and therapists identify strengths and gains, and work on attitude changes that are supportive of a lifestyle that is going to be different from before the injury. A myth once held by some professionals in brain injury rehabilitation was that with enough time in rehabilitation, all deficits will be recovered and the person will return to the life one had before the injury. This myth denies the reality that brain injury is a permanent condition. Certainly, improvement can be made to an injured brain, but as has been stated in many ways already, improvement depends on both healing *and adapting* to permanent change. Improvement and rehabilitation does not mean total return to one's former style of life. Any life catastrophe produces permanent change where, after grief and mourning resolve, a new life course must be charted. The new course must accommodate the fallout from the catastrophe but can neither deny that it happened nor stay mired in its despair.

A related concept is that brain injury rehabilitation means growing *with* brain injury, neither denying it nor giving in to it. Brain injury changes the brain—in some ways temporarily; in some ways permanently. In many ways brain injury is a change for the worse, and with regards to its impact on the individual's life, it is a change most would rather not have to deal with. However, one's choices are to succumb or give in to the loss and be sad and angry about it forever or to move on, accept the change, grow, and adjust.

To be consistent with the concept of accepting and growing *with* brain injury, the term "brain injury" might be changed to "brain *change*." This is not to belie the devastating effect and losses of sudden brain change on the individual's life, it is to emphasize that life goes on—in a positive, productive, personally meaningful way—*with change*.

Brain change—from the catastrophic moment of possibly life-threatening injury to the arduous process of rehabilitation—means life change. This cannot be denied. One of the first steps toward successful rehabilitation is to plan for financial stability. Concurrently, the cultivation of attitudes needs emphasis—attitudes that support growth and the acceptance of change.

Identifying Gains

When one is psychologically ready, an important stage in recovery is to identify personal gains from the brain injury experience. This stage may seem quite odd at first glance. It requires the individual's overcoming the shock of the experience and the focus on loss. It is the evolution into a new level of awareness and acceptance.

One generalized or nonspecific gain that can be accepted following a brain injury experience is that one can, indeed, regain a sense of who he or she is and can actually live peacefully with significant change. There is often a self-satisfying smugness that develops as an individual realizes he or she possesses the key to understanding, based on first hand experience, what brain injury is really all about while others can only imagine. Again, this idea may seem twisted but it really can happen. And when it does happen—perhaps fleetingly at first—it is a powerful first step in regaining for oneself a positive regard and a conquering feeling rather than relinquishing oneself to a victim identity. However tragic the experience of an automobile accident, a fall, or an assault may have been, the individual who emerges from the event with a brain injury has the potential to accept his or her fate gracefully and realize he or she holds the key to achieving a level of understanding that can actually be quite renewing. That understanding, if coupled with respectful rehabilitation, can help a person grow with brain damage, and grow in powerfully satisfying directions, albeit different directions than ever planned for before the injury.

Newness—in almost every aspect of life—is the outcome of readiness and commitment to grow with brain injury. Developing a new daily routine that accounts for needing more time to take care of hygiene, meals, and dressing may need to be arranged. With help, cultivating organizational skills—from one's wardrobe closet to one's desk drawers—will help cut down on misplacements, indecision, and frustrations. New work standards and goals must be identified and attempted, again with professional and family help to learn what feels comfortable and right.

New energies must be identified and used. This might mean throwing out the television so one isn't prone to becoming a couch potato. It means getting involved with some new hobby activity (music, playing cards, raising a dog, whatever). It means finding new things to do that are satisfying. It means learning patience, telling yourself to slow down, relax, take a break. It means starting over, in many respects, to build a life on a foundation of positive values.

One caveat most people with a brain injury find quite useful once they master it is the old adage of the Italian race car driver: "Throw out the rearview mirror." Learning not to look back can free you from always comparing where you're at now with where you think you would have been or should be based on old standards. If you say, "I wish I could do that again" or "I used to be able to do that but now I can't," you are only comparing yourself to an old and now useless standard. Such comparisons keep you down and set you up for constantly seeing losses and failures. Give up looking backward. Look only forward at what you are doing right now and how you will experiment with life tomorrow. Reconstructing the new you is a powerful, exciting, and enriching way to produce new energy and positive change.

Recovering self-awareness after brain injury is a unique process for each individual. The proceeding descriptions do not fit everyone's situation. The underlying theme, however, is that as self-awareness recovers, a search for growth opportunities must prevail over mourning the losses. The scales will tip either way for a while but the prevailing goal must be to count gains, not losses.

Reducing Anxiety

Learning to live with ambiguity and uncertainty is the key to reducing anxiety. Definitely easier said than done! Change of any kind means unfamiliarity and unease. Life after brain injury is a rather constant ebb and flow of change and uncertainty, at least early on. Learning ways to find some solace and comfort in all this change is essential for recharging the batteries, so to speak, and for continuing the journey.

Finding a comfortable easy chair or a shady spot under a tree or a spot on the bank of a creek to where you can retreat now and then is a particularly good way to maintain some balance and a steady keel. However, this special spot should never be a place to go and think negative thoughts, to sulk, or to brood. Go there and be happy, smile, contemplate the goodness in your life—at least relax.

Forming positive attitudes is also key to reducing anxiety. Writing down affirmations—statements of positive (and realistic) beliefs about yourself—and reading those affirmations frequently every day helps in the cultivation of peacefulness, and reduces anxiety.

Values change during the course of brain injury recovery. (The term "recovery" is used in a broad, not strictly medical, sense.) People who make good recoveries are willing to explore value changes in their lives. Learning to be more patient, to take things a little slower, to stop along the way and smell the roses are keys to opening yourself up for the potentials and the growth that value changes allow. Learning some mental balancing strategies such as tai chi or meditation can foster an openness and receptivity to learning and self-acceptance.

Breaking Stereotypes

Answering and honing the question "Who am I?" takes a lifetime for most folks. When you have to start all over in addressing that question because your world has turned upside down after a brain injury, it becomes an immediate, and often irritating, challenge, especially if you are an adult. One of the first tendencies in coping with a brain injury is

---

Box 5-2—Accepting Today...

One of the challenges in brain injury rehabilitation is to avoid looking back and reminding yourself of losses. Looking at what you have today and maintaining a positive stay is essential in reforming attitudes and getting on with life. Today is the most important day in your life. The past is done. Tomorrow, however, depends on today.

These testimonials from persons who have had brain injuries can form the foundation of affirmations.

- Dignity and self-worth stand above being different.

- Experiencing life fully requires creativity and flexibility in thinking.

- Life priorities focus on quality, not quantity.

- Change replaces constancy.

- Challenge replaces defeat.

---

to persist in former ways of doing things, only to encounter frustrations one after another. Breaking the mold of how things used to be done is necessary in order to find new ways of doing things. Expanding one's base or scope of values is essential. If you were a conservative, set-in-his-ways curmudgeon, or, hopefully not quite so immovable, you will probably need to lighten up. Not easy if that has been a lifelong pattern. But, anything's possible and you might need to tell yourself that over and over and over again.

Containing the effects of brain injury into manageable mental compartments is crucial. Take each challenge one at a time to avoid being overwhelmed. You have to learn again what activity, expectation, or plan is comfortable for you, and what isn't. If playing baseball isn't satisfying anymore because you can't run or catch like you used to (oops, don't look back), then you might volunteer to teach T-ball to youngsters or take up less competitive Saturday morning neighborhood games.

Brain injury can be a catalyst that promotes positive and satisfying change despite its otherwise disruptive and unfortunate side. Most people would choose another source of motivation for breaking stereotypes and introducing major change into their lives. However, since the injury has occurred, and major life change is now inevitable, the opportunity looms large to "make the most of it." The alternative is submission, despair, unhappiness, grief, and loneliness.

A significant strategy toward redirecting how we think about an injury and the predicament it has created begins with our choice of words to describe and define it. Language is the vehicle of thinking and if we choose to use words that build positive images, we can, indeed, break through the unworkable stereotypes of the past into the challenge of newness and growth.

The Power of Language

Our choice of words plays an enormously powerful role in forming our personal identities. Psychological research has demonstrated that depressed people say and think worthless things about themselves. Insecure people think bad things will happen to them. Suspicious people describe their world using sinister and evil words. Shy people think other people are better than they are, and say so. Distrustful people believe others are out to take advantage of them. Our thinking, and the words we use to describe how we feel and what we believe, both about ourselves and about others, greatly influences behavior, personality, self-concept, and relationships with others.

The power of positive thinking reminds us that how and what we choose to think or say has a dramatic influence on what we actually do, what we believe, and what we accomplish. Often our choice of words and the effects they have are obvious; sometimes they are subtle.

In our effort to balance losses and gains, good and bad, devastation and growth, we need to be particularly aware of how we express our feelings, both silently to ourselves and out loud to others. Sometimes it's the "What came first, the chicken or the egg?" Do we feel how we describe ourselves because of how we describe ourselves, or do we describe how we actually feel? There is little question that we can make ourselves sick if we keep telling ourselves, and others, how ill we feel. On the other hand, we can make ourselves feel good, or at least better, if we tell ourselves we don't feel so bad.

Good words versus bad words. Language is a matter of choices. Building sensitivity to our choice of words helps diminish losses and promote gains. Affirmations condition how we want to think. Awareness of dangerous words increase our sensitivity to how we don't want to think.

The Language of Affirmations

Affirmations are powerful tools for forming attitudes, beliefs, and actions. An affirmation is a positive statement that we *choose* to make about ourselves, and repeat it over and over. "I am feeling better and better every day" is an affirmation that can have a long-term, powerful impact. Notice how the affirmation is structured. It is in the present tense. It does not say "I *will* feel better...," it says "I *am* feeling better...." Affirmations must be constructed in the present tense so that the effect is now, not later. Affirmations are affirmative; they are positive. They are simple and straightforward. They condition the mind.

There is no denying that an affirmation cannot change objective reality. Saying you do not have a brain injury over and over is delusional. Saying that you are adapting, you are coping, you are feeling positively challenged, you are more and more in control of your thoughts—these are affirmations. They don't deny reality; they form how you react to reality.

Affirmations are self-respecting and offer—actually create—encouragement. They are how you choose to come to terms with something thrust upon you not by your own choosing. They help restore the balance that misfortune tips the other way.

Changing beliefs and attitudes is not an easy task. Often people who vow to use affirmations will abandon them after a few days because there is no miracle cure occurring. Unfortunately, this suggests that the individual used the affirmation in order to change something he or she has no control over. That is not the purpose of an affirmation. Instead, affirmations are tools for gradually molding and shaping our attitudes about something over which we don't have control but over which we can control our reactions.

Some example affirmations include: "I take a deep breath and exhale very slowly when I begin to feel frustrated. I am calmer now." "I am a responsible person. I use my daily planner to remember every commitment I make." "I hold my head up, smile, and people like me." Affirmations imply that while you may not be responsible for your circumstances, you are responsible for your attitudes about them. An affirmation is like the adage, "If life hands you a lemon, make lemonade."

Dangerous Words

Using the positive words of affirmations to shape how we think and feel about something, ourselves, or someone else, is complemented by the need to avoid certain words that carry negative connotations. This vigilance about using certain loaded words is subtle but nevertheless powerful. Certain words carry a hidden message that eats away at our beliefs and attitudes and sabotages rehabilitation efforts. Here are a few words that must be avoided or used cautiously:

Suffering. This word probably needs no explanation. Yes, people injured in any manner do suffer, but to extend suffering forever, as in saying "a person *suffering* a brain injury" only sustains the pain and implies its permanence. Such a word implies an impassable situation. If its use is needed at all, use it sparingly, cautiously, and to indicate a temporary condition.

Victim. This word is showing up more and more in our culture as we describe people who are "victims" of violence, abuse, sexual assault, cancer, brain injury, and so forth. We can all be victims of dozens of things because there are dozens of things over which fate has more control than we do. Like the word suffering, it needs to be put in its place and not carried on forever or used as a permanent descriptor. Using phrases like "a *victim* of a brain injury" essentially implies that the person was, is, and always will be a victim. A victim is a person who has no control. A victim is *not* a person who is in control. Do you want to overcome the passivity, the negativity, and the devastation of the initial impact of a brain injury? Don't use this word.

Loss. People who experience a change in their memory, where they are slower in recalling things or must expose themselves to new information several times before it is sufficiently well retained often reduce their abilities to an expression of total loss. "I've lost my memory," is a paradoxical statement. If you lost your memory, would you know it? Don't talk to yourself or about anyone else as having "lost" something. It is a change, or even, if you must, a diminishment—not a total loss.

Even talking about having lost the use of an arm after a stroke is dangerous because it precludes its use in any capacity at any time. Many people who have a stroke that causes the muscles in an arm never to function again, still may learn to use that arm to help hold papers on a desk, to steady the use of the other arm, to protect a pocketbook by placing the purse between the body and his or her arm, and so forth. It is even possible, with extended time, that some neuromuscular control may return to that arm if it is regarded still as a useful arm. The arm may not be useful in the same manner as before the stroke, but it is not entirely useless either. If you really felt it was useless, you wouldn't mind if it were amputated. Right?

Losses are inevitable in life. The losses (or changes) in function following brain injury are real. It is how we grow with those changes that molds how we accept and adapt to them down the road. The advice here is to avoid or minimize long-term use of words that characterize the negative at the expense of the positive.

Bad. If referring to a *lost* function isn't bad enough, referring to your "bad arm" is twice as bad. That's probably more uses of "bad" in one sentence that anyone should come up with. The point is, why would you want to refer to any part of your mind, brain, or body as "bad?" It is such a bad word!

Deficit. Many people refer to changed functions as "deficits." This is approaching an objective (even statistical) description but still carries a loss, bad, and negative connotation. Neuropsychologists, therapists, and physicians regularly refer to a patient's deficits following brain injury. Why? Because that is what makes one a *patient*—deficits. If you want to be really objective, use the word *change*, as in "her ability to grasp and understand complex problems has changed, and she is taking more time, writing things out, and seeking help from others when she needs it in order to understand some new concepts." Certainly, this is a lot more words, but it is a fair—not a harsh, demeaning, or short-cut—statement of one's modified capabilities. "She has a deficit in abstract thinking" is a comparative statement but doesn't go anywhere other than to state a loss—a bad thing. Such a statement says nothing about the nature of the deficit and how the change might be adapted to. Your mission: "deficit" reduction.

Try. This word needs to be stricken from English and every other language. There is virtually no instance when this word is necessary, convenient, or accurate. "Just *try* to do it" is a statement of failure. Or, worse yet, consider the statement, "I tried; I just couldn't do it." This is self-forgiveness founded in self-righteousness. This is giving up in the face of a belief in your *in*ability. To try has no challenge to it. Nike probably wouldn't have sold nearly as many athletic shoes if their motto were "just *try* it" (instead of "just *do* it").

Train your brain to set off a warning buzzer every time you use the word "try." Figure out what you are expecting yourself to fail at then turn the words around and make it a problem-solving statement, not a defeating statement. The statement, "I tried to pass calculus but I just couldn't get it," can be restated as, "I took calculus and discovered that I do not have the foundation concepts to understand it yet. I will either go back and take some more preparatory mathematics or will change my goals, depending on how much I am willing to work at learning calculus." This says you may take calculus again. It says what you *did learn* about yourself from taking calculus. It suggests you are sensitive to your goals and potentially changing goals. It says you are self-respecting and realistic and that you don't give up. It says so much more than a flat, giving-up statement like, "I tried, but I was a failure so I can stop trying now."

Can't. Here's the granddaddy of all the bad words. As soon as you say you can't do something you have closed the door. "I can't remember that; because I've lost my memory," needs to be replaced with, "That looks like it might be a challenge to remember and will require my writing it down, going over it several times, forming a strong visual image of it, and asking someone to help cue me if I block on recalling some of it later." Again, the affirmative, positive statement uses more words, yet it keeps options open and *enables* rather than disables the individual. You can go through the rest of your life without ever needing to use the word "can't." Try it. Oops, *do* it.

A Statement of Faith

Faith, here meaning trust and belief in yourself, is most powerfully reflected in words that are positive, self-affirming, and honest. Faith is the key to coping with anything and any adversity. Faith is fostered by our choices, words, and deeds. Faith is a peaceful trust in the future, in the unknown, in the outcome of challenges. It is not hope merely in the sense of winning at some competition while others lose, but hope in the sense of personal victory over adversity, where anyone can gain. Faith is the foundation, the trust, the anchor.

Recognition that grief is the natural reaction to devastating change yields to recognition that growth comes from any adversity. Faith is the fuel. Faith is built from realistic expectations that have been constructed of positive value. It is built by avoiding negative words that sustain adversity and defeat. It is the peacefulness of knowing you are taking control back from an unfortunate fateful event.

In the great cosmic scheme, there is always balance. When things get out of kilter, something always happens to equilibrate them. Losses in a catastrophe are a given. Gains come from individual determination to rebalance life, to regain the positive, to meet the challenge. To turn grief into growth requires awareness of the mental processes that turn victim into challenger.

Donald—Real Person

Tuesday, November 16, began as any other day in my life. I had, as usual, a positive attitude. Before heading to work I would give myself enough time for 15 minutes of daily devotions. On this particular day, that's the last thing I remember doing until I "woke up" in a hospital later that day.

I am told by my coworkers at the office that I was busy rushing around preparing for my sales trip to Des Moines later that day. I was hurrying up and down the stairs gathering the necessary equipment for the sales demonstrations scheduled for the week. After completing the set-up of one of the microscopes and placing it into a transport case I attempted one more trip down the very familiar set of stairs with the large transport case in hand. Although I do not remember these events which occurred prior to the fateful trip down the stairs, I know it was the same routine I had repeated many, many times before.

The resulting head injury which occurred from the fall dramatically changed my life. The Donald who regained consciousness in the hospital is now a different person.

The next weeks and months I felt devastated. This sudden change in my life resulted in my being overwhelmed with a feeling of powerlessness. I sensed that I was disabled and was a second class person. I became preoccupied with the idea of what I was before the injury which resulted in sadness and grief. Each morning I awoke I would believe that this would be the day that the old Donald would come back. As the days turned into weeks I began to wonder if I would ever be the same again and was continually comparing present functioning with what was before. This constant preoccupation led me into severe depression. The anger within exploded more and more frequently toward members of my family, against those who loved me the most and wanted only what was best for me. Although my family was disturbed with the changes in me and did not understand these changes, they continued to be supportive and love me.

There continues even now, more than a year after the fall, a veil of confusion like I am in a fog and "not with it" or out of sync. These problems along with several others have prevented me from returning to my sales job. This resulted in additional pressures because our family began to get behind in our bills which produced greater stress.

I was eventually referred to a neurologist who put me on some medication to stop the downward spiral of severe depression. I also started to see a psychologist who immediately began working with me on changing my attitude. She continually reinforced the idea that it was self-defeating to keep comparing my present functioning with what was before. I finally came around to realize it was fallacious to wait for the old Donald to come back. Slowly I accepted the challenge and continue today with what is my lifelong process of change—accepting new ways of doing things and changing my career and life plans. This allows me to accept myself better and has given me a certain amount of satisfaction.

The skills I am now learning have helped me cope with my problems and to condition myself to deal with them without reaching the level of frustration that was encountered early on. I have thrown away the rearview mirror of my life. I am learning creative ways of improving my memory. I am taking responsibility more and more for my life. This "take charge of my life" attitude is inspiring me in goal setting as well as getting organized in specific areas to turn desires into actual goals, and then into actual achievements. Each day my devotions include thinking about my strengths and how I can turn the challenges with which I am faced—which had been barriers—into bridges to the future.

I am committed to improving my attitude as well as to becoming a better organized person. My mental blocks continue to embarrass and frustrate me but I just remind myself to stop and find a way to cope. I have been thinking recently about what the future may be in regards to my vocation. My short-term goal is to determine what possible careers may be available as well as realistic for me. I have decided to take a typing course at the community college. This will help me evaluate my skills and learning capacity. I then expect to enroll in a computer class and possibly pursue a vocation in office systems or computers.

My head injury has virtually changed every aspect of my life. With God's help I have the ability to accept reality, to give tirelessly, to adapt to change, to direct hostile energy into creative activities, to take charge of my new life, and to love. My goal each day is to live life anew, to experience the joy of triumph, to have faith in life itself and in doing so experience that fleeting commodity—happiness.

6

Redefining Normal

An attitude many people develop soon after a brain injury is the idolization of normality. A person may feel he or she has been robbed of being normal and the old, familiar, normal self is longed for. The feeling is not one of being merely "different" but of being "abnormal." Being different is at least neutral but being abnormal definitely can be an uncomfortable and unsettling feeling. Where everything has changed, including how one relates to family and friends, and where everyone else seems their familiar and normal selves, the person with a brain injury can feel left out, abandoned, and helpless.

These feelings are reflections of a fragile self-assessment due to the topsy-turvy experience of brain injury. Brain injury often, at some time and to one degree or another, robs the individual of self-confidence and a positive self-regard. Lack of emotional control and adaptation to a once-familiar personality is now different and unfamiliar. Reactions of family and friends often, out of frustration, become demeaning, controlling, devoid of respect, and distancing because they don't understand the brain injury experience either. The person who is brain injured experiences a sense that others are going on with their lives while he or she is standing still. He or she may feel forced to undergo therapy, pressed to listen to lots of advice from others, and relegated to be the individual to whom care is given but from whom no one expects care to be returned. It is like being a child again only with guilt for regressing to that stage and a sense of discomfort in an alien experience. When the world as you've known it comes crashing down, loss of a sense of normality is not a pleasant experience.

Effectively, having no choice but to accept changes, learn coping strategies, and accept support from others feels like a lot of unnecessary work. Learning to know, all over again, what your strengths and weaknesses are, figuring out your new role in the family, coming to terms with a personality that seems distrustful and not you at all, makes you long for the days when you were "normal."

There is no magic formula to make it all right again. Undeniably and forever more, normal is now going to be different. The choice is to accept the challenge or remain mired in an idolization of a perfect normality that likely never really existed so perfectly anyway.

Three themes of this chapter offer specific ways to help recover a sense of control, a sense of being normal again, even if not returning to the old self. The two most influential changes that brain injury produces are in memory and thinking. Understanding and advice about improving these two key cognitive domains are offered to help rebuild self-confidence and a sense of comfort. The third element in recovering a sense of "who am I?" is through resuming some kind of meaningful work. Self-identity is significantly formed through the work we do.

There are other self-improvement areas besides memory, thinking, and work that contribute to a redefinition of normal. Learning to love, to play, to help are also important. Each person will create his or her own way to cultivate other areas of renewal.

Life may not be like it was before the injury but it can be satisfying. It is a matter of redefining what the new normal will be like. Enhancing memory, thinking, and working skills are practical and concrete ways for doing just that.

Memory: The Lifeline

Without memory, without a sense of what has happened in one's life, without a sense of the continuity and time frame of when things happened, it is difficult, if not impossible, to maintain a sense of who you are. Our memories are our lives. Memory of what we've done, people we've loved, accomplishments we've made, what we like and dislike, what we've thought and said (or refrained from saying), our embarrassments, our moments of joy, our reflections in times of pensive thought, our educational learning, our multitude of experiences: these are who I am, who I was, and who I will continue to be.

Brain injury does two things to our memories. While usually preserving at least some aspects of past experiences, memory may be somewhat clouded for details; thoughts and images of these experiences may not be easily retrieved. Even more disturbing following brain injury is the difficulty in laying down new, moment-to-moment memories.

The neurology of memory processes is exceedingly difficult to understand. Learning new things depends on rich and complex mental (brain) connections with past memories. Using memory depends on retrieving things through immediate recall and through associations among thoughts that share common links. This whole process is slow and unreliable in the injured brain. Memory, the key to self-identity and a personal sense of continuity, is now fragmented.

Sometimes, therapists advise that families show old photographs and familiar objects dear to the individual who has experienced brain injury to help recover memories and restore a link to the past that defines personal identity. This tactic is, indeed, important early on after a brain injury. Family photo albums, familiar tales of experiences, and a chronology of key life events can help old memories reconnect. Writing down in chronological order the places where you've lived, what you did there, who you knew there, and what led to changes in where you have lived is a good strategy to provide a concrete reference that the individual can refer to regularly. Simple exercises of writing down likes and dislikes—about anything from people to food to colors—can also help reestablish a sense of memory and of personal identity. Reconnection with the familiarity of the past helps improve memory and reestablish a sense of personal continuity in life experiences.

These activities are important early on after a brain injury and are especially important for persons who have experienced relatively moderate to severe damage. Persons sustaining milder injury usually do not experience the devastating loss of memory continuity, and spontaneous recovery is typically more complete.

Whatever the degree of brain injury, common to all who experience such fate is a change in how well new memories are stored and retrieved. A key task, then, for any person who has suffered a brain injury is to practice good memory strategies and habits. The suggestions in the boxed text in this chapter offer several concrete ideas for improving day-to-day memory. Often overlooked or underestimated is the need for formal memory training following brain injury. The underlying goal in any effort to improve memory is to encourage the brain to create mental images that can link memories back together and reestablish the framework on which new memories can be added.

The frustrating thing about memory and brain injury is that the person with a brain injury often does not want to go to the trouble faithfully to practice new memory habits so that they become second nature. Partly this is denial (or unawareness) that it is necessary; partly it is forgetting to practice the right strategies. With consistent reminders and support from family, friends, and therapists the person wishing to improve his or her memory can realize a tremendous benefit by regularly adapting certain strategies to one's daily routine. The important thing to recognize is that the brain is functioning in a somewhat fragmented manner until it can regrow adequate connections. It needs to be coached to grow these connections; it won't happen on its own. Even regrown connections won't recover the memory system as reliably as it was before injury. Thus, the attitude of "I'll just wait it out and when my brain heals I won't have these memory problems" is fallacious. Recovering or gaining a good, functionally reliable memory requires work, commitment to consistent strategies, and recognition that faithful application of these techniques actually works.

BOX 6-1—Memory Builders

These strategies are extremely effective in improving mental organization, learning, and remembering:

- Write down the important things you want to remember. Writing things down implants them in memory much more effectively than merely listening to them. Writing something down quadruples the number of brain cells involved in remembering something than just listening to whatever it is you want to remember.

- Repeat back what you want to remember. This gives the brain a chance to rehearse, further cementing the memory.

- Visualize what you want to remember and make up the visualization yourself. Make it vivid, exciting, and unusual. See it in your mind. Most of what we want to remember are things we hear. Our visual sense is very powerful. So, make visual that which you hear in order to remember it much more strongly.

- Keep a calendar. Just one, that is large enough to write lots of things in but not so cumbersome you can't carry it with you.

- Read and engage in substantive conversation (not gossip or trivia). These activities stimulate memory and thinking. An active mind has more links upon which new memories may be built.

- Learn new things and be aware that you are learning. Be actively involved in your learning, never passive. Read, outline, draw, doodle, repeat, make charts—whatever it takes to be actively involved in personalizing learning.

- Literally tell yourself to "pay attention" when you want to remember something. Prime your brain for remembering.

- Never say you have a bad memory, or that you've lost your memory. Maintain a positive focus on what you can do, not what you can't.

- Oh yeah, be sure to write it down!

Thinking: What We Do More Of Than Anything Else

If you think about it, we really do spend more time thinking than we spend doing anything else. Day dreaming, fantasizing, planning, mental organization, mental rehearsing, studying, plotting, ruminating, stewing, brooding, worshiping, praying, contemplating, and wishing are all just different forms of thinking. Brain injured or not, the important question is how much thinking time is productive and how much is wasted, or worse yet, destructive? For something that consumes so much of our time, humans are poorly trained in how to do it well. We often don't use tools for thinking that improve the end results. We spend much too much wasted time in negative thought that produces no problem-solving at all and only festers more negativity. We wish and daydream without formulating realistically workable plans, only to be disappointed by reality.

Brain injury places certain obstacles on our quality of thinking. Sometimes, after a brain injury, thinking time is really empty time. The brain is taking a rest from thinking. Many times a spouse or family member may be bothered by seeing their loved one who has had a brain injury just sitting and appearing to be deep in thought when really he or she may mentally just be shutting down for a while. When thinking is energized it may be fragmented, hasty, ill-considered, and lead to disastrous results. It is important at those times to quiet the mind—to take a break from thinking.

Another problem with thinking after a brain injury is that it is almost always slower than it was before. And, it is usually slower than the people with whom you associate. Keeping up with conversations, lectures, and the usual moment-to-moment flow of information that constantly bombards us is difficult because you aren't thinking quite as fast as the source is delivering. Thinking through problem situations may take more time, all the while those around you are urging you to "hurry up."

The boxed text in this chapter offers suggestions of how to practice productive thinking and eliminate negative thinking. Regularly reminding oneself of these strategies will, over the long run, improve not only quality of thinking but also cultivate a positive attitude toward life in general. Improved thinking builds self-confidence.

Rumination and Destructive Thinking

One of the most destructive kinds of thinking that almost everyone engages in from time to time but which seems unusually frequent after a brain injury is rumination. Rumination is "chewing the mental cud." The term comes from the cow and her first stomach, called the rumen, from where cud is regurgitated and chewed over and over and over. Mental regurgitation of, or mulling over, disturbing or unsettled thoughts is almost never productive in any way. Thinking over and over how someone has done you wrong or what you'll do to get even with someone who has hurt you is rumination. Replaying situations in your mind, over and over, is rumination. Only the most disturbed person will act on some of the crazy, insensitive, and immoral thoughts that rumination produces.

Of course, learning any new strategy or getting rid of an old habit is not easy. It takes time and reminders. A mental bell needs to go off every time you catch yourself ruminating. You have to have a mental diversion to take your mind off what you know you don't need to be thinking about. You have to ask yourself, "Is what I am thinking about going to lead me to a productive solution of what is bothering me?" If you cannot truthfully answer affirmatively, then you need to change what you are thinking about.

Ruminative thinking is usually passive as well as negative. It is like watching the same really bad television program over and over. Rumination is mind dulling. If it leads to anything at all, that is usually negative feelings, frustration, and ineffective emotions.

One way to rid yourself of rumination is to make signs and post them in conspicuous places around the house. The sign might be a cow

BOX 6-2—Thinking Builders

These tips are useful in improving the effectiveness of thinking, managing day-to-day affairs, and problem-solving:

- Be organized. Keep things, papers, and notes filed in notebooks and folders. A place for everything, and everything in its place.

- Slow down and don't attempt to match the hectic pace of everyone else. Do what you can that allows you to feel comfortable. Don't do more than one thing at a time. Make a list of what you need to do; stick to the list; check off one thing at a time as it is accomplished.

- Take time to solve difficult problems. Sleeping on an idea or problem often results in clearer thinking about it later. All problems don't need immediate solutions.

- Practice thinking and visualizing instead of being mentally passive. Sketch out ideas or write notes to help your mind gel ideas. Keep a sketch pad and a notepad handy.

- Keep your brain active with reading, writing, conversation, and drawing. Too much time spent passively watching television or just staring out the window isn't very stimulating to brain cells. Be sure your library card is current—and use it.

- Make lists and review your lists frequently. This will keep you organized and on top of the things you need to do. Making a list will also encourage you to prioritize the things you need to do.

- Balance relaxation with work, always. Be sure you have one thing to do each day that relaxes you: a walk with the dog, listening quietly to soothing music, tending your plants or garden, or whatever provides you peace.

- Keep distractions to a minimum whenever you do anything. Read, study, or pay bills in a quiet place. Don't play with the radio or talk on the phone while driving. Go for a walk in the park, not in a busy city area.

- Don't put off tasks. If there is something that needs to get done, do it now. Then, reward yourself with something enjoyable.

with a bold X through it—you'll know what that means. Or, it might simply read, "No Rumination," or "No Chewing of Mental Cud." When you catch yourself ruminating, or your sign reminds you, consciously shift to a pleasant thought. Plan ahead what that might be such as the memory of a pleasant trip you once took, a fond feeling you have for someone, a favorite flower, picture, food, or place. The objective here is to have some device to help you catch yourself in the act of ruminating and to have a readily available thought to switch to.

Simultaneous Thinking

Productive thinking usually falls into two categories: simultaneous and sequential. Simultaneous thinking is thinking about more than one thing at a time. Of course we really don't do that. Our consciousness can only be aware of one thing at a time but we can switch back and forth, sometimes rather rapidly, seeming to think about more than one thing at a time. The key to being able to do this is to remember what all the things are that you are mentally processing, more or less simultaneously, and to not get lost or forget where you were at in your thinking about one thing when you switched to another. See, it is complicated!

Some people who have a brain injury have difficulty switching from a task they are engaged in to, for example, answering the phone then returning to their original task again. The phone call causes a distraction. This can have dire consequences if the task they were doing when the phone rang was frying something on the stove. Forgetting to switch back to that task quickly after tending to a brief phone call can have smoky—or worse—consequences.

It is essential in memory improvement efforts to become consciously aware of instances of simultaneous thinking and take control over them. Limit distractions. Find a way to remind yourself of what you were doing when you switched to another task so you don't forget what you were doing in the first task, and can return to it in a timely manner. Keep something in plain view or in your hand that will remind you.

Lots of people who have had brain injuries complain about situations such as walking into a room and forgetting why they went there in the first place. This becomes so distracting they then forget to return to the task they were engaged in before.

The key to avoiding lapses in simultaneous thinking is to slow down, limit the number of things you allow yourself to engage in at the same time, and devise reminders (such as a list) for returning to former tasks. Practice being well organized (see the Thinking Builders box). Organization is a significant key to avoiding confusion.

If the phone rings while you are preparing something on the stove, make sure you answer a phone right there in the kitchen—one that has a long cord—so that you can continue tending to the stove. Don't leave the room to answer a phone elsewhere in the house. Let the answering machine get it.

If you must leave the stove for some interruption, carry a cooking utensil (for example, a pot lid and a spatula) with you—*and don't set these items down anywhere*—as a visible and obvious reminder of what you need to get back to *immediately*.

Sequential Thinking

Sequential thinking refers to thinking about and carrying out a sequence of actions that leads to a goal. The simple task of making cinnamon rolls, even from a box mix, involves several steps that must occur in a specific order. Mentally, one must be organized to appreciate the proper order, sufficiently capable of remembering what has and what has not been done yet, and reflective enough to know if you've put all the parts together. You have to remember to preheat the oven before you do anything. You have to remember to add the sugar and cinnamon before you roll up the dough. You have to remember to set the oven timer and stay within earshot of the buzzer that will tell you to take the rolls out of the oven. The steps involved in what seemed like a simple task before the brain injury may seem overwhelming now.

Dealing with that sense of being overwhelmed is a critical goal in brain injury rehabilitation. Occupational therapists focus on helping individuals relearn simple sequences of activity after a brain injury. The need to slow down, plan—*write out*—each step in advance, then pause between steps to evaluate what you've done and what you have next to do are all essential and conscious strategies to avoid feeling over-whelmed.

At first, taking conscious control of sequential thinking that was probably fairly automatic before the brain injury will zap energy. Thinking is tiring. The brain burns lots of energy thinking. That is why often an individual may have good intentions about doing some task but feel overwhelmed with how much energy it requires. With practice and the consistent use of mental organizational aids, as described in this chapter, tasks will gradually be less draining and more satisfying to perform.

Managing the quality of thinking, the ability to shift among tasks, and the ability to think in terms of steps necessary to accomplish a task requires guided practice. Speech and occupational therapists and neu-ropsychologists can extend the basic guidelines given here. Patients and families benefit greatly from such training in their quest to redefine normal.

Work and Right Livelihood

The individual who experiences a severe enough brain injury and who is unable to return to a former line of work faces the challenge of dis-covering his or her right livelihood—the kind of work one does that is consistent with abilities, interest, desire, and satisfaction. This discov-ery can be exhilarating and renewing for anyone. It is sometimes par-ticularly challenging for the person who has a brain injury because the natural instinct of that person is just to get back to normal and proceed with original goals. Once he or she can give up the glorification of what once was and set out on a course of personal discovery, finding one's right livelihood can be one of the most rewarding and satisfying experiences of life.

Right livelihood involves choice at its foundation. People enter jobs and careers in order to earn a living. People enter right livelihoods to earn self-satisfaction more so than money. Sometimes right livelihood earns one adequate financial benefits. Sometimes a job, solely for the sake of financial benefit, must supplement one's right livelihood. The person with a brain injury who is unable to work in the competitive work force might have to supplement whatever his or her right livelihood becomes with disability insurance or social security benefits. This is not compromising the honesty and value of work. First and foremost, work must define and satisfy your deepest, core self. It should not be sought solely for its income status or some other artificial reason.

What one does as a primary occupation of time must be satisfying, self-respecting, and have an appropriate financial reward to it. Even volunteer work, which usually has no financial reward, can be very satisfying and self-respecting if one is unable to participate in income-producing employment as well. Retired people, for example, often volunteer their time to organizations with whom they have a special regard. Volunteering at the local library because you love books and love to read can be a very enriching thing to do. Working two hours a week at a blood bank because you have a special regard for helping save lives or because you have a background in nursing gives yourself recognition that, in some small yet vital way, you are contributing to saving someone's life.

Competitive employment requires the ability to keep up with the normal pace of usual work demands, to engage in simultaneous and sequential process thinking unaided by someone else, and to handle the physical and stamina demands of a job. It also requires the ability to communicate with coworkers and customers and the ability to learn and adapt to changing policies and procedures. While job adaptations can sometimes accommodate a functional limitation and relegate its importance so that it does not interfere with getting a job done, this might not always be possible for someone who has had a brain injury. This is why disability insurance of various forms exists. Such insurance may not make up the financial difference were one able to earn a competitive salary, but it can help take the crunch off a financial hardship.

Right livelihood means getting to know what you like to do, what you can do comfortably, and what mental and personal resources you have with which to do the job well. This means taking serious stock of yourself, of the changes that brain injury may have brought about, and of the resources available to you. A vocational rehabilitation counselor or someone in a similar position should be able to help in this regard. Discovering the right mix of interests and capabilities is necessary to achieve a right livelihood. Sometimes you have to give up a fantasy and get into some realistic thinking. While this might seem discouraging at first, it will be acceptable later on when you find success and peace in what work you do.

Right livelihood means successful livelihood. Not successful solely from a financial standpoint as that is rarely a long-term and satisfying standard. Rather, successful livelihood is satisfying and meaningful. Successful livelihood provides a sense of pride, knowing you are doing the best you can do and contributing to society.

Every individual grows up defining who he or she is and learning, within the norms society accepts, to fit in and feel comfortable. When all that experience comes tumbling down, as the result of brain injury, the process of feeling one's normal self begins anew. Learning to think and to remember effectively forms the foundation for regaining a sense of comfort with who we are. Learning again, and very likely in a different way than before, to define who we are by what we contribute to society—our work—becomes the crowning stage in redefining a new normality.

Redefining normal—our work, our memories, our thinking abilities—is challenging. There is not just one way to accomplish this. The awareness of what one must do is the first step. Then, with the help of rehabilitation professionals, family, and friends, a person can begin the quest to redefine what will become the new normal. It won't happen through wishing or daydreaming. It will happen by experimenting and connecting with people and agencies who can help.

Samantha—Real Person

Hello. My name is Samantha Elizabeth Janes Garland, of Russian Romanoff decent, or so my slightly expansive father has told me. I was born a firecracker on July 4, 1944, in a little town outside of New Haven, on the hottest Fourth on record. In my own right, I've been described as a sparkler, spinning rose, and sky rocket. As a child I thought all the excitement of the Fourth was always just for *me*. Eventually, with some disappointment, I learned the truth. But to this day, I can't imagine having a birthday without bands, parades, glorious fireworks, sparklers, and the Stars and Stripes blowing in the breeze.

My birthright heralds that I am a true firecracker, driven by the fiery determination to make things happen, a strong will to reach for the highest goals, and to achieve the impossible. I am also a loving, passionate, and a bit stubborn person. There has never been anything that I could not achieve if I put my heart and soul into it. As a kid, I was the first up and the first down when several of my family conquered Billy's Baldspot, a small mountain outside the Adirondacks in New York state. I was also sick in bed for three days afterwards.

I discovered that I loved to learn. I made great grades in college and thrilled at achieving academic success. I realized I could get an A in any course I took by just applying myself, studying hard, and loving what I was doing. It was magic.

Spreading my magic to others was my next step. I taught junior high science and loved it—those hungry minds before me. What a thrill.

Eventually, I quit teaching to raise Brad. When he was two I was diagnosed with abdominal pre-cancerous polyps, the details of which I won't go into. I was fortunate to be one of the first to be fitted with an internal ileostomy pouch which I have had to use ever since. I learned how to take care of myself and educate physicians and nurses about it. The surgically-corrected condition and the ileostomy gave me a second chance at life. Again, I was rocketed into passionately embracing life at every turn.

I adopted my second son, Jeff. With Brad six and Jeff two, I returned to college and obtained a degree in sales and business. For three years I survived on no more than four hours of sleep any given night. I graduated with a B average. I then took a job selling ostomy pouches. I knew what I was talking about and felt passionate about helping people in the same situation as I.

I married three years later. Frank is a gentle, understanding and less intense man. He took life more leisurely and quietly than I did. I helped Brad through his own bout with his inherited abdominal polyps and was myself diagnosed with thyroid cancer. With treatment and thyroid replacement medication I'm now good as new, and so is Brad.

A year later I fell off a horse. I don't remember falling off; all I remember is waking up in an intensive care unit and thinking to myself, "I wonder what in-service training I am doing for these nurses today." When Frank, Brad, and Jeff appeared at the door I knew something had happened. I was told that I fell off the horse, broke two ribs, and had a concussion. A friend had come to the stables to see me ride and found me unconscious, lying on the ground, the horse grazing peacefully nearby.

I was taken to the emergency room and admitted for seven days in the hospital. After I went home I didn't give the fall much more thought other than feeling the pain in my side if I twisted the wrong way. After two more days off work I returned to my full schedule.

Strange, though, I discovered I couldn't easily find words that I needed to use when I was working with clients or demonstrating the product. It was like going to the word filing cabinet and having to search for words, never to find them. I found myself being very careful about speaking, but nothing else really seemed strange or different. The next summer I had to make out my first contract for a large hospital. After the home office received the contract they called me and asked where I had gotten some of the product numbers and other figures. I couldn't find an answer for them. Later that year I was assigned a new manager. She began pointing out my using incorrect words and abruptly stopping my speech mid-sentence. I realized I was having these problems ever since falling from the horse. My job was in jeopardy as the new manager couldn't accept my odd speech characteristics. Concern mounted. A social worker friend of mine suggested I get tested by a neuropsychologist.

I will always remember the morning of my testing. I was convinced that I did not have a problem and thought this to be a waste of time. About two hours into the testing, I was feeling so frustrated that I asked the examiner for a break. It took me forever to put together little block patterns that I knew I could have done in a snap a few years ago. There were other tasks I didn't do well on either. I was near tears and then realized that this is exactly how I felt at the end of most regular work days.

The testing marked both the beginning and the end of a chapter in my life: realization of the end of being able to do many of the things automatically that I had done all my life (the end of the firecracker in my life), and the beginning of my facing doing things differently because now I had to.

I knew I did strange things with numbers. Why, it took me sometimes twenty attempts to dial a phone number before I got it right. I realized I would figure out the right questions to ask at a sales meeting twenty minutes after the meeting was over. My self-esteem began to weaken as I realized my thinking was different and I couldn't do things with the confidence and verve I used to.

Throughout the next year, my manager continued to be demanding and I continued to seek help. However, I thought I was the old goal-oriented, do-the-impossible person I had always been. I did not slow down much. This attitude played havoc with me. I was irritable. My family later told me they took to the bomb shelter when I came home from work. I was frustrated and unhappy. My temper was hot.

With help, I vowed to accept the beginning of the second chapter in my life. I am not the person I was before I fell from that horse. I can't always accomplish the impossible. I am setting realistic goals. I don't need to be top sales person for the year anymore. At a recent sales meeting, all the outstanding team players were honored. It was hard for me to say to myself that I had done the best job I could even though there were no awards for my work. I can't climb to the top of the sales mountain at the same speed as my other team members. My customers know they will get service and dedication from me. Meanwhile, I continue to set realistic goals and most of all I take time, slow down, smell the roses, and go forward. This is the hardest thing I have ever done in my life. Way down in my heart I know that there are many blessings from the fall—but there are so many times that I have to remind myself that life is good and that I have many things to contribute to my own life as well as other's lives that I do well. Understanding who I am today and most importantly accepting that new person and embracing her with love and affection will allow her to grow. This is my new challenge. I am meeting this challenge as I have met the others, with the same energy and determination. This is the new, and the same, Samantha Elizabeth Janes Garland.

7

The Special Problems of "Mild Brain Injury"

There is "head injury," and then there is "brain injury." The two terms are not always synonymous, as discussed in Chapter Three. A blow to the head may result in temporomandibular joint damage, facial and skull structural changes, bruises and lacerations, neck injury, stretched and torn connective and muscle tissues (collectively referred to as myofascia), cranial nerve branch contusions, and a host of other possible injuries. Unless the physical force injury is sufficient, however, the brain may be relatively spared from injury when other structures of the head are not. Although the brain is a delicate organ and it does not take too much force to the head to cause mild brain injury, the distinction between head injury and brain injury is an important one for diagnostic clarification and treatment planning.

Pain, dizziness, blurred vision, balance difficulty, poor concentration, and irritability are some of the manifestations of head injury that may not have a direct relation with injury to the brain. Inner ear injury, eye injury, or neck and back injury can cause some of these symptoms. Treatment is dependent on accurate diagnosis, and expectations for recovery are dependent on knowing precisely what bodily systems are injured. The psychological implications from injury are different if one believes his or her brain versus some other part of the head is injured.

Thorough diagnostic assessment is necessary to clarify the cause of mild brain injury symptoms. This chapter focuses on mild brain

injury, specifically, where diagnostic understanding is sometimes controversial, and often difficult to achieve with precision. The qualifier
"mild" implies a relative aspect (compared with more severe brain
injury) and also carries a qualitative distinction of its own. Often, the
term "mild brain injury" implies subtle functional changes that may
have multiple causes, but where only minimal or mild physical trauma
to the brain has occurred. Such conventional thought, and especially
use of the term "mild," may misrepresent the seriousness of the situation because even mild brain injury can produce permanent, life-altering changes.

Neuroscience professionals speculate on why mild brain injury
might present so many lingering problems. Generally, a relatively mild
injury to the head puts an individual in a conflicting position. While
not so injured that he or she cannot carry on many of life's usual activities—perhaps including driving and even return to work—there are
persistent problems that prevent full, comfortable, and unlimited
return to those activities. This situation, coupled with slower than
expected recovery, may actually contribute to increasing pain, frustration, discouragement, and mental deterioration. An individual who
sustains a moderate or severe brain injury clearly cannot immediately
return to most usual activities and sooner and more readily accepts the
need for rehabilitation treatment.

Many individuals who experience a mild traumatic brain injury, and
become increasingly aware of compromised mental and emotional
functioning, may come to think of themselves as "crazy." They, their
families, and some health practitioners fail to realize that changed functioning and the powerlessness to rectify the situation is really rooted in
subtle damage to neural tissue in the brain.

Objective diagnosis of mild brain injury is sometimes difficult to
achieve. Understanding the mild but significant impact of an injury
must be approached from several angles. The neurologist and the neuropsychologist are the health care providers most able to help in such
diagnostic studies. Physical examination of the nervous system is per-

formed by the neurologist. Behavioral examination (language, thinking, social, and perceptual-motor) is accomplished by the neuropsychologist. Between the two, subtle abnormalities can be identified, if present, to support a diagnosis of mild brain injury.

Mild Traumatic Brain Injury

According to criteria established by the American Congress of Rehabilitation Medicine, mild trauma to the head must be of sufficient magnitude to produce at least *one* of the following symptoms of *brain* injury:

- Loss of consciousness of any duration, even brief;

- Loss of memory for events immediately before or after the accident, even a partial loss;

- Altered mental state following the accident, including feeling dazed, disoriented, or confused;

- Focal neurological signs (such as double vision, paralysis, or loss of speech) that may be transient.

In order for any of these signs to fall within the scope of mild brain injury, loss of consciousness cannot exceed approximately thirty minutes and posttraumatic amnesia (memory loss) cannot exceed twenty-four hours. Also, at thirty minutes after the injury, the Glasgow Coma Scale (see Chapter One) should not be lower than thirteen. It is noteworthy that only injury to the *brain* could produce any of these four symptoms. Many other symptoms that are reported after a head injury could be caused by non-brain injury or by psychological reaction, thus sometimes creating confusion about the cause of the symptoms.

The importance of differentiating mild from more severe brain injury is manifold. First, prognosis for recovery is generally better after milder injury than after more severe injury. Although studies have shown high percentages of people with mild brain injury still experiencing some problems after two years, many other studies demonstrate that individuals with such injury report no residual symptoms after three to six months.

Another reason for differentiating the severity of brain damage is in appreciating the treatment required. Mild brain injury typically responds well to psychologically oriented therapy. Individuals are often able to carry on with many of their usual daily activities and employment. However, their weakened sense of self-confidence, slower pace of mental processing, and often lingering physical problems—head and neck pain being the most prominent—respond well to treatment that offers explanation for the difficulties and that offers reassurance. Treatment that teaches practical mental and emotional management skills along with some cognitive skills is usually helpful. Too often, a diagnosis of mild brain injury, or concussion, is minimized by doctors and the individual affected, and treatment is neither recommended nor sought. This reaction belies the need for a restful recovery period which if not accepted can lead to extreme frustration and worsening symptoms. This is why, especially in cases of mild injury, patients should see a neurologist and a neuropsychologist trained in this specific disorder.

In contrast, more severe brain injury usually requires broad and intensive intervention by physical, occupational, and speech/cognitive therapists. Medical management of the effects of moderate to severe brain injury is typically required for such things as muscle contractures, seizures, and intraparenchymal (inside the brain tissue) injuries.

Accurate and definitive diagnosis of mild brain injury is also required due to certain social concerns. Mild traumatic brain injury is often sustained, or suspected, in automobile accidents such as rearend collisions. The chance for whiplash injury is fairly great in those types of accidents, and differentiating the nature and manifestation of injury to the individual is critical for injury claims settlements and litigation. Considerable controversy exists over the issue of whether an individual's symptoms from such injuries might be due to brain damage, or to injury of other structures of the head, or might be trumped up for the benefit of expected financial reward from litigation. Neuropsychological study of the individual is usually crucial in clarifying such differentiation.

Mild brain injury can be caused by many other conditions other than physical force trauma. Mild stroke or asphyxia (lack of sufficient oxygen to the brain, such as from carbon monoxide exposure) can produce much the same clinical pattern as trauma. Recognition and differentiation of symptom sources is, nevertheless, critical for appropriate treatment.

The study of mild traumatic brain injury is a specialty in and of itself. Many health professionals focus their knowledge on the challenging task of differential diagnosis of persons who have sustained head injury where the presence of mild brain injury is equivocal. Even if the diagnostic criteria are met, questions typically remain regarding the source of various symptoms, whether from brain or non-brain injury.

Postconcussion Syndrome

A phenomenon observed in nearly every case of mild brain injury, and in some cases of more severe injury as well, is a set of symptoms collectively known as "postconcussion syndrome." Generally, the syndrome refers to the sometimes vague and rather broad set of complaints offered by the individual who has suffered a relatively mild injury. The source of symptoms is implied to be derived from the concussion, but it is not clear whether that includes *brain* concussion. Symptoms within the postconcussion syndrome may have brain, somatic (bodily), or psychological roots. An individual who has experienced a relatively mild brain injury, who recovers nearly complete cognitive functioning, may also manifest reduced functioning as a result of pain and discomfort, as well as depression or anxiety, associated with other injury such as neck or myofascial injury. Of course, the diagnostic challenge is to figure out whether depression is caused by injury to the frontal poles of the brain (which research has shown can, indeed, cause a neurotransmitter imbalance resulting in depression) or to emotional reaction to the loss one experiences in capabilities, family relationships, and other personal and social factors.

BOX 7-1—Typical Characteristics of Postconcussion Syndrome

The following symptoms are most commonly reported after mild head injury. The source of the symptoms may or may not be due to brain concussion, making the syndrome of somewhat dubious diagnostic value. Symptoms are listed in order of frequency as reported by persons who have sustained mild head injury.

- Headache

- Memory impairment

- Dizziness

- Fatigue and weakness

- Concentration difficulty

- Confusion

- Nausea

- Mental dullness

- Irritability

- Depression

- Sleep difficulty

- Loss of self-confidence

- Visual problems

- Tinnitus

- Hypersensitivity to sounds

- Hypersensitivity to light

Subtle neuropsychological changes occur and present themselves as symptoms following mild brain injury. Virtually any injury to the brain causes at least some degree of slowing in mental processing. When the brain must find detours around injured neurons, that takes time and uses mental energy. Blocking when attempting to find a word to express a thought, absentminded behaviors, or a sense of clouded thinking typically cause frustration, irritation, and fatigue. Subtle and scattered injuries throughout the brain, as well as specific injury to brain stem structures, cause diminished concentration, making focusing on reading, work, or school difficult and prone to errors.

Personality changes from brain injury, even mild injury, include fear and anxiety, depression, depersonalization (a sense that you aren't the person you were accustomed to), derealization (dream-like perception of the world), impulsivity, reduced sensitivity to social graces, and propensity to misunderstand the motives and communications of others. While the controversy exists due to the lack of obvious visibility of brain damage, studies have shown microscopic injury to scattered cells in areas of the frontal lobes as well as throughout the brain that certainly could account for these kinds of problems.

A variety of other problems, which may or may not have their basis in brain dysfunction, include vestibular changes (balance problems, dizziness, vertigo), tinnitus (ringing in the ears), blurred vision, and reduced sensitivity to smell. As a consequence of these problems, irritation occurs and erodes self-confidence, concentration, and the ability to work at one's normal pace and quality.

Myofascial injuries, subtle damage to the first two or three vertebrae, and stretched muscles in the shoulders and neck can be a source of significant pain, including headache. Pain from any source detracts from one's ability to concentrate, think, and function optimally. Thus, the source of symptoms must be clarified in order to treat appropriately.

Posttraumatic Headache

Headache is probably the most prominent complaint that falls within the postconcussion syndrome. Headache, like mild brain injury itself, is a specialty among many health care and medical research professionals. Headache can stem from numerous causes, with only a relatively small fraction caused by actual injury to brain tissue. In fact, brain tissue itself does not contain pain receptors. Any pain that emanates from within the brain is usually caused by distention or dilation of blood vessels, which do have pain receptors. These problems can be due to brain swelling, blood pressure problems, and bleeding within the brain. Migraine headache sufferers experience pain associated with dilation of blood vessels overlying the brain.

Headache following head injury may have nothing at all to do with the brain. Localization of pain in the head is quite imprecise as to the source of the pain. Injury to spinal structures in the neck can be experienced as pain that feels as though it is coming from inside the head. Such problems with "referred pain" make diagnosis challenging. However, nerve blocks in peripheral (outside the brain) regions often cure headaches, at least temporarily, confirming their origin from sources other than the brain itself. A neurologist can usually identify the source of headache.

Regardless of the source of headaches following head injury, persistent pain can have devastating effects on one's thinking, memory, and disposition. Frustration derived from inability to successfully treat headache pain accumulates and evolves into depression and discouragement.

Some headaches following trauma to the brain may be due to changes in brain chemistry. Changes in the concentration or availability of certain neurotransmitters change the way the brain perceives pain. People normally have vastly different tolerances for pain. A person who has tolerated pain well in the past may now, after a mild blow to the head sufficient to cause a specific neurotransmitter toxicity, tolerate pain much less well. Thus, what used to present as mild but entirely tolerable discomfort may now produce heightened sensitivity to light, sounds, and excruciating pain, rendering the individual virtually unable to function normally in daily tasks.

Acceleration-deceleration movement (as in whiplash), when the head is suddenly and violently hyperextended then hyperflexed, can cause a multitude of injuries to the neck, vertebrae, muscles, and even to the brain stem. The momentum behind hyperextension/hyperreflection of the head can cause the distance from the top of the brain to the bottom of the brain stem to extend as well. This stretching movement can disrupt reticular activating and consciousness-maintenance systems within the brain. The confluence of these injuries produces a large component of the postconcussion syndrome and associated headache.

Other, coexisting factors can exacerbate the experience of postconcussion syndrome and headache. Difficulty sleeping, due to pain and discomfort, can reduce one's mental sharpness just as can any cause of inadequate sleep. Muscular weakness or sensory numbness can interfere with normal daily routines and contribute to frustration intolerance. Nausea, which may have many causes including vestibular injury, certainly interferes with one's sense of well being. Any of these persistent, nagging symptoms of mild brain injury can rob the individual of energy and enthusiasm and can heighten the awareness of pain. Again, sorting out the cause of symptoms within the postconcussion syndrome requires private-eye investigative determination in order to understand the interaction of symptoms and to plan appropriate treatment.

Treatment for Postconcussion Syndrome

Treatment for any single symptom following concussion is focused on the cause of the symptom. It is generally futile only to give a patient pain relievers for headache when treatment to restore muscle tissue would address the root cause of the pain. Medications to treat migraine will probably break the cycle faster than medications to dull the senses.

Usually, the physician sorting out the symptoms of mild traumatic brain injury and postconcussion syndrome must identify the nature of symptoms as having orthopedic (bone and joint), myofascial (muscle and supportive tissue), peripheral neurological (body), central neurological (brain), or emotional and psychological causes. Once an hypothesis about the source of a symptom is derived, treatment can proceed relatively well targeted. Sometimes, response to treatment can be diagnostic in itself and help refine the understanding of a symptom.

The emotional and psychological factors that may contribute to the presence or severity of any symptom cannot be understated. Persons who experience mild traumatic brain injury may recover much better, regardless of the causes of their symptoms, when neuropsychological counseling accompanies other rehabilitation and treatment modalities. The individual needs education about the source and nature of his or her symptoms. Particularly when these symptoms involve cognitive, emotional, and personality changes, fear of irreversible brain injury is almost always present. A neuropsychological counselor who is familiar with the mechanism of injury, postconcussion symptoms and the response to treatment so far, and who is sensitive to the array of personality factors which color any reaction to injury can offer understanding, hope, and a realistic grasp on the whole ordeal. Typically, the neuropsychologist and physician (such as physiatrist, neurologist, orthopedist, or other specialist) work together in communicating findings and making sure that information provided the individual is consistent and supportive.

Posttraumatic Stress Disorder

Another complicating problem associated with mild traumatic brain injury that is almost never associated with more severe brain injury is the phenomenon of "posttraumatic stress disorder (PTSD)." This cluster of anxiety-based symptoms stems from the impact of a severely frightening and emotionally traumatic event on a person's life. Many soldiers involved in the Vietnam conflict in the 1960's suffered posttraumatic stress due to their sense of being trapped in unforgiving territory where bloodshed, surprise attacks, language barriers that virtually blocked communications, vague war strategies, use of highly toxic chemicals, and a constant threat to life (to one's own as well as one's companions) hung heavy in the air for days, weeks, and months on end. That, coupled with the lack of societal support, produced a psychological reaction in the soldier of extreme panic, withdrawal, on-edge temper, extreme startle propensity, depression, fitful dreams, flashbacks and often difficult reintegration within one's family, work, and community.

While one's involvement in a car accident or other physically and emotionally traumatic event may seem to pale in comparison with a war experience, people do sometimes develop immediate or delayed posttraumatic stress disorder. Of course, this is fairly easy to understand in those cases where particularly gruesome accident situations occur where one feels trapped and incapable of helping, and where a serious threat exists to one's life or safety.

The diagnosis of posttraumatic stress disorder is probably overused in cases of relatively mild head injury but at least an anxiety reaction can reasonably occur following a sudden and frightening accident where one feels helpless and vulnerable. Being trapped in a wrecked car where the odor of leaking gasoline is strong, for example, can produce extreme panic that the person will remember probably forever and may produce lingering anxiety symptoms that meet the diagnostic standard for posttraumatic stress disorder.

One of the requirements for PTSD is a memorable event upon which the anxiety symptoms are based. So, the controversy lingers over whether one can experience both PTSD and brain injury simultaneously. If, by definition, brain injury requires some level of amnesia of events surrounding the accident, how can posttraumatic stress develop? Because the amnesia is often incomplete in cases of mild brain injury, the person may remember the moments before an accident, but not the actual accident itself. The panic of seeing another car headed right for

yours can be terrifying. Furthermore, the amnesia surrounding a physically traumatic event may be incomplete, which only adds to its terrifying nature. Incomplete or vague memories that have a frightening stem
are often woven together with embellishments consistent with a "near-
death" or other exaggerated interpretation. This, coupled with lingering and uncomfortable postconcussion symptoms can fuel and sustain
anxiety reaction to the event.

As with any illness or injury, diagnostic labels are often simplistic
and used liberally. Sorting out the symptoms from any injury requires
sensitivity to the multiple potential causes of those symptoms and
addressing each of them individually. To say that PTSD and MTBI
can *never* exist concurrently may be too simple. To say that the complex interaction of symptoms might produce *both* PTSD and MTBI
requires that the symptoms be sorted out and understood in terms of
their effects on the individual's life.

Connective Tissue Disorders

Numerous musculoskeletal and connective tissue disorders appear to
be related to body trauma in general, but manifest rather frequently in
cases of mild traumatic brain injury. This adds to the conundrum of
the disorder. Persons who suffer chronic fatigue syndrome or fibromyalgia after a minor accident may be suspected of malingering their disorders as the manifestation of the condition is often vague, poorly
understood by medical specialists, and often not able to be objectively
confirmed by medical or psychological diagnostic tests.

Persons who experience accidental injuries, which may or may not
include head (or brain) injury, may suffer lingering and permanent
musculoskeletal and connective tissue diseases, including fibromyalgia,
arthritis, osteoporosis, gout, rheumatism, or neuropathic arthropathy.
Certain viral or viral-associated diseases have been linked to somatic
trauma, particularly chronic fatigue syndrome. Some people become
more susceptible to immune deficiency disorders (particularly viral diseases) following severe body trauma.

Describing each of these problems and linking them with possible brain injury is beyond the scope of this text. The point to be made here is that injury to the body and brain, no matter how minor it may seem, can have far-reaching and life-changing effects. The first line of defense in minimizing the effects of trauma is emergency medical care in order to minimize the cascade of further injury and to facilitate the body's own defenses and healing processes. The second line of defense is to attack the psychological and emotional reactions often produced by significant injury. Learning to accept injury, to do what is necessary to facilitate the body's healing powers, and to adapt to any permanent changes are challenges required by anyone in the course of a lifetime. Finally, rehabilitation designed to improve what can be improved and help teach acceptance of and adjustment to what cannot be improved makes successful management of brain injury possible.

Respect for the infinite system interactions within the body and how those systems individually and collectively may fail following body and/or brain trauma is essential. While medical and neuropsychological science seems ever to reach new heights, we have a long way to go in understanding the human body. Medicine, psychology, and rehabilitation are still arts, relying on science wherever possible. Ferreting out the sources of pain, fatigue, sleeplessness, confusion, depression, weight loss, loss of self-confidence, memory weakness, poor concentration, and other symptoms observed following concussion is the challenge posed by mild traumatic brain injury.

June—Real Person

June 15, 1995, will be a day to remember forever. It was a hot evening, filled with happiness and anticipation. My husband, Sean, and I had been house hunting. We found a great ranch style home in excellent condition. The property was fenced and perfect for my two young sons, Lonnie and Mark. The best part is we had the down payment already in savings.

On the drive home from looking at the house, we discussed our decision to make an offer the next morning. Lonnie was at home and Mark was still at the babysitter's house. Less than one mile from the babysitter's home a slow-moving three-quarter-ton farm truck pulled out in front of our 1993 Toyota. Sean braked hard and avoided a collision. Seeing no oncoming cars ahead, Sean pulled out to pass the truck which then started weaving across the road. Horn honking alerted the driver and Sean braked again and pulled back into his own lane. Moments later as he pulled out to pass again, I couldn't believe my eyes. The truck turned sharply left directly in front of us. Sean slammed on the brakes and I closed my eyes hard and thought to myself, "This is going to hurt."

The next thing I remember was sitting on the hot pavement gasping for air because of the chemicals in the air bag. Sean had pulled me from the car. The front passenger side of our car had slammed into the truck's back left wheel. I remember the driver of the truck asking, "Where did you come from?" I had no idea what life had in store for me from that moment on.

Before the accident I had been an insurance agent for nine years. In addition to my managing a small agency, my husband and I had just opened a small antique store 15 days prior to the accident. We had been married a few years and were totally crazy about our six-month-old, Mark. Life seemed to be going great for us. I was a "take care of business" type person. Sean had really liked that feature in me.

Immediately after the accident I felt shaken up. X-rays showed no broken bones or bleeding. I went on in to work the next day with aches and pains throughout my whole body, including a splitting headache. (I never had headaches before.) It was Friday and I was thankful for that and thought that after the weekend I would feel better. By Sunday, I felt drunk and tired. I went to work on Monday anyway but I left early to see my doctor.

By Friday, I was miserable and still in pain. I could barely read or write, much less remember simple things. The doctor ordered a CT scan of my brain. Meanwhile I had to deal with a company supervisor who seemed to care as little as possible about what had happened to me. I felt totally helpless and alone.

My problems kept getting worse. My doctor told me it could take days, weeks, or even months for all this to go away. I only heard "days," and months later I couldn't understand why I wasn't just like my old self again. One doctor told me I was just overstressed. Meanwhile, my supervisor insisted I was putting everyone in a pinch by not working.

My doctor then ordered neuropsychological testing. The diagnosis: mild brain injury with residual postconcussion syndrome. Finally, someone understood that my problems were not just "psychological." Meanwhile, I received a nice termination letter from the insurance agency.

Over the course of several months, my physical problems gradually disappeared. My abilities to read and write (and spell correctly) have improved. I am still working on getting back my ability to do accurate math again. I still have headaches but they are not as severe as they used to be. My memory is an everyday issue but I'm writing everything down now and that is helping a lot. I think my greatest problem is dealing with everyday common stress. It seems to mount up and cause an eventual explosion. I have always had a positive attitude and actually continue to have one. This is despite the charge from my insurance company that I am "malingering." This from someone who has never met me, never even talked to me.

I have learned to slow life down by a pace or two, or three, or four. I am working for a new insurance company now and enjoying it. They feel I'm doing a good job and so do I. My highlight of the day now occurs when a former customer wants to switch his insurance to the new company I'm working for. Our antique store is doing great despite a slow beginning. I could barely make out a deposit ticket for months after the accident but now I can do it, actually without mistakes. Sean sometimes gets frustrated because I'm not the same, but I am beginning to like myself again. I'm no longer a door mat and am getting a little more of my "take charge" characteristics back.

I doubt the driver of that farm truck knows the troubles he caused and I'm certain my former boss will always expect the worst from people. The dream of getting our new home was within hours of becoming a reality but is now on hold. The financial losses caused by the accident and the endless fights with getting insurance coverage has forced a hardship on us. Our hopes for a new home in the near future are out of reach. Sometimes I struggle to remain positive but a smile from Mark always helps. Despite my misfortune I continue to be thankful for my good fortune.

8

The Never Ending Journey

The paradox of brain injury is that you don't remember the event that changed your life but you know you aren't the same person ever again that you used to be. Traumatic brain injury is a sudden, dramatic, life-changing event that you can't remember, and can never forget.

Brain injury begins a journey—a lifelong commitment to learning and discovering the uniqueness of who you are and what life has to offer. This quest is the key to overcoming, or at least managing, the changes caused by brain injury. There is an excitement that accompanies new learning: the joy of overcoming obstacles, the discovered truths that lend a little more contentment to a frustrating world.

Brain injury or not, scientific research consistently demonstrates the benefits of a mentally active lifestyle in order to stimulate intellectual capabilities and growth. People who are mentally active maintain an openness to new attitudes and values and feel positive about their ability to grow connected with the rest of society.

While living, itself, may be described as a never ending journey of discovery, the journey with brain injury becomes particularly keen. There develops a conscious, driving desire to find ways to enhance life, to feel good about yourself and about life.

The never ending journey through life after a brain injury is an opportunity for self-discovery that is often not paralleled in "normal" people; cultivating patience to overcome pain and disabilities; learning new and better ways to accomplish old tasks; acquiring wisdom through overcoming the pain of losses; making it through walls of negativity and emerging with a smile; constantly growing in emotional maturity. All these challenges have the potential to overshadow the losses, the financial strains, the frustrations, and the periods of confusion. Driving it all is a commitment to a *positive* attitude—not one of helplessness and victimization, but of renewed strength and dedication to a new life that fate bestowed.

Like Dorothy in the *Wizard of Oz*, who had the capability to go home all along, we each hold inside ourselves hidden capabilities that need to be released. Dorothy just had to use the resources she had all along and didn't need to go through the terror of the haunted forest, the witch's castle, and the winged monkeys to find someone to help her. It's all in the attitude. It's all in building faith in yourself and discovering who you really can become. While we may not have the magic red slippers Dorothy had, we can begin anew life's journeys with our own unique resources.

Many people who reflect both insight and contentment in their lives are ones who have been through and have overcome major adversity. While the charmed life of a fantasy princess may seem enviable at times, being a member of the *common* human race provides a potential for genuine strength, composure, and empathy. These qualities often emerge from adversity. Remember the adage, "What doesn't kill you makes you stronger." While any negative life experience—even as catastrophic as a major brain injury—can lead to bitterness and unhappiness, the choice to conquer and emerge victorious is much more satisfying.

Some people who experience a brain injury never seem to get to a point of satisfaction with their lives. They condemn the experience, resent others whom they loosely blame for their ills, and never seem to learn to take charge of their own lives. Of course, there are plenty of people in the world who have not had a brain injury who fit this description. It is the premise of this book that despite brain injury, the life journey can be a positive one, filled with many moments of satisfaction and contentment.

The question "Why did this happen to me?" fades into oblivion as inevitable grief and self-pity are overcome. The reason this question is asked in the first place is because of feeling helpless. Overcoming that feeling and accepting the belief that "life is worth living" is a conscious commitment *anyone* can make. To question whether life after brain injury is worth living is to sustain being mired in old expectations, in sadness that it happened, and in feeling the victim. The brain injury experience is, without doubt, a life-altering experience none of us would wish on anyone. To experience it, however, and rise above it, can leave one enriched in ways not possible had the injury not occurred.

This chapter looks at some of the processes, ingredients, and values that make life worth living after a brain injury—more than just worth living, a real opportunity to live with a depth of appreciation of life and of values that pass many people by. As such, life can be an exciting, enriching journey. Time to click heels.

Recovery, Remediation, Rehabilitation

With no help at all, some degree of spontaneous recovery of mental functions will occur after a brain injury. This is the brain's natural effort to reestablish itself, without formal help from outside, in order to get on with life. Anyone who has experienced a brain injury knows, however, that passive reliance on spontaneous recovery is inadequate. Just as a newborn would not learn to become a responsible, socialized adult left on her own, so an individual experiencing brain injury cannot be left to fend for herself without help from others. That is what brain injury rehabilitation is all about.

After a brain injury, the first level of intervention is, of course, to save the life. Usually, rather soon after medical stabilization, the individual enters into rehabilitation—the rebuilding of life. This may involve a formally designated, hospital- or clinic-based program, an outpatient service, or something one does on her own at home. Rehabilitation following brain injury is a *necessity*, whether the injury is mild or severe. Rehabilitation is the concerted effort to reverse and/or mini-mize the effects of neurological damage. Rehabilitation is also, and just as importantly, the foundation for letting go of losses and for building a new life. It is hard work; it requires commitment; it is never ending.

Recovery of Lost or Damaged Skills

A rehabilitation team at the early and intense stages of recovery can consist of physical therapists, occupational therapists, speech therapists, music and art therapists, psychotherapists, nurses, doctors, social work-ers, chaplains, friends, parents, siblings—virtually anyone who contrib-utes to helping a person recover lost or damaged skills. With practice that mimics how we teach an infant to learn to walk and coordinate her body, so rehabilitation therapies teach a person whose neuromus-cular connections have been damaged (but not beyond repair) to recover those functions, at least to the extent the injured system will allow.

The focus early in rehabilitation is to recover whatever skills the ner-vous system will allow. Seemingly endless repetitions of body move-ments, torturous practice at repeating words, rehearsing over and over again the basic activities of daily living, practice in the logic of how to perform essential activities—these are the foundations for reestablish-ing the neuromotor links and brain connections that will help restore basic skills. The goal is recovery of whatever functions can be recov-ered.

Remediation of Deficiencies

Remediation refers to correcting a deficiency. It is a bit broader con-cept than that of recovery and includes learning strategies for minimiz-ing the effects of a deficiency if the impaired function cannot be completely recovered. Walking, for example, that cannot be com-pletely recovered can be remediated (i.e., aided) by the use of a cane, or

BOX 8-1—Rehabilitation Specialists

Modern rehabilitation is represented in an interdisciplinary team of specialists. The variety of specialists reflects the complexity of knowledge about brain injury which cannot be the responsibility of just one or two persons. Specialists include:

Behavior Therapist: This individual specializes in recognizing the antecedents of behavior problems and the kinds of controls that might be necessary to maintain emotional and behavioral stability in patients who have significant difficulty doing this on their own.

Case Manager: Usually a nurse or social worker, either on staff with the facility, or provided by the insurance company, who acts as a liaison between the patient/family and virtually all the other care providers, insurance companies, rehabilitation equipment suppliers, and other agencies that are or will become involved with the patient.

Chaplain: The spiritual needs and desires of patients and families are usually challenged in times of crisis. Helping families to accept what has happened and to make it through the uncertain times is provided by the chaplain.

Consulting Physicians: Depending on other injuries, a variety of specialists may be consulted for pulmonary, orthopedics, cardiovascular, or other problems.

Neurologist: This physician often takes over when the neurosurgeon has done his or her job. Neurological evaluations monitor recovery, and particularly address potential problems such as seizures, headaches, and other neurologically-based physical symptoms.

Neuropsychologist: Evaluation of brain functions as reflected in behavior, emotions, and cognitive abilities is the job of the neuropsychologist. He or she provides primary information for coordinating the psychological and social reintegrative aspects of rehabilitation.

Neurosurgeon: This physician is the key coordinator in emergency trauma treatment. He or she directs the intervention to save the life, perform surgery when needed, prevent further injury, and begin the physical healing.

Nutritionist/Dietician: Proper diet is essential for optimum body and brain recovery. This specialist knows foods, nutrition, weight-control, and the interaction of nutrition with various medical conditions.

Occupational Therapist: Using the body to accomplish the familiar activities of daily living is the responsibility of the occupational therapist, including regaining use of the fingers and hands, eye-hand coordination, self-care skill building, eating, and bathing.

Physiatrist: The physician specializing in physical medicine and rehabilitation often takes over primary care of the patient once out of acute care and in rehabilitation. This physician directs and coordinates many aspects of the physical and medical aspects of rehabilitation.

Physical Therapist: This individual focuses on restoring physical use of the body, teaching walking, posture, balance, endurance, strength, and coordination.

Psychiatrist: This physician, who specializes in the application of medications in mental health, is sometimes called upon to help the patient deal with troublesome emotional and behavioral problems.

Recreation and Activity Therapist: Teaching the patient to make the most of leisure time, to enjoy relaxation, and to gain self-confidence for balancing work and play is the goal of the recreation and activity therapist.

Rehabilitation Nurse: The nurse cares for the patient on a moment-by-moment basis and coordinates routine daily activities, carries out the doctor's orders, attends to the patient's needs, monitors the patient's medical condition, and participates in patient and family education.

Respiratory Therapist: Patients experiencing breathing problems, particularly those on respirators, need assistance in adapting to such equipment and in gradually learning to carry out automatic, independent breathing again.

Social Worker: This individual assesses the family's needs and risks, helps to plan for discharge, makes referrals to appropriate community and government resources utilizing applicable laws and regulations, and helps to coordinate benefits. The social worker role may act as the case manager.

Speech Therapist: Restoring language and thinking skills is the job of the speech therapist. Motor-speech, reading, hearing, and talking are retrained in order to further development of higher level cognitive skills.

Vocational Rehabilitation Counselor: Once a person is sufficiently recovered from the acute phases of trauma, this specialist may be of great benefit in helping individuals make alternative work plans.

a leg brace, or some other assistive device. Therapy aims to recover first, then remediate what cannot be recovered.

Cognitive remediation is a term heard frequently in the course of rehabilitation. It refers to teaching an individual how to overcome shortcomings in memory, thinking, mental organization, and performing such basic skills as reading, writing, and arithmetic. The quality of those cognitive functions will change to some degree after a brain injury and may never completely recover to their pre-injury quality. In order to enable the individual to function despite permanent changes, remediation strategies are taught to help the individual perform these functions better and more effectively than had remediation strategies not been taught. (Many examples of these were provided in Chapter Six.)

Lifestyle Rehabilitation

Rehabilitation is the overriding concept that includes recovery and remediation, but has yet an even broader scope. The portion of the word that derives from "habitat" means living space or the interactive community where one normally lives. So, *re*-habilitation implies recovering a satisfactory lifestyle within a satisfying community. Rehabilitation doesn't imply getting back to where one was before the injury nearly as much as it means getting on with life in a satisfying, worthwhile, and self-respecting way, functioning fully, likely some ways differently than before. We know that life after a brain injury is never again the same. Thus, rehabilitation in the context of "brain injury rehabilitation" must take on this broader and more enlightened meaning.

Brain injury rehabilitation isn't just about achieving optimum functioning or maximum potentials. Most people never achieve these lofty goals in their entire lives. Rehabilitation is about recovering *and about building new* skills, attitudes, behavior styles, self-respect, and self-concept that enable a contented—and energetic—life journey. Constantly focusing on achieving pie-in-the-sky maximum potentials may compromise the experience of prideful contentment right now. Strive always and only to perform better and you may never achieve your goal. The journey can be just as important as the destination.

Our culture rather constantly places expectations on its citizens to aim high, perform 110 percent, achieve the best that we can. Striving for personal best is excellent as long as it does not interfere with satisfaction in the moment. Brain injury rehabilitation is a balance of the two: achieving potentials and enjoying the journey of learning and discovery.

Avoiding Dependency

Very early in the course of recovery from a brain injury, there is an impressionable period where family, nurses, doctors, and others are supplying every need the injured individual may have. People who are taken care of may learn a form of dependency that exacerbates whatever deficiencies they have. An individual recovering from coma is directed when, where, and how to do just about everything, from taking a shower to eating a meal, to practicing arm and leg exercises, to visiting with family and friends. The brain is vulnerable to this kind of regimentation and dependency and, if allowed to proceed too long, virtual dependence on others may become an expectation. "Learned dependency" needs to be avoided or it will interfere with rehabilitation in general. Although rehabilitation is really a lifelong process, the first year or two following the event that caused the brain injury are the most vulnerable for negative experiences or expectations to set in. This is why rehabilitation must, from the outset, focus on functional *inde*pendence and attitudes that encourage self-confidence, self-respect, and self-reliance.

Family members can aid in an individual's recovery of responsibility. By encouraging the person to fend for himself or herself as much as possible—while providing encouragement and guidance when necessary—the individual will avoid developing dependency. Being able to take care of yourself as much as the body and mind will allow helps foster positive self-regard and confidence. Families and care givers must restrain their desire to take care of someone when, perhaps with only a little help, the person can take care of himself.

A major philosophy in this book is one of accepting change and making choices to make the experience positive—at least sometimes. At every turn, with every therapist and every opportunity, the person with a brain injury must be perceived as a whole person. This simply means that the effect of the brain injury must be kept in perspective. The individual must never be perceived as an invalid—someone who cannot do anything for himself. (Just think of the word: "*in*-valid"!)

One must never assume a person with a brain injury cannot do something or other. In fact, the attitude must prevail that the individual can do whatever he wants. The rehabilitation process aims to discover whatever special modifications, practice, or adaptations might be necessary in order to accomplish a particular activity—from walking to making a bed, to writing a check, to understanding a written passage, to preparing a simple meal, to interacting with a family, to performing work. Brain injury rehabilitation requires a balance of strategies to recover functioning, techniques to adapt to functional changes, and an attitude of acceptance and commitment to continued growth and discovery.

Coping, and Liking It

One of the questions asked, sometimes with a resentful snarl, by a lot of people in the thick of rehabilitation is, "With all this coping I am expected to do, how can I *like* it?" Of course, this question bespeaks considerable frustration. Anyone who states defiantly that he is, indeed, coping, but not liking it, hasn't crossed the line yet into self-acceptance. Crossing this line is not easy. To many individuals, just accepting that their lives are different and that they must constantly do things differently, and remain eternally patient, acknowledging that their old selves will never return, ought to quality them for martyrdom. Getting to the point of saying "Hey, this is me, I'm different, I like myself again, and I actually find this journey a positive challenge" seems at first an absurd impossibility, a candy-coated Pollyannaish self-deception at least.

The first step in learning to cope, *and liking it,* is to realize that in any situation or confrontation, whether with someone else or within yourself, you have two choices. You can give in to weakness (we call that "succumbing") or you can meet the confrontation headstrong and willfully overcome it (we call this "coping"). Coping means analyzing the situation, figuring out what you can do about it, then just doing it. Coping with a disability does not necessarily mean getting back to the way you were before the disability. It means figuring out how you can minimize the effect of a disability, do things differently, and get on with life *despite* the disability. It definitely does not mean giving in to a weakness or a disability.

A writer who experiences a brain injury might find that keyboarding is now a slow and tedious effort, producing many more mistakes. Also, thinking isn't as fluid as it once was and so writing requires many more rewrites than before. The writer undergoes months of rehabilitation. While many aspects of her life have recovered or have been remediated, no effort has undone the brain injury sufficiently enough to allow her to write as prolifically as she used to. Remembering that she was taught to throw away the rearview mirror (see Chapter Five), she develops a plan to daily write down ways she can cope with the changes in her abilities so that she can still write enjoyably and productively. This goal is the first step in coping. Had she succumbed to her idolization of the rearview mirror of her life she might have given up her love of writing altogether with nothing to replace it, only to become bitter and resentful.

An individual who does not keyboard easily, does not think fast, and makes several spelling mistakes is evaluating all these things with respect to some "former" standard. By throwing away the standard and starting over, coping can and does evolve. First of all, thinking is the key to writing well. The individual who has trouble organizing thoughts might do well, for instance, to learn the skill of "mind mapping." This is a strategy for drawing one's thoughts out on paper in an organized and pictorial (but not linear) manner. There are many books, videos, and audio tapes on the subject that the individual could acquire and learn from.

Having learned to take control of thinking and feeling satisfied that mental organization is under control, putting thoughts on paper is the next aim. Whereby keyboarding might still be a practical strategy, one might need to adjust expectations of speed and accuracy, and rely on a personal computer with spelling and grammar checkers. Technology provides tremendous aids to rehabilitation in that it offers multiple and alternative ways to accomplish the same task. Advancements in speech recognition software might enable the individual to speak to her computer now instead of keyboarding. Or, going back to longhand writing and employing the services of a typist might be the answer. The issue here is that the rearview mirror must be discarded and an attitude of discovery accepted in order to cope, successfully, productively, and satisfyingly, with the change in how one writes. Not an easy task, but entirely possible.

Rehabilitation does not imply that if you just keep going through the mechanics of coping, and telling yourself to like it, you will eventually be able to do anything you want. Sometimes, all the adaptive strategies in the world won't work to restore some function or to learn a skill. In the earlier example of the writer, it might just turn out that she will not be a writer anymore—at least not in the sense she used to be. If the degree of brain injury interferes so much that writing can no longer meet the demands of an editor (from whence the paycheck comes), it might be necessary to drastically alter career expectations.

Due to psychological denial (dreading the loss of one's livelihood and vocational joy of self-expression), or due to inadequate ability to self-monitor and self-judge one's own work, writing as it used to be may be lost forever. Adjusting to that loss may be excruciatingly painful and take a long time. Eventually, however, the time may come to write with a different standard, or to exchange it for some other form of self-expression altogether, perhaps photography.

Forcing yourself to cope isn't coping. Adopting an open-minded attitude and taking serious stock of your strengths, weaknesses, and options is the beginning of coping. Finding out what works and sticking with a plan to make it work is coping. And if something isn't working, do something else. When regrets creep into the mind, replace them with something positive. Keep track of successes and find new joys and adventures on which to build new successes. Remember to smile and be the kind of person you want others to be. These are examples of the ingredients for coping. Coping, and liking it, happens when you once again start to like yourself.

Insider vs. Outsider Perspectives

Many people adapt an outsider perspective to their own disability. This means, essentially, that in their now alien experience they feel self-pity. They haven't owned up to themselves. They feel sorry for themselves just as we might feel sorry for someone who is down on his luck. A disability from the outside arouses feelings of pity, sorrow, loss, avoidance, and other negative emotions. People see others' disabilities (from the outside perspective) wondering how anyone could possibly adjust to such misfortune. By seeing yourself in a pitying, or at least sorrowful, way as other's might perceive and feel sorry for you, coping is not possible.

Eventually, most people come to take their disabilities in stride—to accept the new challenges as a part of their nature. People generally learn to accept what used to be considered shortcomings—shyness, klutziness, physical blemishes, hair loss, short stature, brain changes, or whatever—as a part of themselves.

To experience a disability from the inside is to own it and make it a part of you—without resentment or self-loathing. It is to integrate, get used to, or relegate the disability so that its negative impact is minimal or neutral. Actually, a disability from the inside experience ceases to be much of a disability at all. Coping is possible when one's disability starts to become a more or less comfortable and natural part of life. To cope with disability it must become a part of you. It must be accepted in a manner that does not deny its presence but does not let its presence overshadow life either.

Keys to Coping

Time is the greatest healer. In our impatience, we tend too often to forget that. We can augment the healing power of time by cultivating a few very effective coping attitudes.

Pride. Whatever it takes, cultivate pride in yourself. If you think, "How can I be proud of myself with all these scars on my face," you are using self-defeating thinking patterns right from the start. Don't look for the negative things you want to overcome. Look for the positive things you like (or, could like) about yourself. Your affable personality, an artistic skill, unique knowledge about some subject, your warm smile, your capability to love and care for someone or for animals or for the environment, some possession that has a great deal of special meaning—any of these can be the foundation for a feeling of pride. Too often pride is smothered by a focus on something negative, something lost, or some fault or shortcoming we dislike about ourselves.

Identify one thing you like about yourself: a talent, a specialized knowledge, a hobby or activity, a personality trait. Ask yourself how you can share what you like about yourself with others. How can you expand your special gift? Developing pride starts with just one thing. The more you exercise your prideful feelings, the more those feelings will spill over into other areas of your life.

Positivity. This has, of course, been a theme throughout this book. In order to accomplish anything, positive thoughts provide the foundation. That does not mean that if you have strong enough positive thoughts about winning the lottery it will happen. Thinking positive only influences *you*, not some external chance event. Being positive means owning your feelings in a commanding, satisfying, prideful manner.

Whenever you feel a little down, a little stressed, a little tense, a little angry, it is probably because you have slipped into a negative mode. Recognizing these signs is important so that you can get back on track with a positive attitude, a positive outlook, a positive determination to find a way to accomplished what you need to accomplish.

Remember to use affirmations (see Chapter Five). Like pride, positive feelings grow with practice and become infectious. The more you consciously practice being positive, the more it occurs automatically.

Hope. The idea of hope must not be confused with the concept of a wish or a desire. These are vastly different things. Hope is confidence and trust. Its popular use has been twisted to reflect a wish for something desired. Hope in its truest sense is not a wish for something but a peaceful trust in oneself, the future, one's family and friends, and one's well-being. It's one's capability to accept the cards life deals. We know by now that we cannot direct fate. We know we can cultivate an expectation that will set a course for our lives that is as independent as possible from fate, but never denying that fate forces upon us burdensome change and challenges at times when we least expect it. This attitude is the foundation for hope. It is self-assuring. It is a faith in our own strength, within the realm of the unknown.

Hope is related to the concept of faith (see Chapter Five). Hope, trust, faith, confidence—these are foundation attitudes. They are not created overnight. Many people spend years or even a lifetime cultivating a sense of peace and contentment built on these attitudes.

One method many people find extremely helpful in developing hope and faith is to find a hero. Identify someone, living or dead, who you admire and respect for his or her courage and personal strengths. Find ways to practice those attitudes and characteristics in your own life. Read about that person, write down the things you like about that person and are making a part of your life.

Contentment. This is an ingredient of hope, positivity, and pride. It deserves recognition for its own value in fostering a coping lifestyle. Many people find contentment in being in a peaceful place, meditating, painting or making music, taking care of a pet, or escaping in the fantasy of a novel. Finding means and ways to cultivate contentment is an essential ingredient for coping. This does not mean that day-to-day life will always be filled with contentment. It means that when life doesn't feel particularly contented, you find something to balance things out.

Likely apparent by now, pride, positivity, hope, and contentment are not mutually exclusive ideas. One complements the others. They are all attitudes, or values, people strive to achieve and improve upon. Each person, through reading, talking with others, and contemplation, finds ways to strengthen these ideals in his or her own private way.

Reinventing a Sense of Peace

Often, after some tragedy, everything that goes wrong gets blamed on the tragedy. Things do go wrong from time to time. Always have; always will. It's just convenient to have a scapegoat on which to blame things. However, blaming something or someone for everything that goes wrong just isn't healthy. Such a habit erodes self-determination and confidence and further turns one into a victim.

We've all heard the saying, "bad things happen to good people." This is to remind us that unfortunate circumstances do not bespeak our badness or that we deserve some kind of punishment. Things just happen over which we have little or no control. It is just as reasonable to say, "good things happen to bad people." We evaluate things and people as good or bad, and badness has to be blamed on something or someone. Not so.

There is no such thing as a charmed life. The fate of Princess Diana is a prime example of that. The fact is, life is an unfolding journey, most paths of which are unknown to us until we start down them and then they yield unpredictable events. Sure, there are some events we'd rather not have to contend with, but should one of those events (such as a brain injury) become part of our journey, we can either deal with it (cope) or wish it to just go away (deny it). Choosing the latter will lead to anger, resentfulness, self-loathing, self-rejection, and a mushrooming negative experience for the rest of life.

Gaining awareness of how our minds deal with pain and change and develop positive attitudes and peace is crucial for coping with brain injury. Often, a relationship with a therapist who can guide development of this awareness is helpful, if not essential. Psychological professionals understand the imposition of brain injury and how that may make self-awareness and the cultivation of appropriate attitudes challenging. While several suggestions have been given for self-directed discovery, learning from someone with specialized training and experience can be beneficial.

Accepting Uncertainty

One of the most difficult things some people face is acceptance of uncertainty and the unknown. Uncertainty confronts us every time we wake up and get out of bed. An abnormal fear of the unknown is the disease of anxiety. A sense of contentment, safety, and satisfaction replaces fear and anxiety as we learn to accept uncertainty. When we no longer feel overcome with uncertainty, we can relax and begin to feel contentment.

Brain injury, by virtue of creating many aspects of a new environment and a new lifestyle, can cause anxiety due to uncertainty. There is no magic formula for coping with ambiguity. Awareness that it is an expected component following brain injury may make it a little less disturbing. Anxiety gradually subsides with time, coping, and a positive attitude.

Worry is a symptom of anxiety, uncertainty, and a sense of powerlessness. Worry is a negative reaction that leads to more anxiety. It is akin to rumination (see Chapter Six). If we know how the future will turn out, we wouldn't spend time fretting and worrying about it.

Like so many attitudes and behaviors, to worry or not to worry is a personal choice. Look back on some incident you were very upset and worried about and you can now see how unnecessary the worrying was.

You might even be disappointed that you lost so much time and mental energy stewing and brooding about it. Make the choice to accept the notion that uncertainty is a part of life. Embrace it with faith and positivity.

Reducing Stress

Learning to accept uncertainty without succumbing to its anxieties is a hallmark of emotional maturity. Of course, being careful and responsible helps control untoward eventualities but never completely eradicates them. This is why we must be mentally adaptable to whatever befalls us. This requires flexibility, adaptability, a sense of hope and trust, and strategies to promote relaxation and a comfort zone—in short, reducing stress.

While it is capable of the most ingenious creations, the mind is sometimes negligent in dealing with the stresses it creates. One of the designers and developers of the Empire State Building—an architectural, manufacturing, and engineering feat of magnanimous proportions—is said to have suffered an irreversible nervous breakdown during construction because he could not cope with the pressures of bringing to fruition the imagination his brain created. Learning to diminish stress, control anxiety, and find contentment is a challenge of living for anyone. Finding ways to relax and accept the unknown is essential for mental health.

Numerous suggestions are presented throughout this book on how to reduce stress and anxiety. As with any cultivation of personal change, no one method works best for everyone. Each, in his or her own way, must experiment with thoughtful ways to increase coping, pride, contentment, faith, hope—in short, emotional maturity.

Lessons in Negative Experiences

Many creative people have said in one way or another, "If it weren't for the failures, I wouldn't learn anything." There is a rare breed of student

---

BOX 8-2—Emotional Maturity is...

- The ability to deal constructively with reality.

- The capacity to adapt to change.

- Freedom from tensions and anxiety.

- Finding more satisfaction in giving than receiving.

- The capacity to relate to others with mutual satisfaction and helpfulness.

- The capacity to direct one's energy into creative and constructive outlets.

- The capacity to love.

—adapted from The Criteria of Emotional Maturity
by Wm. C. Menninger, M.D., 1899-1966

---

who has never had anything but As in every course, every semester. Then one semester, the student gets a B. She is devastated. Her perfection is blemished. Instead of seeing the experience as a feedback about reality, she takes it as a personal failure and is devastated. This example applies only to the rarest of us, but illustrates how we can become so overwhelmed with an experience which we brand as negative that it loses its potential creative and constructive value. Not only could the student who received the solitary B learn more about what she needed to know and do in order to get an A, she might learn a more powerful lesson that there is no such thing as perfection. The belief in perfection is a trap because nothing is perfect. Even the most perfect and beautiful rose will develop a mold spot or two and will eventually wilt away. Nature does not support perfection—only momentary, teasing glimpses of it.

A negative experience might hurt really bad at first. Recognition of that hurt needs to be grasped as early as possible. One can either go down the path of succumbing to the negative experience and relinquish control to fate, or one can feel bad but recognize the positive value that is emerging from the feeling. It is essential always to ask the question, "What can I learn about myself from this experience?"

Family and Friends

The journey with a brain injury taxes family and friends as much as it does the person who has experienced the injury. Nearly everyone who has experienced a brain injury also experiences a major change in family and friend relationships. There is often a distance that grows between people, a sense of not connecting. Anger and division may develop within the family, leading to divorce and alienation. There is a push-pull conflict within the family and among friends: wanting to be supportive, but at the same time feeling so devastated by the nature of the changed relationships that they become befuddled, often resulting in pulling back. Just as with any major change, recognition of the dynamics of what is happening is the first step toward dealing with it.

Despite the stress-induced, disintegrative effects on the family, it is entirely possible to pull through stronger and more loving than ever. Rehabilitation of brain injury is a family affair. Just as commitment is required from the person with the injury, so too is commitment required from the whole family. This is commitment to learn, to talk frequently and openly, to listen carefully and objectively, to cultivate patience, to participate in the rehabilitation activities, and to practice positive attitudes. Life plans and personal values usually must be reevaluated to make room for the drastically altered plans of the family member who is injured.

Just as important as the family is in this journey, so too are friendships. The stress of brain injury also affects these relationships as well. As the person who has a brain injury must be the teacher who helps others understand, so the person with the brain injury usually must initiate the cultivation of new friendships and the sustaining of old ones.

Finding and Keeping Friends

After the smoke has cleared and the healing well underway, the person emerging with brain injury sometimes finds himself gradually more and more alone. By and large, family and friends have gone their own familiar ways. Loneliness creeps in and sometimes consumes the individual's life. Attempts to deal with the loneliness may be ineffective because the individual really only wants things to be like they were. He isn't willing to change how he goes about cultivating and sustaining friendships to ease the loneliness. After all, throughout life, relationships for most people have a way of just evolving without much effort. For the person with a brain injury, familiar relationships have ebbed and new ones just aren't materializing. This vacuum of human contact often adds a barrier to coping.

Some individuals may seek desperately to make new friends by showering them with recognition, phone calls day and night, invitations to do things and go places—a real show of neediness. Sometimes, the tendency is to talk incessantly about one's injury experience, smothering relationships with self-centeredness. Or, an individual may reject others because of his prevailing negativity. Persons not brain damaged may be seen to have it all. The person who has a brain injury may be reminded too much about his own losses and self-perceived shortcomings that "normal" people might perceive as undesirable. Thus, being a loner feels safer.

Finding and maintaining healthy, mutually supportive friendships is a key component to coping. Accepting yourself and cultivating a tolerance for the imperfections in others is a start. Projecting a smile and a sense of warmth is a good next step. It is not possible to force a friendship with someone, but it is entirely possible to lay the groundwork and then let nature take its course. The boxed text provides some suggestions for encouraging the development of healthy relationships.

Sometimes, it is necessary to put yourself into situations where friendships might develop such as through a church or other organization, recreational activities, or volunteer services. It is essential, how-

BOX 8-3—How to Find and Keep a Friend

Here is a sampling of some suggestions for building good quality friendships. A great exercise would be to extend this list with another ten or so suggestions.

- The Golden Rule overrides all suggestions: Do unto others what you would have them do unto you.

- Remember to smile—not a big Cheshire grin, just a warm, gentle smile. Smile at others as you pass by; smile at coworkers in rehabilitation or on the job; smile for your family. While it won't guarantee one, a smile lays the foundation for friendship.

- Put yourself in places to meet people. Church activities, community events, night classes, hobby events, family and neighborhood gatherings, support group meetings, educational conferences, musical events—these and other places will not guarantee that a friendship will emerge, but a friendship will definitely not emerge sitting alone at home.

- Have something to say to someone. A brief compliment or remark about the weather would be better than asking a question. Asking people questions as a way to "break the ice" often has the effect of putting them on the spot and may make a person feel uncomfortable.

- Give more than you receive. Give briefly, however. Be patient. Don't force it. Don't appear needy. Quality friendships take time to evolve.

- Be confident in yourself and have something to offer a friendship. Kindness, warmth, patience, and understanding can be a tremendous gift for a relationship.

ever, that these are not entered into with specific expectations. Be the kind of person you'd like to meet and let nature take over. It will take time. Oh, that demon, patience again!

A journey with brain injury eventually fades into, simply, a journey through life. The existence of the brain injury takes a back seat to the whole-again person who has emerged. No journey is free of bumps so early preparation through the practice of patience, positive attitudes, and openness to alternative plans can make the ride at least smoother, if not truly enjoyable.

The journey never ends. Once on a path that first requires incredible amounts of energy and new learning, the journey takes on a comfortable momentum of its own. Discovery—without regrets from the past—becomes the fuel that sustains the journey.

May—Real Person

Before my stroke, I managed a small dress shop. I juggled the responsibilities of being a single parent to ten-year-old Adam with making enough money for us to survive.

About a month before my stroke I developed a severe headache. But I kept working anyway. I carried ice packs and medicines to work every day, hoping the knife-like pain in my brain would finally go away. I made several trips to the emergency room, only to be sent home with pain reliever medicines that didn't work. A friend took care of frightened Adam for me because sometimes I could barely talk or swallow, had blurred vision and numbness in my hands, and could hardly walk. The doctors just told me to go home and "sleep it off."

On my third visit to the emergency room in about two weeks, I was given a CT scan, MRI, and arteriogram. I was treated with blood thinners and pain killers. Only morphine seemed to work. I was finally told I had had a blockage in an artery. The blockage eventually cleared but my thinking, frustration, and anxiety didn't. I felt, and still do to some extent, dazed, detached, and depressed.

I look back on the weeks of speech and physical rehab and I miss seeing that outgoing, energetic woman I used to know. I am now timid, slow, and cautious. I recall fragments of the "other me," like I am looking back at the memory of someone else, not me.

Despite the changes I felt inside, I was yet unaware of the changes that lay before me. I was so happy to be with Adam again, to see my parents, and to finally be home. I felt thankful to be alive!

I had a seizure ten years ago that left me unconscious. Five years after that my car was struck and my head broke the windshield of my car and I had a mild head injury. The effects of those events seemed minor compared with the stroke. It took me months to find the courage to drive again. I thought I had had enough crises for one lifetime.

Mostly, I have looked for the good in every situation, or the "lessons to be learned." The past year and a half has been the toughest for me to keep an optimistic attitude as I struggle to find meaning to this latest life-changing event. I lost my job and friends drifted back to their own lives. I felt I was a liability to everyone. I kept the faith that someday I'd pull through this, however, but I can't tell you how I did it.

Everyday tasks—things I accomplished with ease, speed, and efficiency—were now done with great effort. I would drop things, burn food on the stove, trip over my own feet, and walk into walls. Adam thought I was losing my mind, and sometimes so did I.

I had to start driving again to take Adam to school and his activities. I kept getting lost, had several "close calls," and usually forgot where I had parked. I couldn't keep my checkbook straight, figure out change, or find my keys half the time. These things gradually improved to the point where I could deal with them without too much frustration.

My neighbor urged me to do volunteer work and to join a stroke support group held at a local junior college. Slowly, somehow, I started to redefine myself. One important thing is that I learned to see myself as a survivor, not as a victim. Through new friendships I began to find new hope, a new outlook, and strength to keep on going.

I can't jog, ice skate, or run up and down the stairs anymore. I can enjoy, with Adam, the beauty of a sunset, the peaceful sounds of music, and making flowers grow in my garden.

I still face financial strains and relationships with my family are frustrating. It seems as though I constantly have to convince them that the changes in my life are not due to my being lazy. God, I work harder than I ever have in my life. I have to help them, as I caution myself, not to compare myself with who I was before but to go forward with who I am today. I think a deep faith in God, a sense of humor, and keeping things simple—definitely keeping things simple—has given me hope that life is a journey to be appreciated each day, not merely a destination. I accept changes every day. I know I have the courage to see myself in a positive light. I know I have crossed a vital threshold because I no longer fear losing that courage.

9

Return to Community: Finding and Using Resources

One of the most frequent comments made by people whose lives have been touched by brain injury is that they feel all alone in the experience. The family feels overwhelmed by something that few people know much about, much less have gone through. The period of uncertainty of outcome may last for months. The individual, himself or herself, who eventually comes to realize the effects of brain injury also experiences a sense of alienation and loneliness in the experience. Making use of community resources is vital in combating these feelings and establishing a path for reentering life and becoming a family and community member once again. Expanding the realm of contact with people who care and who hold the keys to resources must be a part of every rehabilitation program.

While the resources in the initial treatment and rehabilitation of brain injury are readily available, primarily through hospitals and rehabilitation centers, as one progresses through the later stages of recovery with brain injury, resources may seem few and far between. While most larger communities have organizations and individuals who can help with returning to work, education, and socialization, finding those resources sometimes requires a bit of sleuthing.

A primary focus of any rehabilitation plan is return to functional activities at home including such essentials as self-care skills, ambulation, hygiene, dressing, and communication. The rehabilitation plan should also include return to mainstream life activities of work, school, leisure, family, and socialization. This chapter helps identify some of the resources that will be useful throughout the rehabilitation process as the individual reestablishes connection and interaction with his or her community-at-large.

Returning to Work

For most adults, work defines who we are. It determines to some extent who we associate with and how we see ourselves in the larger community. The workplace is where we find and make friends. Once we leave school, work becomes the primary social structure for friendships and personal identity. We are typically defined by our jobs. When we meet people for the first time, a common question asked is, "What do you do?".

Adults in their working years often feel left out when not employed. Work can include a wide range of vocational activities including home-based self-employment and homemaking as well as traditional office, factory, industrial, and retail settings. For homemakers, just as for people who work outside of the home, there is a sense of incompleteness when one does not return to the familiar homemaking roles and activities. What one does to contribute to his or her family and to society at large provides meaning and a sense of value to life.

Over the past two to three decades, research has shown an increase in the percentage of individuals returning to work after brain injury. Studies report that between 15 percent and 50 percent of persons with brain injury return to employment. The rate of return to work, of course, is related to severity of injury and residual functional changes and disabilities. Greater changes in memory, mental processing speed, and motor functions appear to interfere the most with the potential for returning to work. Individuals with mild brain injury and fewer cognitive changes are more likely to return to work than those with more severe injury who are left with greater cognitive and functional changes.

The potential for return to work is related to the type of work one was doing at the time of the injury. It is much more difficult to return to a complex job entailing a great deal of responsibility and requiring extensive organization, problem-solving, quick thinking, and broad skills regardless of the severity of the brain injury. Thus, the likelihood of returning to one's former job is highly related to the type of employment and the skills necessary for successful performance of that work.

When the potential exists for return to work, an assessment of the work demands and the individual's capabilities is undertaken. Work factors assessed include but are not limited to: specific tasks that the job entails, available supervision, work speed required, safety factors (such as use of power equipment or climbing), new learning required, management responsibilities required, and necessary motor and sensory requirements (such as use of both hands or extensive speaking). Once the job is assessed, then the rehabilitation team and individual can evaluate current cognitive and motor capabilities for potential achievement of work goals. A neuropsychological evaluation is typically used in assessing cognitive functions to help provide the individual with critical information regarding work potential for short-term as well as long-term vocational planning. When the rehabilitation team helps the individual begin to return to his or her former job, reduced job duties on a part-time basis are often recommended, at least initially.

Returning to employment, if not to one's former work setting then to some kind of work, is usually done on a gradual basis that may take a year or two. The brain needs time to reestablish the connections and the comfort level for performing to the work standard required by the job. Sometimes trial and error might provide the best clues as to what work capabilities might be reasonable. Occasionally, a failure experience in work might be necessary to reveal that the brain just isn't up to the demands of a particular job. For these reasons, a guided vocation plan with trained counselors to help smooth the bumps along the way is important.

Resources for Employment Opportunities

Most formal rehabilitation programs include or have access to vocational rehabilitation services. A key source of assistance for many individuals is the Vocational Rehabilitation Service offered by state governments. That agency's mission is to return individuals with disabilities to gainful employment.

The rehabilitation program and treatment team recommends vocational evaluations to assess job readiness, entry level, and assistance needed in order to begin a work reentry plan. Where the individual begins in his or her work reentry does not necessarily indicate the final job attainment. Many individuals are distressed at returning to a much different (usually lower) job than their former work level. Willingness to work with the vocational team and gradually rebuild job skills is a critical component in successful work reentry. The team and individual must work together to understand the factors that drive the job reentry process. A highly supportive working relationship is necessary between the individual returning to work and the vocational rehabilitation team and supervisors who work with that individual.

There are several levels of employment to be considered in planning for return to work:

Competitive refers to mainstream employment where there are no or few major modifications to the job or job site required. This includes the wide range of typical employment from work that requires less than a high school education to work that requires an advanced college degree.

Supported employment is usually considered to be competitive vocational activities but with assistive and supervisory supports provided. The degree of support varies and may include the use of a job coach whose role is to work with the individual to learn and successfully complete a job. It is an intensive one-to-one form of job placement assistance and, at times, includes on-the-job training. A job coach may be used on a temporary basis to provide additional individual assistance in becoming successfully established on the job. Having reached a level of independence, the job coach gradually withdraws and the individual is then working on a competitive job.

Long-term supported work may be an alternative for individuals who find it difficult to manage in competitive or potentially competitive employment. Such positions may involve full or limited job duties and job modifications. Such individuals work as paid employees but with greater assistance provided than is available in competitive employment.

Sheltered workshop employment is a highly structured job setting where an individual works on a simple one or two step job with production rates that are less than typical for competitive employment. A supervisor or job coach is always present and provides structure for the workday.

The boxed text shows the job skill demands characterized by competitive, supported, and sheltered employment.

BOX 9-1—Job Skills Required for Types of Employment

The job skills listed below range from low to high, depending on whether the employment type is sheltered, supported, or competitive.

SHELTERED	SUPPORTED	COMPETITIVE
Low Skills Required		High Skills Required
	Organization	
	New Learning	
	Processing Speed	
	Problem-solving	
	Job Independence	
	Attention to Detail	
	Social and Awareness	

There are times when the changes caused by brain injury require that an individual be retrained for a different job. Jobs with a high degree of stress, or which demand high production or fast judgments may be ill-suited for the individual with residual cognitive compromise due to brain injury. A job may be found with the individual's previous employer, but one requiring fewer demands that would otherwise sabotage successful return to work. Many employers recognize the value of the individual as a loyal and dedicated worker and are willing to work with the vocational team to find an appropriate position within the company. There are many reasons for staying with a familiar company including job benefits, social structure, and the possibility for additional advancement within an employment setting that knows the employee's job skills.

Overcoming Barriers to Employment

Naturally, there can be psychological barriers to the job reentry process. Some individuals are resistant to return to a job that is perceived to have less status, even if it is the initial reentry activity with a plan to move toward the individual's former position with the company. As mentioned in earlier chapters, a problem frequently associated with brain injury is the individual's decreased awareness of the cognitive changes that have occurred. An individual with a moderate to severe brain injury may not recognize that changes have occurred, precluding return to his or her previous job and therefore failing to understand why stepping directly right back into the previous position is not possible. This reaction can be seen at the Rancho Scale level IV (see Chapter Three). At this stage of recovery the individual is not yet oriented to the changes produced by brain injury. The individual may insist that he or she is fully able to resume work, driving, and other activities. Even at more advanced stages of recovery, diminished awareness of cognitive changes may make it difficult for an individual to accept different work and lifestyle capabilities. Also, an individual with memory difficulties may forget that he or she forgets and thus not understand concerns about aspects of returning to a previous job where problems with memory could be dangerous, or at least interfere with acceptable job performance.

An integral part of rehabilitation is to improve self-awareness and understanding so that the individual may participate effectively in realistic goal setting. Family involvement and support is also paramount. Just as the team and psychologist work with the individual in understanding functional changes as they relate to job performance, family education and involvement are also crucial for support and encouragement.

There are times when return to employment is not a timely or appropriate option for the individual. Even so, adults enjoy and profit in being productive citizens in the community. If paid employment is not an immediate goal, then the rehabilitation team, along with the individual and family, might explore avocation options such as volunteer work. There are many organizations in communities that rely on the volunteer work force to help carry out their services. Libraries, animal shelters, self-help organizations, hospitals, community and government agencies, civic organizations such as orchestras and museums, and other entities rely on the volunteer work force. The volunteer is a necessary and cherished member of these organizations. Such organizations include a variety of duties and serve as an alternative work environment for social as well as productivity and identity needs of the individual. Volunteer-based organizations are often willing to work with individuals with special needs by having other volunteers serve as job coaches and providing job duties specifically tailored to the needs of the individual. As a volunteer, the individual can likely set work hours with greater flexibility and may be able to use transportation alternative to the volunteer site as opposed to driving. Volunteer work often serves as training and as a springboard for future employment if that is a potential goal.

Returning to School

Young adults injured while in high school or college continue to look forward to completing their educational training before entering into work. A number of individuals who sustain brain injury choose not to return to work but, rather, to explore college or training aimed toward a different vocational goal. A similar process is utilized in considering the steps for returning to or entering college as is utilized for work reentry. Again, a neuropsychological evaluation provides valuable information regarding cognitive capabilities as these relate to potential for college training and at what level. When an individual is recommended for return to school, it is common to begin at a level with a fairly easy curriculum. A university setting typically has a competitive student population, a challenging curriculum, and high expectations for achievement. There are likely to be demanding entrance requirements as well. Many college settings, in contrast, offer four-year degrees but may include a less competitive student population as well as a less difficult curriculum. A junior or community college typically includes two-year degree programs (either academic or vocationally-oriented) and greater willingness to work with students with special needs. A student may begin school reentry at a junior college with an eye toward eventually entering a college or university program at a later time.

Returning children and adolescents to school poses different challenges. Children with mild to moderate brain injury may evidence little if any substantial change in achievement scores, especially in reading, although diminished arithmetic skills can be due to changes in attention and mental processing ability. Children who do not evidence significant change in expressive communication or motor skills may be perceived as having no impairments from brain injury. The plan may be to return the child to his or her original classroom without modifications and see how he or she does. Sadly, the child usually fails before getting the necessary special attention to subtle, but very influential, changes due directly to the brain injury (such as subtly slower process-ing speed, memory lapses, attentional and learning problems).

A neuropsychological evaluation provides a thorough description of the mental status and educational needs to meet any changes in aca-demic potentials or capabilities. The educational and rehabilitation team may need to provide teachers and other students with informa-tion regarding a child's injury and the special learning and social needs the child will face on returning to school. Because children continue to develop, it is important for the family to closely monitor progress throughout the school years. As the child progresses from grade school through junior high and into high school, course work becomes more demanding with regard to level of independence in managing one's learning. A child may not evidence significant difficulty returning to early grade school after a mild to moderate brain injury but may expe-rience increasing difficulty as he or she progresses into higher grades. Repeat neuropsychological evaluations should be obtained periodically or when difficulties are observed, in order to aid the child, parents, and teachers in determining what modifications to the learning environ-ment might maximize success at the next level.

Educational Resources

For children and adolescents, resources include the special education personnel of the child's school and the rehabilitation team. Together with the parent, this expanded team can recommend the need for an Individualized Education Plan (IEP) or a 504 Plan. An IEP is the stan-dard system used for all students, regardless of type of disability, that have special educational problems and needs. Such a plan involves spe-cial services such as speech therapy, extra tutoring, or other individual-ized help. A 504 Plan involves minor modifications in the classroom that do not involve the special education team, such as providing a spe-cial desk or writing device.

The IEP is monitored and established by the special education spe-cialist with the parent's involvement. A justification for special services is determined due to the child's needs (such as caused by brain injury), and specific educational resources are recommended. The IEP must be written and monitored over time to assure students are obtaining the special resources to meet the special needs.

The rehabilitation team can also serve as a valuable resource for identifying state and local resources. There are advocacy programs in states that provide additional assistance to parents in negotiating services with school districts. Schools are allotted limited special education funding to provide services across a broad spectrum of disability groups. While every parent with a child with special needs wants the full range of services available, few school districts have the funding and therefore the personnel and equipment to meet every parent's request. Some programs are fairly aggressive in their approach whereas others may try to develop better partnering relationships with other resources. Parents and program representatives should be very clear with each other regarding roles and approach strategies. Specific advocacy program representatives can be identified in a specific locale through the child's school, the local, state, or national Brain Injury Association, medical centers, pediatricians, and others who work with special needs children.

Various states offer guidance through such entities as the department of education and the department of mental health. Parents should contact the state affiliate of the Brain Injury Association for additional resources offered in their state. Local support group chapters may include parents experienced in working with local schools as well. The child's physician should be able to provide documentation necessary in obtaining school services including occupational, physical, or speech therapies. School therapy programs usually are not designed to provide the degree of therapy offered through a comprehensive rehabilitation service. Their mandate usually requires assisting children to reach independence in functions necessary to adapt to a school setting. School based speech therapists, for example, are often trained to treat phonation and may not be able to offer cognitive therapy for improving attention, memory, and other higher mental processes, the latter often just as central to the child's needs. Thus, resources from other agencies and services may be needed to supplement what the school might provide.

Parents may utilize the counselors of their child's school as well. The child who has had a brain injury is likely to have changes in social skills due to cognitive and personality changes. Changes include heightened emotional reactions, acting out in frustration, poorly controlled impulses, poor social judgement, difficulty tracking conversations, insensitivity to social cues, difficulty responding at developmentally appropriate levels, and impaired self-confidence and esteem. It is important that the parents, school, and rehabilitation team plan for ways to help the child meet social needs as he or she returns to school. This may involve assistance from the school counselor, psychologist, or social worker. Teachers are encouraged to monitor social adjustment as well as academic progress. The parents and team may wish to educate classmates on brain injury to help them in their reaction to the student returning after an injury and to provide appropriate help to the student.

Disabled Students Services

Student special services departments of colleges and universities offer a range of services to the student population. Options and services may include but not be limited to: note taker, special tutorial labs, individual tutoring, un-timed tests, computer equipment and various in-class modifications (such as more seclusion or smaller class sizes to cut down distractions). Before identifying the school of interest, contact a number of schools to determine what services are available to the student and what experience they have had in working with students returning after brain injury. Some educational institutions offer specialized course work for at-risk students. The course work may have as a focus the identification and enhancement of skills necessary for college success such as reading for content, study skills, math skills, and writing skills.

The individual and family should contact the State Department of Rehabilitation for guidance in planning college programs, and for information about funds for books, tuition, and transportation.

Achieving Independence in Living and Housing

After a brain injury, individuals typically want to return to their previous level of adult independence. An essential ingredient in this is one's place to live. Those living in family environments will typically return to roles that allow them to be productive members in the family structure once again. This includes homemaking skills needed to live independently including doing laundry, cooking, cleaning, and basic home maintenance. At discharge from the acute care hospital, it is common for an injured individual to live with some family member, even if not living with that individual previous to the injury, as he or she often has a need for supervision and assistance, at least for a while. Over time, individuals strive to live independently, or to return to their former living arrangements, if they did not return there directly from the hospital. Returning home includes determining the need for home modifications in order to accommodate any changes in physical functioning (e.g., ramps, wider doorways to accommodate a wheelchair, elimination of the need for stair climbing). The rehabilitation team typically visits the home and provides recommendations for changes that allow access to the home, bathroom, and appliances and workspaces. In looking for a new home or apartment, such modifications must be a consideration as well. The team measures doorways, steps (number, depth, and presence of hand rails), number of floor levels in the home, placement of appliances and cabinets, room size, and other layout challenges.

Housing Resources

Federal and state governments have agencies available for helping individuals with disabilities locate housing and, in cases where financial need is demonstrated, assist with funding for housing. Unfortunately, there is often a waiting list for such specially funded housing. Such programs may be able to provide lists of other housing options in the community which are modified for the adult with special disability needs. The rehabilitation team and state brain injury association can usually provide assistance in identifying state and local agencies available to provide assistance.

Some communities have group housing for individuals who have certain challenges with independent living skills such as dressing, eating, and self-care who need supervision and assistance with these activities. Such group living is an option when living with family is not possible and the individual cannot live independently.

The highest level of need and care is available in a nursing home. This is an option to be considered when the individual requires a high degree of ongoing nursing care that cannot be provided in the family home for whatever reason. Nursing home placement is not an easy decisions for the individual or family because of the stigma often attached to nursing home placement. If nursing home placement is considered, the family and individual should consider that it need not be the final placement but rather the current placement until additional resources and appropriate housing options are located or until further recovery occurs. Nursing facilities and group homes have advantages. In addition to providing the care and supervision needed at each level, there is a social structure available. Most facilities provide regularly scheduled structured and supervised activities for socialization and recreation. Such facilities may also provide and arrange for transportation to appointments and work sites.

Participating in Leisure Activities

Returning to recreation and leisure is a vital part of the return to community for adults and to the home for children and adolescents. Various members of the individual's rehabilitation team can be a resource for helping identify leisure and recreation resources. Leisure activities might include participation in sporting events, cultural activities, or recreational events such as camps or craft classes. Help might be enlisted for finding people to play chess with, participation in community festivals and holiday events, or volunteering on other social activities. The YMCA and local parks and recreation departments usually offer a variety of seasonal activities.

The individual who used alcohol or drugs in the past will require counseling regarding these problems. Drugs and alcohol can have a profound and harmful effect on the brain whether or not a brain injury has occurred but certainly so after an injury. Not only will the individual be counseled to stop or greatly reduce alcohol use and cease use of all illicit chemicals, the individual may require special treatment or counseling to avoid activities and friends which might encourage the use of alcohol and drugs. Individuals who have a history of drug use prior to a brain injury are at high risk for returning to that behavior—a risk that can have severe consequences for a person whose brain is already injured.

When extensive motor and/or cognitive changes seem to preclude return to some past leisure activities, the rehabilitation team can often identify modification that will allow the individual's participation in the activity once again. An individual who loved golfing may be able to golf with different assistive devices. There may be a psychological barrier to not returning to an activity exactly as it was previously enjoyed where competitive play may no longer be possible. This unfortunately often leads to isolation and depression.

Resources for Leisure Time

Local chapters of the state brain injury associations usually meet regularly and include scheduled leisure activities planned by the individuals who have experienced brain injury and their families and friends. Local governments, park departments, junior colleges, YMCA/YWCA, and similar youth organizations usually provide activities that include persons with various disabilities.

State brain injury associations may be able to provide information regarding respite programs for families of individuals with brain injury. This may range from alternate temporary housing to a structured program of camp with trained staff and appropriate leisure activities. Such programs encourage the individual to participate in new leisure activities as well.

Parks and recreation departments, community colleges, and other organizations offer classes for learning new skills, crafts, and sports. With guidance from one's physician and the rehabilitation team, the individual can likely participate in a wide range of leisure activities.

Meeting Financial Challenges

A frequent effect of brain injury on the family is a change in finances. In addition to the injured individual's lost work and income, family members lose work time during initial hospitalization, lose work time providing transportation to therapies and appointments, and must stay home to provide supervision and asistance. Application for social security disability may be initiated. Even though the rehabilitation program is not complete, disability status should be applied for because obtaining this financial assistance is typically a lengthy process, usually taking a minimum of one year to quality. Benefits such as short-term and long-term disability may also be available from the individual's employer. State Medicaid funding for medical expenses and aid for living expenses might be another option for some families where private health and disability insurance resources are minimal. Social workers and the state brain injury association usually have information regarding financial resources and options. The services of an attorney may be helpful, especially when complex issues arise around child custody, guardianship, accident litigation, and other matters that will have a significant impact on financial stability. Most communities offer emergency services for food and clothing. Local churches may have similar services or provide information for obtaining such services.

Agencies that work with children with disabilities of any nature can provide family members with information regarding the range of services and help available to families that include children who have experienced brain injury. Veterans may qualify for assistance through their regional veteran's administration hospital or clinic.

Resources for returning to a satisfying lifestyle after a brain injury depend on the individual communities. The resources outlined above are general but provide a starting point to seek opportunities unique for each community. Rehabilitation of brain injury is a lengthy process with resources shifting from agency to agency along the way. Finding the right resources might require some aggressive effort, but isolation without these resources will only lead to despair.

Sharon—Real Person

When I remember my past it is important for me not to glorify who I think I once was. I know that I excelled in math and English. I think that whatever I do today I could have done better before. I'm not sure that is really accurate. I know I was an organized person and capable of doing the things I set out to do.

For the past 16 years, since I've been married, I ran my home, handled the finances, took care of the kids, held down a good job, and kept up my home. I enjoyed my life, planning activities for us all, preparing meals, and having numerous get-togethers for family and friends.

While driving back to work after lunch one day, another car ran into the side of mine. The first thing I remember after the accident is of this man pacing back and forth throwing his arms up in the air and

BOX 9-2—Return to Community: Resource Checklist

Individuals, families, and helping professionals may need to contact several organizations and agencies to find the right help at the right time. This checklist provides a starting point. Use a local phone directory to make the specific contacts in your community. One contact usually generates several more possibilities. Also, many communities have a central resource network that brings a wide variety of agencies together to benefit its citizens. Your local or state Brain Injury Association should be able to direct you to that agency.

Education
Community colleges
Special education services in public schools
Disabled student services
Adult education, local public schools

Employment
State Vocational Rehabilitation Services
Vocational services connected with rehabilitation provider
Volunteer agencies
Former employer's human resources department
Goodwill

Financial
State Medicaid Office
Social Security Administration

General Assistance
Local affiliate of the Brain Injury Association
Catholic Community Services
Church and ministries organizations

Housing
Housing Authority of local government

Recreation and Leisure
YMCA/YWCA
Parks and Recreation departments

yelling. By the time the police got there I had a headache. I didn't feel that I was injured, though. It wasn't until the next day when I woke up that I realized how much my head and neck hurt.

My doctor assured me there was nothing wrong. After two weeks of blurred vision and headaches so severe I could barely walk, I insisted that, *yes, there was* something wrong. He said I needed to learn to live with this and it would go away. When I went to my eye doctor, she found a loss in my peripheral vision and wanted an MRI of my brain. My family doctor said this would not be necessary but referred me to physical therapy, "just to ease my mind."

Eight months after my accident my head, hand, and arm pain lessened but was still there. Another doctor manipulated my bones and added more physical therapy. I began to feel a little better.

Aside from the seemingly never ending physical discomfort, I seem to have lost my self-confidence. Several things have led to this: my inability to concentrate, loss of my short-term memory, and the long time it now takes me to understand almost anything. The periods of time that I seem to lose completely have been very unsettling. This is happening less and less. Whether this is because I am getting better or because I have chosen to avoid a lot of the things in my life that would cause me frustration, I'm not sure. When I am told that I have done things or that things have taken place that I was a part of yet have no recollection of, it is very frightening. Much time passed before I actually believed anyone that these things were happening. To make things more difficult, I don't sleep well at all since the accident. Sometimes my short sleep periods are filled with violent nightmares.

After so many defeating experiences, I have developed some negative habits. I found that by avoiding anything that caused me frustration or extreme stress, I could lessen the number of incidents where I was failing. Even being active socially has become difficult. In even small groups of people it is very hard to keep up with the pace of things. By the time I think of what it was I wanted to say the subject had long ago changed.

Making even a simple decision has become difficult. I find that doing what used to be fun, like going to a new restaurant, can become overwhelming. A long menu is just too much to bear. If I go to a store and need to purchase a gift, I can be there forever, and then come home with several things, to make my choice later when I am not under any pressure to hurry. (Maybe I'd remember to return the other stuff later.) I'm always the odd man out—always the last to catch on to something.

I guess all my life I have had a negative image of a disabled person. And, yes, I am rigid in my way of thinking. To me, there was always a right and a wrong way to do things and not much room in between. I think that has had a lot to do with why I am so sensitive about my injury and why acceptance of the new me has been so hard.

My life has become a struggle. I felt that it was important for me to continue working no matter what. I think that I felt that as long as I am still working then there couldn't be anything really wrong with me. Getting up every morning knowing the challenges that I will face is exhausting in itself. It seems my whole life has now become trying to stay at the peak of my performance for my job. Although my family has always been the most important thing in life, I find I have little or no time or energy left for them at the end of the day. I once knew everything that was going on with my family. Now I feel I am unable to keep up. It's like I was on automatic pilot before—everything came to me so easily and now so much thought must go into the least little thing.

With the help of friends, doctors, and a special cognitive training course for persons with brain injury, I am learning I am not alone in the way I feel or the things that have happened to me. It is reassuring to know that there are biological reasons for the things that I am experiencing and it is not just all in my mind as my first doctor would have had me believe. I know in the beginning I felt that I must have lost my mind. I have to devote some of my energies each day to reminding myself to think of something positive. I need to ignore the remarks and prejudices of others that have affected my self-worth.

I know I must become comfortable with my new self. I must accept the changes that have taken place. This is the most difficult thing for me to do. I may be quitting my job to have more energy for my family. I'm having to figure out priorities I never had to be concerned with before. There are constant questions in my mind that I haven't come to terms with yet. I've still got a ways to go.

Note: The major content of this chapter was prepared by Terrie L. Price, Ph.D., The Rehabilitation Institute, Kansas City.

10

Practical Care Management—for the Family

When flight attendants demonstrate the use of emergency procedures, passengers are told to put on their own oxygen masks first, then assist those seated nearby. While at first glance this may seem a little like clamoring to be first to jump into the lifeboat, assuring yourself of oxygen first is necessary so that you are then able to help others. If you pass out because you didn't immediately put on your own oxygen mask, you are no good to anyone. If you put your mask on first, you are then able to help someone who is too young or who is having difficulty, even though they may have passed out already from lack of oxygen.

This advice to "take care of yourself first" is appropriate in any situation where you may need to take care of someone else. If you are not strong enough or capable enough you will be of little help to anyone. In the situation where you are called upon to help take care of someone who has had a brain injury, it is critically important to make sure you are prepared and able to help.

While taking care of a person who has sustained a brain injury may not be as immediately life threatening as the sudden need for oxygen masks aboard an airliner at 30,000 feet, it is just as important to maintain a cool head, a clear mind, and a strong constitution. In fact, the ongoing demands and challenges in caring for someone struggling to make sense of a world from the perspective of a damaged brain requires grounding and a realistic and helpful perspective of the situation.

Take Care of Yourself First

Taking care of yourself first means that you maintain the emotional strength to consider your values, make decisions, and stand by your commitments. The emotional demands in a family where a loved one has a brain injury can be huge. Families are sometimes torn apart when the stresses become overwhelming. Finding ways to "regroup" and step back from the intensity of the situation is critical. When you feel over-whelmed in a situation, it's time to pause, reflect, and regain perspec-tive.

Find quiet times to read, reflect, and relax. Talk about problem-solving (not just griping) with others and stick to a plan to solve a problem. Remind yourself that love is the foundation for caring about another person. Find time to laugh. Make time to be quiet and clear your mind. Practice all the values that you hold dear in your soul—honesty, respect, nurturance.

Family members sometimes find themselves mired in the day-to-day trials and tribulations of dealing with a person who has a brain injury. Periodically letting go of these times is essential to "clear the air" and gain a different—and renewing—perspective. Seek help from others to share in the responsibilities and to give yourself a break. Going it alone, without help and without breaks, can quickly erode relationships and energy. Don't be timid about reaching out for help.

Families may alter their plans and activities if a member becomes brain injured. However, if at all possible do not give up goals that are near and dear. Find a way to keep working (perhaps cutting back to half-time for a while), maintain social contacts and activities, continue attending a night school class, or whatever activities are important. Maintaining a balance within each caregiver will help maintain balance within the family.

It is so easy, in so many situations, to become entrapped. This dis-couraging and energy-draining predicament quickly undermines patience, perspective, and power. While there is no universal response to the situation, the key is to cultivate an awareness of feeling entrapped. By being aware—as early as possible—that you need to step back from a situation, regaining perspective and a foothold will be easier. A walk in the early morning fresh air, going alone to a movie, coffee with a trusted friend, writing a song or poem—a diversion from the routine can often help restore balance.

Sometimes, caregivers and families become entrapped in worry. Insidious worry creates inner turmoil and a sense of helplessness that can destroy efforts to stay positive. Worry is nonproductive rumination. It is easy to worry about the unknown future and what will become of a loved one who has become brain injured. Losses must be grieved and the new person accepted unconditionally. When you become aware that you are worrying, distract yourself and literally tell yourself to stop it! This is not to imply that the challenges of dealing with brain injury should be denied. In fact, if concerns, emotions, and plans and strategies are discussed openly and frankly with others, worry will take a back seat and productive, problem-solving attitudes will prevail.

Practice Positive Patience

Dag Hammarskjöld, Secretary General of the United Nations from 1953 until his death in a plane crash in 1961, wrote a wonderful and powerful affirmation[1]: "If only I may grow: firmer, simpler-quieter, warmer." To attain and maintain this goal grounds one's patience. It is all too easy to get caught up in the chaos, the confusion, the uncertainty, and the barrage of demands in dealing with anything complex. Hammarskjöld carried the weight of keeping peace in the world. Most of us carry a much less heavy burden. Such an elegant reminder to stay strong, to be quiet, and to exhibit peacefulness benefits any situation, whether spanning the globe or within the walls of one's home.

Being firm means taking care of yourself and maintaining a conscious effort to do what is right in a tough situation. It means building

---

1.   Hammarskjöld, Dag. *Markings*. New York: Alfred A. Knopf, 1978, pg. 93.

confidence to remain self-secure and anchored. A person who has had a brain injury needs consistent direction and a model for strength and stability.

Being quiet, taking time to reflect, seeking advice from others, acquiring information—all these things contribute to taking care of yourself. It is so easy to get caught up in the moment of chaos when emotional stability evaporates. Keeping things simple and straightforward underscores peace.

Without warmth and a sense of genuineness, taking care of anyone becomes mechanical and tiring. Warmth beams from a determination to look into the eyes of the other person and see—*and share*—his or her suffering, consternation, and bewilderment. By cultivating the empathy of warmth, you preserve your own confidence, integrity, and strength without crumbling under the weight of someone else's troubles.

Hammarskjöld presents what may seem like a contradiction: to be firm yet simple, quiet, and warm. To be firm means not to be weak or uncertain. It means to maintain a fixed course in the face of resistance. To be simple, quiet, and warm complements firmness with elasticity and genuineness. It is a thin line that the caregiver walks in this regard and requires resolve with every stumble to get back on course.

Everyone has his or her own way of cultivating patience. For many it is not an easy commodity to come by. For others it seems all too easy. Wherever you are in your own ability to demonstrate and maintain patience, it is crucial to keep working at it. Patience is the foundation for offering help to anyone in any situation. You need a clear head, a steady hand, a genuine smile, and calm eyes.

"Frustrating" is the word heard most commonly from family members when telling the tales of woe in attempting to help their loved one cope with the demands of a brain injury. An individual with a brain injury is prone to making judgment errors, to being quick and impulsive, and to being stubbornly stuck on one goal at the exclusion of even reasonable alternatives. These characteristics impede communications and create barriers to mutually supportive relationships. Unfortunately, such behaviors become infectious and inflame the ire of others.

Analyzing the behaviors that produce frustration and irritation within the family and figuring out what to do about them must be done within a framework of patience. Therefore, whatever your strategies, practice positive patience: Balance each day with rest, meditation (a walk, reciting affirmations, or formal meditation practice), exercise, alone time and together time, and energetic time. Learn how others cope by participating in a caregivers support group. Read affirming materials that leave you with a sense of peace and a sense of renewed strength. Help from a mental health professional who can remain objective is often invaluable.

Family members have found other techniques for cultivating a sense of balance, positiveness, and patience. Keeping a dairy or journal that focuses as much on the caregiver's experience as on the patient's can aid insight. Writing down basic family regulations and agreements to define everyone's personal time and responsibilities can provide a concrete reminder to respect each other's needs and family contributions. Definitely do not forget the little things that help diminish the heaviness of the situation. Celebrate every holiday, birthday, and other special days you can think of (even Arbor Day and Groundhog Day). Have a little party with cake, punch, theme decorations, laughter, songs, pats on the back. Fold the laundry in the family room with everyone pitching in. Take a quiet family walk around the block after dinner every night. Even fifteen minutes in the fresh air can help clear the mind.

Behavior Analysis

One of the most challenging tasks that face families with a member who has sustained a brain injury is the ongoing need to figure out the meaning of some new (and often troubling) behavior. Whether strange, combative, obsessive, obstinate, peculiar or delusional, cruel and hurtful, or even dangerous, understanding this new person in the family can be an exercise that may seem unattainable at times.

Practical care and management of a person who has had a brain injury requires a deeper level of understanding than do most situations of interpersonal interactions. The nature of brain injury is such that clear and comprehensive thinking just isn't always possible, or at least isn't in sync with society, and what results is sometimes words and behaviors that reflect the jumbled and irrational thinking produced by a damaged brain.

Ideas and thoughts can come out quite confused when the ability to express language is impaired. Behaviors may appear aggressive, selfish, hostile, or in some way inappropriate because the thoughts that produce the behaviors may be incomplete and jumbled. Brain injury produces words and behaviors that are unfamiliar to others and that are prone to misinterpretation.

Analyzing behaviors produced from the vantage point of the damaged brain requires patience and an attitude that guards against defensiveness. Behavior analysis requires empathy and understanding. As with maintaining a sense of personal balance, a mental health professional may be needed to interject objectivity in understanding confusing and troubling behaviors.

"No-fault" Behavior

Many states have adopted a provision that automobile accidents are to be considered "no-fault" and that each person's motor vehicle insurance pays for the respective damages without casting blame and without seeking compensation or damages from the other side. Of course, there are limitations and exceptions to the no-fault policy. The essential theory behind it is that by avoiding figuring out who is to blame for a minor accident and each insurance company paying for their policy holder's damages both parties will get back on the road quicker and without the cost of litigation. It eliminates blame. It is a matter of getting things fixed and getting on with life.

Behavior is the product of a multitude of brain and mental processes. Behavior may be errant, based on factors over which the individual may have limited control or over which the individual may have not yet learned control. Thus, the idea that behavior produced under certain conditions, such as brain injury, is "no-fault" implies that it is free of sinister intentions and, despite its troublesomeness to others, is the "best effort" one has to give. Brain injury causes behavior that is not often produced by choice; the behavior is not the person's fault.

Within the brain is stored knowledge, values, awareness of choices, learned decision and logic strategies, goals and motivations, and a host of personality and intellectual characteristics. Behavior, in the form of words and actions, is produced through a coming together of these resources and mental processes at any moment in time. These resources are not infallible. We all make judgment and reasoning errors from time to time. The individual who has damaged brain circuits becomes prone to making more of these judgment and reasoning errors, getting stuck on ideas without the ability to entertain flexibility in thought or even to be aware of errors in his or her thinking.

By appreciating that a damaged brain will have limitations in access to or availability of mental resources, behaviors that might be less than optimum or even irritating at least can be accepted a bit more objectively. This is not to imply that maladaptive or erroneous thinking should be unconditionally accepted, but it must first be understood and appreciated for what it is—the product of a damaged brain. Then, ways around the behavior can be sought to assist in bringing it more in line with acceptable, productive, and satisfying results. Chastising a person—assigning fault—for inappropriate behavior produced from faulty brain circuits is a common error made by loved ones. Worse yet, it is likely to worsen the behavior. The person who is blamed for the behavior will feel unfairly accused, and unable to be aware of why the behavior is inappropriate.

An individual who has hallucinations, who truly believes there are bugs crawling all over his skin, is basing his perceptions on sensations being received by the brain and processed by brain chemicals and neural circuits. It is futile to challenge an individual who is experiencing such hallucinations with the expectation that such challenge will make him "wake up" to the fact that there really are not bugs crawling all over his skin. Logic from someone else whose brain-basis for perceptions is vastly different will not change the complex sensory and perceptual processes at work causing the hallucinations.

While such hallucinatory thinking is "faulty" in that there is a mismatch between experience and reality, the faulty thinking cannot merely be corrected by someone else's judgments. It is critical to respect what is going on in the brain and mind that produces the hallucinations. Only by respecting the brain and mental processes and even empathizing with the individual in attempting to understand the individual's experience can we begin to be helpful. Helpfulness in this sense is aiding the individual to find a better match between experience and reality. The hallucinatory behavior is "no fault" behavior in that it is not willfully caused. The behavior needs to be accepted as the product of what is producing it—a faulty brain. Coercing the individual to change his or her behavior is futile without first understanding the mental processes that are producing the behavior. The behavior is "no fault" but the brain may, indeed, be faulty.

An example of how to respond to such hallucinations would be, first, to acknowledge the person's *experience*. By this, you are not acknowledging bugs but are accepting the person's experience of uncomfortable tactile sensations that are truly bothersome. Thus, you aren't challenging the experience and eroding communications. Helping the individual to analyze the experience in more basic sensory terms rather than through metaphor (that is, bugs crawling) will help maintain the validity of the experience and respect for the individual experiencing the sensation. Professional help will usually be valuable to get to the source of the sensation and, hence, eliminate it and the bothersome interpretation of the sensation.

This brief explanation is the foundation behind the psychological process of "behavior analysis." If we are to help people adapt to the changed ways the brain processes information, we must respect the processes behind the behavior and avoid immediately finding fault in it. Usually, when we attribute fault to someone's behavior it is based on a mismatch between what we would have done and what the other person did, presuming both persons have the same brain and mental foundation from which to work. This just isn't so in persons who have sustained brain injury.

Brain injury not only alters how one perceives reality, it renders the brain more vulnerable to subtle changes that may produce erroneous thinking sometimes but not at other times. This variability in quality of brain processing—due to scattered neural disconnections—also fuels judgment from others that one's behavior at times is faulty and that the individual could, if he or she really wanted to, change that behavior. In a dynamic brain the mix of neurons, chemicals, and circuits is ever-changing. During a time when brain healing is attempting to produce more consistency in how thought is processed, thinking is vulnerable to glitches over which the person has little or no control.

"No-fault" behavior means that the behavior is not the fault of *intentional* or careless or reckless judgment. When we cast blame onto someone for his behavior choices we are assuming he has the capability to make more reasoned choices. For most people this may be true and eventually the individual will recognize (i.e., learn) to consider ramifications of choices more carefully and produce behaviors that have more socially harmonious results. Sometimes, however, if the individual lacks capability (i.e., has not learned how) to consider ramifications of choices or who misperceives situations or intentions of others because of a damaged brain then it is difficult to pronounce his behavior as careless or reckless.

The concept of "no-fault" implies that behavior is the product of one's best effort at the time and is not based on carelessness or recklessness. While this implies noble judgment, we know all too well that behaviors of many people are often not the product of best effort. However, it is futile to jump to such conclusions immediately in the case of the person who has had a brain injury without first having analyzed the factors that produced the behavior. By doing so we can avoid defensiveness and judgment. By avoiding defensiveness or a judgmental reaction, we avoid locking in the behavior that is undesirable and can identify the brain, mental, and environmental factors that might need to be tweaked in order to help the individual avoid such undesirable behaviors in the future.

If behavior analysis seems complex or too demanding for regularly occurring problems, it may be. However, at the very least, it is certainly possible, and even essential, that the behavior of an individual who has sustained a brain injury be respected for what it is—*the best effort at thinking given the changed brain and mental resources one has to work with.* Seeking objective and professional help from a behavior analysis specialist—a neuropsychologist—will very likely be necessary in order to understand the complexity of the behavior and for planning strategies for responding to and changing maladaptive behaviors.

Figure 6. Therapy can help all members of the family learn to cope with and accept the losses and changes brought about by brain injury.

Dangerousness

The concept of *dangerousness* refers to behaviors that are potentially harmful to the individual or to others. Consistent with the ideas behind behavior analysis, dangerousness stems from the product of faulty perceptions, poorly controllable emotions and impulses, narrow choices, limited logic resources, and the host of personality and situational variables accompanying brain injury that influence behaviors in a potentially harmful way. Dangerousness is based on the judgment of others that an individual's behavior may be injurious to himself or to others because of erroneous thinking.

Impulsivity, anger, perceptual distortions (i.e., misinterpretations of reality), frustration, and defensiveness can contribute to potentially dangerous behaviors. Helping an individual avoid such behaviors requires awareness of the ingredients of dangerousness and the elimination of as many of the ingredients as possible.

The family who suspects dangerous behaviors should contact a health professional immediately for help and guidance. Never attempt to deal alone with behaviors that might appear dangerous. These behaviors usually reflect a brain condition that does not reverse itself easily without some professional intervention. Never assume dangerous behaviors will eventually just go away without help. Even with professional help, weak self-awareness, faulty perceptions of reality, and stubbornness often inherent in frontal lobe damage cannot be optimally changed.

A most frustrating and impenetrable condition of some cases of brain injury is the development of persistent impairment in reality testing. Simply put, significant brain injury, often combined with persistent stress, causes progressive distortion in one's interpretation of reality. Strong suspiciousness, anger, resentments, even severe withdrawal can lead to psychotic behaviors. This severely disturbed state requires professional attention. If an individual's thinking becomes so distorted that he or she is not rational, resulting dangerous behaviors become very high risks.

Failure to accept one's changes due to brain injury, use of illicit drugs, social engagements that foster gang or unsavory behaviors, lack of strong family supports—any of these things can exacerbate the effects of brain injury well beyond usual expectations, These are powerful sources of stress that lead to lying, evasive behaviors, irresponsible acts, all of which only dig the hole deeper and distort reality further. These situations are constantly stressful and frustrating for the family. Professional guidance, supportive individuals and groups, and continuing education can help allay these frustrations. Incomplete understanding of brain and behavior repair is a social problem still undergoing scientific investigation. Families must not go it alone and must seek community resources.

Fortunately, most people who incur brain injury do not develop behaviors to such extreme that fears of dangerousness are aroused. However, if this happens a thorough behavior analysis and professional intervention is necessary to correct the situation. Anyone, brain injured or not, is not going to respond affirmatively to a family member or someone else telling him or her merely to shape up. That doesn't make any sense to a brain that is constructing a reality that very likely may not include the person, himself or herself, as part of the problem.

Improvement in self-awareness is key in brain injury rehabilitation. Unfortunately, often due to damage to the frontal lobes of the brain and other associated brain structures, regaining realistic self-appraisal is frequently not possible to the extent desired. Brain injury rehabilitation programs place significant effort at helping the individual accept a realistic self-appraisal, even if that appraisal must be created and defined by others for the individual. Sustained group and professional influence is often necessary to help a person adopt a perception of self that the damaged brain is not capable of creating on its own.

Crisis Prevention

The primary ingredient in preventing crisis situations where emotions and reasoning run amuck is anticipation—anticipation of the ingredients that ignite such situations. Encouraging an individual to produce logic consistent with your own may very likely produce very strong defensiveness. Failing to regard the limited resources for logic in the individual with a brain injury lays the foundation for a possible crisis situation. The first reaction to defensiveness is to fight. If your ground is challenged you take up arms to protect it.

The first rule in crisis prevention is to avoid defensiveness at all costs. Respecting where an individual's logic comes from and acknowledging that it differs from your own lays a more productive ground for resolution than does insisting the individual think like you do. The latter merely says, "I'm right; you are wrong." Nobody likes to hear this and usually reacts with immediate defensiveness. So, avoid challenging and confronting someone's logic in such a way that a torrent of emotional defensiveness might be unleashed.

It is very difficult to "let go" and allow an individual opportunity to learn and discover reality on his or her own. Sometimes a person who has had a brain injury needs to fail—sometimes several times—before an alternative approach is taken or a more rational logic explored. Attempting to protect the individual from the pain or inconvenience of these discoveries by confrontation runs the high risk of creating defensiveness.

The second rule in crisis prevention is redirection. Essentially, this means to defuse a potentially explosive situation. If an individual is expressing adamant views that are inconsistent with your reality but consistent with his or her perception or interpretation of reality, encouraging that individual to think like you do becomes fuel for the fire. Instead, redirect or defuse the situation. Mention something neutral or redirect the focus of attention to something else, something pleasant.

While redirection may not always work, it is at least possible to shut down the pursuit of an argument or escalating emotions. By refusing to engage in the emotions of a crisis, or potential crisis, you are defusing the situation. The point in any such circumstance is to avoid getting caught up challenging an individual's logic when that individual is having trouble with logic because of faulty brain functioning.

Children eventually grow to the age when they think the only word their parents know is "no." If conflicting logic escalates between an individual with a brain injury and his or her caregiver, this same situation can arise.

If, before the main meal, a person asks, "Can we have dessert now?" a typical retort, especially if the question had already been asked a dozen times, might be a sharp, "No." An alternative response might be, "Yes we can, right after everyone is through with the meal." This response is affirming. It reminds the person of the order of things (meal first, dessert second). It reflects a positive and supportive attitude. It is firm, simple, and warm.

Parent, Spouse, Therapist: All-In-One

Caring for an individual who has had a brain injury drastically changes roles. If you are a spouse or a sibling, normally enjoying a peer relationship, you are now cast in the role of parent and therapist as well. If you are a parent, normally facing the challenges of teaching a child to become an independent adult, you now must add the role of therapist. The individual with a brain injury no longer thinks and behaves as you are accustomed. Your role now must consider the drastic changes in your loved one's ways of thinking and behaving.

Part of the definition of being a therapist is to be emotionally detached sufficiently to impose structure in a relearning situation, to be objective. A therapist does not depend on emotional support from his or her patients. A therapist doesn't even have to be liked as long as he or she is imparting successful relearning. Unfortunately, the combined role of parent or spouse and therapist is awkward, to say the least.

However, it is essential to maintain a certain level of objectivity and therapeutic distance in order to be optimally helpful to a loved one who is struggling to recover some sense of order in brain and behavior processing. It is vital during this period for spouses and parents to seek emotional support from outside the marriage or parental relationship. The family member who has a brain injury may be less able to provide the sensitivity or to meet the emotional needs of others as he or she once could.

The foregoing several pages introduced some pretty hefty challenges in dealing with behavior problems, crisis situations, dangerousness, and just working around awkward behaviors. Never hesitate in these situations to seek help from professionals who make it their life's work to understand the complexities of brain and behavior relationships. Going it alone can be lonely, and perhaps ultimately disastrous to the family.

Not all family situations with a person who has had a brain injury will result in a constant flow of major problem behaviors. It is valuable, nevertheless, to appreciate where any behavior is coming from—the brain—and the fact that it is not necessarily able to be willfully controlled if only the person would just try harder. Recovery with brain injury almost always benefits from carefully considered guidance and a cool and calm model.

Rehabilitation at Home

Presented below are specific principles and several ideas for optimizing the social and physical environment for a person who has had a brain injury. Of course, in order to be fairly comprehensive, this advice covers the range from mild to severe brain injury. Families should recognize what principle is appropriate for a given level of injury.

The overriding principle in figuring out how to interact and how to help a person with a brain injury is to "get inside the brain" of the person with whom you are relating. The first nine chapters of this book offer a level of understanding about physical brain injury and the psychological consequences directly due to that brain damage. Keep that understanding always in mind. The world for the person with a brain injury is, in many respects, interpreted differently than before the brain injury. The Native American proverb, "Do not judge a man until you have walked two moons in his moccasins," certainly applies in this case. The interpretation of the world is unique for each of us but certainly bears especially careful consideration in the case of the individual whose interpretation of the world is founded on fragmented information due to a brain having difficulty with moment-to-moment continuity.

Guidelines for Interacting With a Person Who Has Had a Brain Injury

The following suggestions bear consideration as general guidelines useful throughout the course of rehabilitation. Each individual is different, of course, and needs more or less help in specific areas. Management of the effects of brain injury is a joint venture among the individual, himself or herself, and family, friends, and therapists.

- Encourage rest or break periods either when frustration or fatigue appears or often enough to avoid their onset. Breaks or rest periods will help avoid discouragement and temper control problems. Attention span is improved when a task is interspersed with breaks because the injured brain's ability to sustain focus fades rather quickly. As attention fades, frustration mounts.

- Keep activities and surroundings relatively simple and orderly. Too much, too fast, too soon leads to confusion, feeling overwhelmed, and poor emotional control. Overload can occur easily in a brain that is having to work extra hard just to maintain the basics. Sensory overload can stress anyone. A brain whose ability to translate sensory input into meaningful perceptions and react appropriately is now slower and more prone to error.

- Accept setbacks, both as a normal part of life and as a part of rehabilitation. Giving abundant encouragement and making light of setbacks assures overall growth. A sense of humor helps relieve tension and discouragement. Sometimes you have to accept the shrug of the shoulders attitude of "whatever."

- Write things down that you want the person you are helping to do. Whatever is written down becomes an extension of memory. It is unfair to expect that he or she will remember to carry out more than one or two steps or tasks without this written, visual assistance. This assures the person of what is expected. Provide praise and reward abundantly, but without condescension, when tasks are, indeed, successfully carried out.

- Give honest feedback, with equal attention given to praise for desired behavior and brief, supportive (not punitive), to-the-point, constructive criticism for undesirable behavior. The same principle applies to helping a person with a brain injury as applies to training a child—positive reinforcement goes much further than punishment does. Real sensitivity is required to achieve this balance. Anyone learns much more effectively with praise than with punishment. Don't tell someone his or her behavior is inappropriate. Talk around the problem in a way that offers alternatives and praises the use of appropriate behaviors. For a person whose brain produces limited choices in the first place, simply telling him or her the behavior is inappropriate reaches a deadend. Give alternative and appropriate choices and demonstrate how an alternative behavior might get better results than the "inappropriate" behavior.

- Surroundings should offer familiarity, predictability, and consistency, with regularly scheduled meals, activities, and rest. Knowing what to expect in a familiar environment and consistency in routine gives the brain a rest from always having to make decisions or be vigilant to the unexpected.

- Do not surprise the person who has had a brain injury. Explain activities fully before initiating them. Write down plans. Draw charts. Use maps and calendars. Devise whatever strategies you can to serve as reminders of what is to come. There is a strong sense of discomfort in the unknown—for anyone, but particularly for the person with a brain injury. The unknown future cannot be thought through so easily so it is best to avoid expecting the individual to do so.

- Minimize confrontation or the use of argument for correcting misbehavior. Redirecting the person's attention to something else is much more effective than either arguing or expecting the person to engage in a logical discussion. A damaged brain does not entertain logic, alternatives, and options easily. Once thought lands on a path that *seems* logical, even if it isn't logical to others, it may require too much mental work to alter that path. Alternative thinking about choices and cause and effect can occur only after the brain has had a chance to rest and when the person doesn't feel threatened or defensive. Diversion to some other topic, activity, or focus will help introduce that rest.

- Defuse irritation and anger. Rather than reacting to someone's irritation with your own irritation, model calm, smiling behavior that is neither condescending nor contradictory. When the going gets tough, just sit down for a while. The individual who exhibits irritation and anger can be encouraged to follow this model and be rewarded for it. This takes commitment to patience. Everyone has to slow down, to "stop and smell the roses."

- Being a model of calm confidence provides a sense of sureness and stability that the person with a brain injury wants and needs in order to rebuild his or her own self-confidence. The person with a brain injury depends on others to help him or her relearn how he or she should be acting or thinking, especially in times of stress when behavior easily can get out of control.

- Providing specific choices from which to choose is more effective than requesting an open-ended, ambiguous decision about something. Persons with a brain injury can select from among things relatively easily, but they have unusual difficulty coming up with a decision spontaneously without specific choices to choose from. Left to a spontaneous decision, the choice may be quite inappropriate, or may take an eternity to make—or may be so spontaneous as to be poorly reasoned. Providing a selection of appropriate choices provides the foundation for praise.

- Use wall charts, reminder boards, calendars, labels, notebooks, journals, and other visual memory aids abundantly. Praise frequently when these tools are actually used by the person you are helping.

- Do not encourage excessive challenge or unrealistic competition which places the person with a brain injury at a considerable disadvantage with others. There is no need to increase either the chance of failure or the fear of failure, which leads to anxiety and defensiveness. Competition also encourages comparative thinking, something a person recovering from brain injury does not need to engage in. Comparison with the behavior—and successes—of a person not brain injured can reinforce discouragement. Instead, encourage individual challenge and realistic goal setting consistent with the person's capabilities.

- Do not say or imply that the person you are helping will recover to being normal again. This future-oriented expectation is not dealing with the immediate moment and may give false hope. What is happening right now is what is important. Focusing on a pipe dream is not really productive thinking for anyone. Awareness of what and how you are accomplishing a task right now keeps a person focused, encouraged, and rewarded. It does not support the idolization of some unattainable normality.

- Do not compare the person you are helping with others, just as it is not healthy to compare siblings. A comment like, "Your brother would never do a thing like that," will probably only reinforce the behavior the parent is attempting to eradicate. Respect an individual for who he or she is without comparison to some perceived better or worse standard. Each person deserves respect and understanding for his or her own uniqueness.

"At Home" Cognitive Rehabilitation

Several activities can be used at home to provide or augment cognitive rehabilitation. Activities that are designed to stimulate brain cell reconnections, to help the individual improve memory, to produce an enjoyable experience in thinking and problem-solving, and to increase self-awareness and self-control in a positive manner are all within the scope of "cognitive rehabilitation."

These following suggestions may be used as appropriate given the level of injury in the person you are helping. An occupational or cognitive rehabilitation therapist can assist families in identifying additional ideas and resources.

- Play strategy board games. Games should be relatively short and/or should be played with lots of stretch breaks to keep attention from waning. Games should require some strategic thinking. Good ones are Monopoly (the time-limited version), Scrabble, Battleship, Chess, Checkers, and the like. Games should be selected based reasonably on the ability level of the person who has had a brain injury. Games of pure chance, unless requiring some strategy in planning and memory, are likely of little value for cognitive improvement.

- Hold planned conversations. Fifteen or twenty minutes after a meal or some other relaxing time can be used to focus on the day's happenings in the news, what's going on in the family, and so forth. Such conversation must not be judgmental, or artificially structured or complex. Everyone engaged in the conversation should be equal. Everyone is entitled to his or her opinions and perceptions without argument or challenge. These conversation times should be kept relatively brief. If thoughts are too far from reality, redirecting to a different topic would be a good idea. Deep philosophical or abstract conversation should definitely be avoided.

- Activities that require planning should be done in a relaxed and non-rushed manner. A shopping trip, a family gathering, a picnic, an outing to the museum, or whatever should be planned—on paper—with times written out, objectives or goals for the event stated, routes planned to get there, persons involved, how long it will last, and so forth. This encourages anticipatory thinking, that is organized, thus helping reduce anxiety and providing an opportunity to start building confidence that the task can be managed well. Such activity also helps in learning to use transportation (e.g., mass transit) schedules.

• Making and reading maps can provide good exercise in spatial reorientation. Of course, the maps should be simple and relevant to some activity. Planning a short car trip can be done with a map first. Drawing a map—of the neighborhood or a complex building such as a hospital—builds a sense of spatial organization. Learning to use maps of public transportation systems has an obvious practical value. If a person has specific damage to the right portion of the brain, map making and reading—or any visual-spatial task—might be very difficult or even impossible. In such cases, the individual might be helped to rely on verbal information to help him or her get around spatially.

• Constructional activities such as putting together jigsaw puzzles, assembling model airplanes or cars, or building birdhouses should be encouraged but at a level of difficulty that is not too challenging yet not too simplistic either. (Again, depending on the location and severity of brain injury, constructional tasks may be quite difficult or impossible.) Use of power tools must be avoided, of course. Hobby kits are a good source for constructional activities. As usual, select items that are of appropriate difficulty level. Often, a person embarking on such activities will benefit from a coworker who can help plan the order of steps, without being intrusive, to achieve a successful construction. He or she can aid in keeping the work site orderly, and prompting for rests and breaks if the going gets tough.

- Games, from simple video games to pickup sticks, are great for fostering eye-hand coordination. Dribbling a basketball or foot-dribbling a soccer ball regularly along with some noncompetitive play helps reestablish motor pathways. Eye-hand coordination, motor control, motor anticipation, action planning—none of these are achieved by passively watching television. So, the corollary here is to connect the video game to the television and leave the antenna off.

- Collection hobbies are often good for teaching order, organization, and categorical thinking. Stamp collecting, for example, requires one to learn history, develop a sense of time continuity, and acquire a sense of categories. Stamps are issued during particular historical events, as commemoratives, or in theme sets such as birds, flowers, people, and so forth.

- In any activity, whether collecting stamps or building a model car, time should be set aside specifically for these activities or else they will probably be substituted for by passive activities such as sitting in front of the television. Encouraging activities with another participant is most helpful to develop motivation and cooperation.

- Playing a musical instrument helps cultivate a sense of rhythm, timing, and self-satisfaction. Music is the universal language. Engaging in singing or playing an instrument can be a very absorbing activity. Instruments should be chosen that are relatively easy to play at first such as a harmonica, guitar, or even drums (the silent, electronic pad type where headphones must be worn are probably advisable). Even an electric keyboard, especially if the individual has some prior keyboard experience, can produce good quality and satisfying music with little practice.

- Reading should be a daily activity. Both planned time and "filler" time can be used for reading. Even for persons who were never much into reading to begin with should set aside ten or fifteen minutes to read every day. Reading helps stimulate thinking and attention maintenance. Ideally, talking with someone about the material just read should follow the reading period. This will reinforce what was read and require the individual to translate visually-acquired language into spoken language.

- Photography can be an excellent medium for sharpening visual perception. A beginners class in photography that focuses on composition rather than the technicalities of complex cameras or photo developing would be desirable. Learning to sharpen a sense of awareness of light and dark, shadows, background and foreground, action, emotional tone and picture content, simplicity and complexity, shapes and forms all help improve perception. A simple camera should be used, at least at first so that the composition of the photograph is the most important concern, not the operation of the camera.

- Relatively simple socialization activities should be planned as frequently as desired. Simple outings with a friend or family member, preferably with someone other than those with whom the person who has had the brain injury interacts every day, will encourage social awareness and reestablish comfort being in social environments.

The ideas and suggestions for interacting with a person who has had a brain injury, and the cognitive remediation activities, must be balanced with professional help and guidance when necessary. None of the suggestions provided alone will benefit the individual if he or she is still attempting to cope with (or hide) the depths of despair. Nor may these activities break certain habit behaviors like verbosity or self-centered talk or hallucinatory and delusional thinking. Such behaviors require professional intervention right away.

The individual who has had a brain injury is forced to go through a terrific rebuilding of self-concept and self-control. It is easy for this task to get bogged down. If that is suspected, and none of these suggestions seem to work, seek neuropsychological help so that the home-based activities will have a higher chance for success.

Lori—Real Person

Kyle was 18, handsome, smart, funny, and talented. He played guitar in a rock and roll band and was on his way to stardom when it happened. He was out partying late one night with some friends. They had been drinking and found themselves racing on a deserted country road. No one really remembers how it happened but alcohol was involved; Kyle was a passenger, and all those involved in the crash walked away from the hospital in a matter of days—everyone except Kyle.

We all got the call in the middle of the night and we swarmed the hospital confused and scared. Each of us in the family recalls the phone call and the next forty-eight hours in a very detailed and surreal way. Sometimes even now when we get together, we talk about those early hours.

The doctors didn't expect Kyle to make it through the night, but he did. They said if he came out of the coma, it was highly likely that he would exist in a vegetative state. None of us believed he would die and none of us believed he would be a vegetable. We rallied around him with our love and waited and prayed and hugged for endless days. The days turned to weeks and we moved into the hospital with him, and quit our jobs or juggled our schedules to be there. We were there for him. Some of the hospital staff was less than tolerant of our constant presence, but we didn't care. The talented nurses, doctors, and therapists understood the value of our presence and encouraged us. The distressed staff resented our constant intrusion, prompting, and involvement in his care.

As Kyle emerged from the coma what we saw was a severely brain injured man sitting in a wheel chair in a diaper, his head tipped to the side, a constant stream of drool running down his chin and soaking his shirt. His eyes flitted back and forth in an unnatural way and he had no control over the left side of his body. The muscles on his left were so tight that it was impossible to straighten his limbs. He could speak a few mumbled words and respond with yes and no. That gave us great hope.

The family bonded during those weeks. We came together to will his recovery with our own combined will. We began reading and what we found in books was too technical to fully understand, but we read nonetheless. The stark reality of the situation was sinking in. His doctors said his recovery would be limited but we refused to believe that as well. We wrote him a song, and performed it at a benefit concert for him. We videotaped him daily. And each day he gave us small signs that he was on a journey of recovery. One day he told a mumbled joke, the next he tapped his fingers on a plate to a tune on the radio.

One day someone asked him why he was wearing a diaper. He looked down at it in slow motion. He did everything in slow-mo. Then he lifted his head half way up, still tilted to the side and said, "Get this thing off me." We took it off and took him to the bathroom. It took five minutes to transfer him from the chair to the toilet. His limbs would tremble violently and he did not have the muscle control to sit erect, but he went to the bathroom, and then said, "There."

The day after the diaper incident, someone asked him why he was tilting his head and gave him a hand mirror. He held it with his right hand and studied his reflection for a long time. It took him a week to master holding his head up straight and the drooling stopped altogether. After that, each piece of his recovery was kind of like that. He would notice something that wasn't right, would fight hard, whip it, and move on to the next thing.

And then the intensive physical therapy started. He spent hours each day in repetitive therapies simply working to straighten his limbs. It hurt and his physical condition was very weak but he fought hard and began to focus on each task giving it a hundred percent. And when he wasn't in physical therapy, he was listening to the song we wrote him, over and over and over. He drew courage and strength from it. And we watched and filmed as he began to come back to us.

We watched what was happening and urged him on. It was similar to a butterfly coming out of a cocoon. It was like seeing a baby become a toddler. It was incredibly slow and painful but bittersweet and victorious at the same time. Most of all, our family feared for his future. We feared that he would never be capable of leading a normal productive life. Each step along the way, our family would discuss his progress and rationalize. Then we would agree that if his development went no further, he would still be able to live his life with some sort of meaning and perhaps even feel joy.

We all worked together to achieve acceptance of the new Kyle. It was crucial, we knew from our reading. It was our challenge, but it didn't stop us from pushing him and motivating him, and helping him set and achieve his goals. One of our biggest challenges was not to baby him, to refrain from doing things for him. We helped each other each time we saw it happening with a soft reminder that "helping him won't help him." It was a mantra of sorts. A privately shared sentence understood by all that loved him, which had a profoundly deep impact on his recovery.

It's been eight years now. Kyle learned to walk after hundreds of hours of therapy. His grandest moment was walking down the isle and standing up for his brother's wedding just eight months after the injury. He continued his therapy and would often stay up all night working out. His speech steadily improved. He talked slower, but he could communicate effectively. And he had a strong sense of humor that was contagious. It was a success story in every sense.

Three years after the accident he had a girlfriend, and shortly thereafter a beautiful daughter. That is when his new life brought him exceptional joy. He was a wonderful loving father and because he did not work, caring for her gave him great meaning.

But my brother's story was not over. The family eventually began to notice that he was backsliding. It was apparent both physically and mentally. He was slower, weaker, and unable to focus and stay organized. He got frustrated and angered easily. He was displaying inappropriate behavior. We soon found that he had been smoking marijuana and sometimes using more serious drugs. His recovery came to an abrupt halt. My brother is fighting again now. The drugs on top of the brain injury have placed new burdens and challenges on him, and on his brain.

This new stage has brought us all to a new place. Different yet the same. The old mantra, "helping him won't help him," is still true. All we can do is rally with our love and support just like we did in the early stages. That is so easy to say, but extremely difficult to do. So we seek professional advice and read about addiction to arm ourselves with the facts so we can support him the right way. As he fights to stay off drugs we all know the strength he has and that if anyone can win he can. His early recovery has showed us that.

As a family, one of our biggest challenges was accepting the change in Kyle and not compare the new Kyle to the person he was before the brain injury. For the most part we have been able to do it, even if we needed to remind ourselves on a regular basis. Time helped us get there.

As we support Kyle now and in the future, we continue to arm ourselves with knowledge in the field of brain injury recovery. Once long ago, we might have thought of "recovery" as a definite time when he would be healed but time has shown us that this is not the case. Brain injury recovery is ongoing and our challenge as the family who supports him is to recognize and help Kyle recognize the next step in the recovery process.

11

Practical Life Management Strategies—for the Individual

What is the secret to success, or to happiness? Many late night television hucksters promise the secret to instant success and happiness, ready to reveal a formula for instant financial wealth (their secret to success and happiness)—for a fee, of course. It is never quite that simple. There are no secrets. Knowledge, skills, determination, attitude, a good plan, and the ability to constantly assess where you are in your pursuit of success and happiness are infinitely more valuable than any quick-fix "secret." Just as counting on winning the lottery is not a good life plan, counting on some secret that will make life an easy bed of roses is not a good bet either.

There are innumerable aspects of life, some of which we have no control over, which determine our life experiences—happy and successful ones, or otherwise. Luck or "secrets" may be among the aspects that influence destiny; however, our own decisions, choices, and adaptations are most powerful. How we react to, cope with, and conquer the ups and downs of life is entirely up to each of us. A person determined and in charge holds the keys to his or her own happiness. Magic secrets, luck, or fate play little part in the life of the person who can roll with the punches and remain determined to be happy with whatever comes along—even brain injury. Happiness is a decision, not a stroke of luck.

A brain injury causes a change in how one feels and thinks, remembers, works, and does just about everything. The initial reaction to brain injury, understandably, is usually not a happy one. While brain injury can produce a significant loss of function, eventually the feeling of loss must be replaced with determination to get on with life and find satisfaction. The task of adapting to major life changes is inevitable after a brain injury. The willingness to accept change and meet the challenge opens doors to a satisfying life.

Many people, whether having had a brain injury or not, blame bad luck, others, the government, their genes, their parents, or something or other for their failures, unhappiness, or shortcomings. This is bogus. Blaming anyone or anything makes you a victim, and victims are a helpless lot. Victims perceive themselves as having no control. Only through acceptance that the world in which we live is far from a perfect place and that unfortunate—even catastrophic—things happen to people all the time, can we learn to pick up the pieces and get on with life.

We develop strategies to manage the ups and downs of our lives. We make choices about things we can control. We accept things we cannot control. We adopt attitudes that allow us to accept changes. We cultivate self-respect in order to love and be loved. We grow to know who we are in an ever-changing world, and regularly reexamine who we are. We accept our aloneness and take care of others so they won't feel so alone, and in turn receive care from others so we won't feel so alone.

After a brain injury, self-management means entering new life territory but the same principles apply. The struggle may seem greater while guidance to muddle through it all may seem less available. Throughout history, virgin territory may be challenging to explore, but the rewards of conquering new ground can be exhilarating. The choice to make this journey drudgery or exciting is up to you. The last pages of this book provide some guidance for making it exciting, or at least more satisfying.

When bad things happen—regardless of who is to blame, if anyone is—the aftermath involves choices. Through no intention of our own, a brain injury occurs. How we react to it, how we pick up the pieces of our lives and once again reexamine life, depends on choice. One can remain the victim or one can become the conqueror. The road to recovery is not always well charted, is often rocky and bumpy, and takes turns we don't always expect. Determination to proceed and to discover life along the way is a choice.

Compensation, Coping, and Competency

Adjustment to anything—including to brain injury—means learning to compensate. This means learning to do things differently. If you break your right arm and it is in a cast, you have to learn to do everything left-handed for a while, unless, of course, you are left-handed in the first place. It is awkward. Handwriting is sloppy. Handling a fork probably means you jabbed your lip a few times. Manipulating the video game joystick means your video game scores tumble. You grudgingly accept these inconveniences because you know your right arm will eventually heal and the cast will come off.

Brain injury, too, requires adaptations to doing things differently, but this time the adaptations will probably have to be permanent. These are examples of general adaptations that are usually required following a brain injury: Learning to be more orderly to avoid confusion, learning to slow down what you are doing so you can do it correctly and without so much frustration, learning to be simpler in your lifestyle to avoid feeling overwhelmed, and learning to find alternative ways of doing things that simply cannot be done like they used to.

Whenever frustration, anger, or any sign of failure becomes apparent, it is time to take a look at how you might need to compensate for some activity or former way of doing things. This might seem quite inconvenient and irritating at first, having to change the way you live your whole life. The other choice is not to adapt and, hence, experience more frustration.

Coping is the psychological process we use to accept doing things differently in order to compensate for some weakness or obstacle. People talk about coping with lots of things such as a mean boss, having too little money, a jalopy for a car, a bad snowstorm, the death of a loved one, a damaging earthquake. It's one thing to keep on complaining and quite another to decide to accept the inevitable adversities in life and not let yourself be overcome by them. When asked, "How do you manage such adversity?" we often hear someone reply, "Oh, you just cope." The first step is attitude.

Of course, brain injury is a permanent situation, not temporary like some of the examples above. However, the principle still applies: you either succumb to the situation or you cope with it. It's sink or swim. To succumb means to give in or give up. It means letting the situation at hand fuel the self-pity that is the foundation for unhappiness. It means never achieving victory over adversity.

Healthy recovery with brain injury requires developing coping strategies. By creating positive approaches to dealing with adversity you gradually regain and build competence to be effective in managing life.

Competency—at anything—means being at your best. It means conquering and being in control of the situation the best you can do it. Competency comes from the attitude that you "can," not from the attitude that you "can't." Competency is gratifying and self-respecting. It is work and determination. It is faith in finding the resources to conquer adversity.

The rub in achieving—or *not* achieving—competency comes when you deceive yourself. To be truly competent you must know your strengths and your limitations, honestly. You must know and have a handle on your resources. You must be realistic. Aspiring to become a brain surgeon after you, yourself, have had a brain injury is probably not realistic. To return to school to study something you do feel comfortable with and something the aptitude tests suggest you can handle would be realistic.

In summary, learn compensation strategies to minimize the inconveniences of a brain injury. Cultivate attitudes of coping and acceptance. And, finally, find your realistic competencies: those niches in life where you can excel and be proud of yourself. The suggestions in the next several pages should help you compensate, cope, and define your competencies.

Practical Management Strategies

A mutually positive and cooperative attitude between the person with a brain injury and those close to him or her is certainly desired for optimum rehabilitation. Recovery with brain injury is dependent on committed and persistent effort from everyone involved. The following suggestions have been culled from dozens of persons who have learned how to cope with brain injury. They represent the foundation of the "can do" attitude that sustains a positive life direction.

- Keep a detailed calendar of things you do and plan to do. This builds self-confidence, independence, memory reliability, and self-responsibility. Use one calendar that has all your appointments and plans. More than one calendar and you'll risk confusion.

- Ask questions, but ask yourself the question first to see if you can figure it out. Don't let your brain get lazy; ask for help when you do need it. Asking too many questions makes you dependent and not responsible for yourself and does not encourage your own critical thinking. Find ways to actively get answers instead of passively just asking someone.

- Write things down. Keep a journal with lots of notes. This helps achieve multimodal learning: hear it, write it, and see it written all at the same time. Just writing something down greatly helps you remember even if you don't ever look at your notes. Always carry a pen and notepad. This says you are ready, willing, and *able* to learn and remember. You'll say with confidence, "Here, let me write that down."

- Use no drugs or alcohol. These not only dull the brain they can interfere with the recovery of neurotransmitters and cause great mental problems. Respect your body and its natural state; don't pollute it. (See extended content about drugs below.)

- Do not use mental delinquents like "I can't" or "oh, no." They remind us of negative thinking about ourselves and throw up a wall. Be positive about what you can do; don't immediately be intimidated by something challenging. As soon as you say "I can't" you've closed a door.

- Do not use weasel words like "later," "maybe," "try," or "kind of." These words are vague and never commit you to anything. Be definite. You'll know where you stand and so will others. Instead of doing something "later," set a time and date to do it. Instead of thinking "maybe" you'll read that book, start by reading the first page. Instead of trying, do. Instead of feeling "kind of" interested in a walk in the park, take the walk—with determination.

- Keep a daily schedule. This establishes routines and helps make life predictable and easier to manage.

- Have goals and be realistic. Keep reassessing these goals to make sure you are actually achieving them and they are not just pipe dreams. A goal will never be attained without taking the first step. Don't talk about goals in the future, talk about what you are doing right now toward achieving your goals. A vague plan to start to exercise more to lose weight is nice but doing it right now is goal-*achievement*.

- Know yourself and what you can and cannot do. Be honest and realistic about this, and always make sure you are aware of what you are doing. Believe in yourself. Seek feedback and guidance from others to help discover your real self.

- Be on time. This shows self-respect and respect for others.

- Always be open to learning. Recognize that your brain needs to be open and flexible in thinking in order to accept new ideas. Willingness to learn is a commitment to grow. Start with learning about your injury, the brain, and your potentials.

- Always consider the optimistic side of things. Attitude is everything. Daily affirmations remind you to stay positive.

- Be willing to do new things. Don't just "try." Do!

- Be outgoing to get along with others. Accept others for who they are. Do not judge others. Respect individuality. Care about others. These are the ingredients to making and keeping friendships. Without friendships, loneliness will erode growth. This was in a Chinese fortune cookie: "Your kindness will lead you to happiness."

- Be organized. Make a plan. "A place for everything and everything in its place" is a good habit that will keep your life orderly.

- Do not be the center of attention. That gets old real quick.

- Strive for honest communications. Find family or friends who are honest with you. Accept people for their honesty and you will grow to respect yourself.

- Do not be afraid to accept help. Remember that you don't need to be defensive; you just need to be gracious.

- Listen, *really listen*, to others. If you shut someone out before you've really heard what he or she is saying you won't keep yourself open. After all, there just might be something to learn. Respect others and you will respect yourself.

- Slow down, relax, and have fun. Pace yourself. Do not let yourself get overwhelmed. And if you do get overwhelmed, let people know you are stepping back to regroup.

- Wear a watch. Time disorientation is a common problem following brain injury. Frequently checking the time will help you stay on task and anticipate when events are upcoming throughout the day. It adds to being responsible.

- Accept change; it's a natural part of life.

A Word Or Two About Drugs

Use of heroin, cocaine, marijuana, amphetamines, and a host of other street drugs is a significant problem for some people who have had a brain injury. Just one taste of the effect of these drugs can hook you fast and hard. These drugs essentially enhance the brain's natural neurotransmitters. However, such drugs also create a chemical dependency that causes the brain to want more and more of them. Some street drugs also cause the individual to feel such a sense of escape from reality that he or she gradually pulls away from the reality of family, friends, and responsibilities, relying on the effect of the drug to feel good. Once the hole is started, drug use only digs it deeper and deeper.

The brain—even the injured brain—strives to maintain a balance of chemicals that enable it to work properly and optimally. Sometimes, prescription drugs are given to provide brain chemicals that are missing or in short supply because of damage or biological malfunction. Street drugs at first might seem to do the same thing. Users innocently and deceptively call this "self-medication." The difference is that street drugs are not controlled. They are used in excess of what the brain needs—and they can cause even greater damage to brain tissue. They create a dependency that calls for more and more of the drug. They also introduce chemicals that are not needed but that feel good anyway.

At first, use of a street drug—just like alcohol—takes all your troubles away. This temporary relief from the stresses of life seems okay. Soon, another hit is needed to maintain the feeling. Not just another hit, a bigger hit. Within weeks, or even days, an individual can create in himself an addicted brain—addicted to street drugs that sustain the addiction, create additional damaging effects on brain tissue, remove the individual further and further from reality, and create all sorts of new problems such as how to pay for the escalating costs of these drugs. Within days or weeks the street drug remedy to life's travails is out of control and progressively more and more destructive—biologically, psychologically, and socially.

Two kinds of people believe the above description: those who have been there and conquered the drug habit, and those who have never used drugs and are committed to never using drugs.

The kind of person who doesn't believe this description is the person who thinks he'll try it once or twice and won't let himself get addicted—like just one really powerful martini, only better. First, the initial use of the drug may seem so wonderful that it is virtually impossible to believe that anything bad could come of this chemical. The feeling is just too wonderful. Second, the chemical reaction of these drugs creates a biological dependency; it is not something one can control willfully. The only way to control the biological craving for more and more of the drug is to get more of it or to go through withdrawal. Withdrawal is next to impossible without the help of professionals trained in managing the body and brain's horrible reaction to now having to manage without the drug. This terrifying withdrawal may last for days or weeks, or even months or years.

Find a high you can make yourself—holding hands with someone you like, watching a peaceful sunrise or sunset, listening to a child at play, hiking along a wilderness trail. These highs are reality. You maintain complete control over them. They can make you feel energized, pure, contented.

According to those who have used the drug, a hit of cocaine can provide a rush that surpasses any feeling you've had before, there is no denying that. Following the rush—days, weeks, or months later—the awful consequences come crashing down: Neglect of self and others, drained bank account, rejection by friends and family. More brain damage, maybe hallucinations and paranoia. And then there's the feeling of being at your absolute rock-bottom worst when you need another hit but you're out of dope.

Coping with brain injury—or any of life's challenges—is not accomplished by street drugs. Drug use magnifies the trauma many times over. It seals one's fate as victim to drug dependency. It creates loneliness beyond any loneliness felt so far. It destroys further any sense of hope, faith, or trust.

The rule of approaching life with vigor and determination is: Just do it.

The rule for assuring a life and avoiding the devastation of drugs is, "Just don't do 'em." Drugs can cause further brain damage by poisoning neurons. Drugs definitely slow the recovery from traumatic brain injury.

Adventures in Brain Travel

Anyone, whether having had a brain injury or not, is welcome aboard the exciting adventure into brain travel. The brain is the great frontier of science. While it is the most important organ of the body, we still know precious little about it. Only a few highly specialized physicians are able to open up the skull and perform surgery on the brain to remove blood clots or cancerous tumors. Scientists and doctors are able to resolve some illnesses that plague the brain but not most. We still don't have a good understanding about mental illness or criminal behavior. If we did, our mental institutions and prisons wouldn't be so overcrowded. We continue to seek understanding of how the brain can be best educated and how creativity can be fostered.

The fact that our world suffers from behaviors produced by the brain—murders, robberies, swindles, and a host of other nasty and vile things—means we really have a long way to go in learning how to correct undesirable brain behaviors. Educational reforms haven't really produced much gain in human learning potentials over the past century. There is continued distress caused by depression, anxiety, and mental illness. There is general agreement among many neuroscientists that humans still have not learned how to use the "other 90 percent" of the brain's potential that Einstein told us a century ago that we aren't using.

We yet have a long way to go in learning about the brain. Having had a brain injury puts a greater burden on the task at hand. You can become an adventurer into this vast challenge. Studying about the brain and exploring new technologies may open doors for you. The premise of science and discovery is that no stone should be left unturned. Simply put, there are great potentials for learning about the brain and improving its function that we have not yet tapped. Most situations of brain damage still leave the individual capable of learning and discovering. As a person who has experienced a brain injury, constantly seeking new knowledge and understanding about brain functioning can help greatly in conquering your own challenges. Einstein would be pleased!

Certainly intended to whet the appetite, the ideas for exploration offered here are practical, have already shown promise, and might hold keys to greater accomplishments.

Neurofeedback

While still somewhat controversial and under continuing exploration, the use of biofeedback techniques specifically targeted to changing brain electrical activity may hold promise. We know there are people in this world who have mastered great control over bodily functions that are not supposed to be within the realm of self-control (such as minimal or no bleeding when the skin is pierced or slowing the heart rate to a couple beats per minute). Neurofeedback is the relatively new study of how we might be able to control brain waves to achieve greater activity in certain brain areas that have become relatively dormant, or subdue out-of-control activity in other areas. For instance, neurofeedback might be used to reduce the kinds of brain electrical activity that cause seizures. It is a whole new field that may hold promise or might lead to new ideas yet undiscovered.

If you are interested, explore these ideas through reading and through discussion with a legitimately trained and certified biofeedback professional. Beware of fly-by-nighters that offer promises that have not been borne out through scientific research or demonstration. Seek advise only from professionals recognized by professional organizations and standards.

Meditation

Actually, biofeedback has its roots in meditation. People learned centuries ago that focusing the mind on one thing and shutting down intrusive thoughts from other sources can lead to a peaceful feeling and a renewed sense of energy. Meditation has taken on many forms, from formal study, as in Zen sitting and meditation which is intended to clear the mind and open it to insight, to transcendental meditation intended to promote deep relaxation. The value of meditation has been touted as a way to steer clear of becoming mired in the moment-to-moment stresses and emotional quicksand of life. Its value has been espoused by tens of thousands of devotees for centuries.

As with biofeedback, explore meditation with a legitimate trainer. Read books, attend informational lectures, and learn from those who have a reputation of quality. It's all about gaining control over the brain and mind, a way of getting back some of what injury may have taken away.

Foods and Nutrition

Almost daily it seems that some new information is coming from a laboratory somewhere in the world about the value, or lack of value, of some food, mineral, herb, or vitamin. In fact, there has been a resurgence of interest in ancient herbal medicine that people relied upon centuries ago. Of course, ingesting anything should be done with caution and with information. And, most of all, the addition of any food or nutritional supplement to a well-rounded diet should be done in moderation. There was the craze a few years ago about megavitamins where people would ingest huge amounts of certain vitamins. Many people became quite ill from this activity as certain vitamins can accumulate to toxic levels in body tissues. Obtain and follow tested advice from trusted sources.

Even drinking too much water can be bad for you. Extremely excessive water in the body (consumed through forced drinking) can interfere with electrolyte balance and may even cause a seizure. The body must function within a balance of all nutrients. Excess in just one thing can throw off the balance. Again, it is crucial to explore, learn, and get advice from a trusted and experienced individual.

Recent studies are suggesting that certain vitamins, such as C and E, are particularly useful in helping the brain rid itself of oxygen-free radicals. These byproducts of chemical reactions in the brain are suspected to contribute to diminished brain functioning, and even perhaps to Alzheimer's disease. No research is conclusive as yet, so heed the advice to use any substances in moderation, and with informed choice.

There are numerous books, lectures, audio and video programs, and government reports that teach about the latest findings on foods and nutrition as these relate to brain functioning. There may be real value in being sensitive to how and what we feed our brain. *Open your eyes, ears, and brain, however, before you open your mouth to put anything in it.*

Exercise

The brain needs abundant amounts of two things: glucose and oxygen. Without these key ingredients, it won't live long at all. Aside from exercise that enhances oxygen to all tissues of the body, including the brain, exercise also stimulates the production of other chemicals in the body that have life-enhancing benefits. Again, it cannot be stressed enough, get advice from a doctor or other health professional before you begin any particularly strenuous exercise program. Remember, anything in excess has more potential for harm than good.

Use It or Loose It

Many individuals and groups of individuals have demonstrated that staying mentally active prolongs mental agility. If you languish in front of a television every day you can pretty much count on your brain turning to mush. If you read, engage in conversation, solve problems, pursue artistic activities, and maintain an energetic outlook on life your mind will flourish. Science has demonstrated that even people with a propensity towards developing Alzheimer's disease can head off symptom development for years if they maintain an active brain—an active, exploring, inquisitive lifestyle.

There is no age limit nor intellectual requirement for creativity. To be creative and enjoy the benefits of mental agility you must use the ol' noggin.

Never be a wannabe. As soon as you catch yourself saying, "I want to be (do)…anything," start being or doing whatever it is you are wishing for. Then you can say, "I *am* being (doing)…whatever." Years and even lifetimes are wasted on wishes and pipe dreams. Use your brain. Or, lose it.

The Future

The future in neuroscience is still wide open. Of course, the dramatic discoveries about the brain that lie ahead will probably be made in rigorously controlled scientific laboratories. However, that certainly does not prevent each of us from making our own smaller discoveries. Respect the brain for all the potentials and wonderful things it has to offer. Too many people accept the brain passively, thinking that they have no control over what the brain thinks, how it functions, or the behaviors it produces. They are dead wrong. It is amazing how much control each of us can develop. It takes dedication, research, and learning. Be a part of the future with your own brain. Learn from reliable and ethical sources what you can do to enhance your own brain. This is not intended to spite brain injury but to take control of life despite brain injury. First and foremost, accept the premise that it is you who has control, not damaged cells, genetics, the government, or something else. It is you!

Libraries and bookstores, the Internet, adult education programs, public lectures and demonstrations, science museums—all these are great resources for learning about neuroscience. Remember the words of Auntie Mame, "Life is a banquet and most poor suckers are starving to death."

Now, You're the Teacher

Most people don't know the first thing about their brain, let alone about brain injury. Now that you have first hand experience and are gaining knowledge and control daily about your own brain experience, you already know a lot more than most other people. This puts you in an especially important position of being the teacher to those who know little about how the brain works, how injury causes the brain to work differently, and what must be done to compensate for and cope with that injury.

Many people are afraid to tell others that they have had a brain injury. Of course, there is the fear of prejudice, which is always based in ignorance. The more confident you are about your own success at conquering brain injury and learning to cope with it, adapt to it, and develop competencies despite the injury, the more resourceful you are in teaching others about the effects of brain injury.

Because you have learned to do things differently, perhaps more slowly and carefully, and because you might need to interject more structure and order into your daily activities, others who do not understand your new functioning must be educated. People make assumptions all the time (usually wrong) about other people's behavior. As you probably know from your own experience, making assumptions usually leads to feeling foolish. It is generally best to be honest and up-front about who you are and why you might be doing things differently than you used to.

People who need to know about brain injury and need to understand your new lifestyle, need to be taught. This situation is a paradox because often it is you who has the brain injury who must do the teaching to others. You have the burden of learning all these heroic adaptations yet it is still you who must then educate and break down the stereotypes, misunderstandings, and prejudices held by friends, employers, teachers, and others with whom you have more than casual contact.

It seems unfair but that's life. Fortunately, teaching others can be a tremendous way of learning for yourself. Here are some hints about telling others about brain injury, and about your brain injury:

If someone makes any comment suggesting that he or she doesn't understand your need to write things down, to be orderly, or to take things more slowly and cautiously, tell him or her that you have had a brain concussion and that you need consciously to help your brain do its work more than you used to. Using the term "brain concussion" is a little less emotionally traumatizing to others because most people are familiar with the term "concussion" and usually relate it to a passing thing. The term "brain damage" carries a more scary connotation to those who don't know much about it. The term has been used in a derogatory manner, as well, and you might want to avoid it.

If a person asks you about brain injury, or brain concussion, be honest and tell him or her what you know. *Always*, however, emphasize what you are doing to adapt and compensate in a positive manner. Never, never, never describe brain injury in terms of what you cannot do or what you have lost. Describe it in adaptive terms such as "change" and how you are coping. A positive and supportive comment might be, "I had a brain concussion when I fell off a horse and my head hit the ground pretty hard. I was unconscious about a half-hour. I now write things down and am more careful in not overloading my brain as it needs more time and organization to do its work. I'm pretty satisfied with how I am adapting."

Providing a positive and empathetic attitude will help anyone learn about brain injury. Again, it is paradoxical in some ways that the person who has had the brain injury must be empathetic and understanding of the person who has not had the brain injury. Since most people know nothing about brain injury and because most people who have had a brain injury do not physically look like they have any injury, it is easy for uninformed people to conjure up all sorts of misperceptions and wrong ideas and judgments.

It is difficult to let someone into your life if you, yourself, don't feel comfortable with your life. By learning as much as you can and practicing the ideas presented in this book, it is entirely possible to reformulate a positive, self-accepting image. With a smile and a sense of pride in what you have overcome, you can teach others about your experience in a positive manner. This is not to imply that brain injury is overcome in the sense of eradicated. Rather, the overwhelming change that brain injury causes can be contained and life can once again be lived with pride and acceptance—just lived differently.

Again, A Whole Person

Through the devastation of losing your brain to total unconsciousness, even for a brief while, to the gradual realization that thinking, behaving, and relating are now more prone to error, demand more energy, and sometimes cause great insecurity, the journey through brain injury is complex. Horrible feelings of loss, anger that this was certainly not your choice, and constantly evolving change in every aspect of life characterize the journey. With support, from people who love you and from people who are trained in the art and science of how the brain works and doesn't work, the journey can take a turnaround. Loss gives way to realization of gains. Sadness gives way to feeling love again. Overwhelming mental confusion gives way to accomplishing little things and then bigger things once again.

The misfortune of brain injury brings with it certain opportunity. There are many people in this world who never achieve a state of wholeness in their lives. They are fragmented, unhappy, disorganized, and unsuccessful. They never had a brain injury but they never learned much about the powers that lie within themselves either. Sometimes it takes adversity to wake up the spirit.

Being a whole person means being integrated, being all together, balancing assets and liabilities, maintaining emotional and intellectual resources, and having the capability to step back and look at yourself and make adjustments in what you see. Of course, the specter of brain injury makes this difficult. The injured brain does not easily examine itself and its behaviors. Sometimes it requires help from others to see clearly. To accept that kind of help from others takes real strength and courage of conviction that you do want to know yourself better, and want to make the changes in your life that enhance your capabilities and your happiness.

Faith in nature or a higher power, in yourself, and in others who love you is the first step. The second step is to trust that whatever befalls, one's place in life can lead to harmony, despite however discombobulated things might seem at first. Brain injury inevitably means an interruption in a life plan that was already well underway. It is no small obstacle. As soon as possible in the healing process, begin a program of renewing faith in your capability and your courage to accept the cards life deals and play your hand to its fullest.

Jane—Real Person

I am a sister to ten brothers and sisters. I am an aunt to fifteen nieces and nephews. I am an accomplished ICU nurse. I've flown a single-engine Cessna and scuba dive a couple times a year. I water-ski and snow-ski every year. I enjoy traveling to Europe and the Caribbean. I enjoy sports cars and have driven several. I enjoy a variety of outdoor activities from horseback riding to golf, tennis, and bicycling. My life has always been one of adventure and gusto.

A year ago a lady pulled out in front of my car and I hit her front quarter panel. I was knocked unconscious and fractured my sternum, back, and neck.

I still describe who I am in the present tense but I haven't done any of those things above since the accident. Every aspect of my life has been affected. I have almost constant back and neck pain, headaches, and sinus congestion. I've had to modify all activities and have gained weight due to lack of exercise and being on steroids. I have to pace myself and not take on too much at one time. I stop when the pain gets too great.

I've had to hire people to do chores that I used to do without help. I'm impatient and I really hate to bother other people to help me cut the lawn, spray the trees, or do any heavy lifting.

I must constantly work on myself and my thoughts to regain my self-confidence and sense of self-worth. I'm working on accepting the fact that I've had a brain injury and am allowing myself time to heal. I need to be more patient and kind to myself. I have to catch myself making negative talk in my head and just stop it. Practicing positive messages to myself does work.

I need to remind myself to get more sleep and expect less of myself in terms of what I want to get done in a day. I'm afraid I'll forget something really important, especially at work, so I write things down all the time.

A week ago I bought some luggage with rollers on it and a book telling me how to pack light. I'm going to take another trip soon, but probably not to Europe. I'll practice closer to home first.

I work on staying focused on what I am thinking about. I see tasks I start all the way to their completion now, no matter how long it takes or who I have to ask for assistance. Yes, I still feel some anger at times about the pain and the changed life I now lead. I was determined and full of life before and I am now practicing—doing things—to be full of life again. I usually made my own choices in the banquet of life. Now, if I want to continue with the banquet, I have no choice but to accept a dish I didn't ask for.

I still have a lot to do. I can still love and care for my brothers, sisters, nieces, and nephews. Sometimes the little things I took for granted before now soar to new heights of meaning and emotions.

I've found a less stressful job in a surgeon's office. Some days I thank God I don't work in an ICU anymore. I'm beginning to like the people I work with—and the patients too. My boss is a perfectionist, so it is still necessary for me to be ever-vigilant of my stress level and to be sure I get adequate sleep. I can forget easily and feel very lightheaded at times. I have to take care of myself or I'm of no use to anyone else.

Appendix A

Hospital Equipment

arterial line. A catheter placed in an artery, used to monitor blood pressure in the arteries and to allow for access to arterial blood for laboratory studies.

catheter. A hollow tube placed into a part of the body for the removal of fluids or to allow fluids to be introduced into the body.

central venous pressure (CVP) line. A catheter that is threaded into the right atrium of the heart. The CVP reading directly reflects the right ventricular filling and diastolic pressure in the right atrium of the heart.

chest tubes. Tubes that are placed into the chest to drain fluid from the body.

endotrachial tube. A tube that is inserted into the trachea through either the mouth or nose to ensure an open airway.

Foley catheter. A catheter that has a small inflatable balloon on the end, usually inserted into the bladder. The balloon is inflated to keep the catheter in the bladder so that urine can be continuously drained into an external bag.

halo. A metal ring used with patients who have spinal cord injuries to preserve proper alignment of the neck and spinal columns. This helps keep the patient still and the body aligned during healing.

intracranial pressure monitor. A monitor, inserted through the skull, that measures pressure of the fluid inside the brain and skull.

intravenous (IV) line. A small catheter placed into a vein, which can be used to give a patient fluids, drugs, or blood; also used to monitor venous blood pressure.

intravenous board. A board that is used to hold an extremity immobile so as not to dislodge an IV line.

monitor. Any machine that gives a reading of vital body processes, such as cardiac (heart) monitors or intracranial pressure monitors.

nasogastric tube. A tube inserted through the nose into the stomach, through which to feed a patient, to give medications, etc.; used if a patient is unconscious, has severe jaw injury, or is unable to swallow.

respirator/ventilator. Machines that either assist a patient with breathing or actually breathe for him or her by forcing oxygen into the lungs.

space boots. Large, soft protective shoes used to support muscles and tendons during coma.

Swan-Ganz catheter. A catheter that is threaded into the heart and wedged in a pulmonary arteriole; used to measure pulmonary artery pressure and pulmonary capillary wedge pressure, both good indicators of left ventricular function.

traction. Traction devices apply a pulling force to reduce, align, and immobilize fractures; to lessen, prevent, or correct deformity associated with bone injury and muscle disease; and to reduce muscle spasms in fracture of a long bone or in back injury.

transducer. A device that changes input energy of one form into output energy of another. For example, physiological energy such as the heart beating is changed from beats to lines on a strip of paper that can be read.

ventriculostomy. An operation that is performed to drain fluid from a ventricle of the brain to treat hydrocephalus.

Appendix B

Common Medications

antibiotics. A category of medications used to control the infections to which injured persons are prone.

baclofen. Relieves muscle spasticity and muscle tone problems; available in a pill and implantable pump.

Botulinum toxin. Injection used to reduce spasticity and muscle spasms.

bromocriptine. Helpful in dyspraxia problems

BuSpar. Used to alleviate anxiety without much sedation.

Dantrim. Relieves muscle spasms, cramping, and tightness of muscles; a surface acting antispasticity agent especially useful in children.

Decadron. A cortiosteroid used to reduce inflammation and improve brain functioning through reduction of brain swelling.

Depakote. Antiseizure medication also treats mood swings.

Dexadrine. Cortical brain stimulant.

Dilantin. Used to control or prevent seizures and convulsive disorders.

Haldol. Used to calm agitated, combative, anxious, or tense patients, usually during the relatively early stages of post-acute treatment.

Inderal. Used to calm agitated head injury patients.

Lasix. Used to reduce excess water from the body and help reduce intracranial pressure, water in the lungs, or sluggish kidneys.

laxatives. A category of drugs used to encourage bowel movements and to relieve constipation.

Maalox. Used to help prevent stomach ulcers or stomach discomforts that hospitalized patients are prone to develop.

Mannitol. Removes water from the brain, used to decrease intracranial pressure.

morphine sulfate. Used to reduce pain and to reduce bodily reflexes through sedation.

Mysoline. An antiseizure medication, often used if other similar-acting drugs fail to work.

Nembutal. Used to reduce intracranial pressure and reduce pain.

Neurontin. Antiseizure medication, also treats mood swings.

Nicotine skin patch. Used as a brain stem stimulant.

Pavulon. Used to relax skeletal muscles to help keep the patient from struggling, usually while on a respirator.

Paxil. Antidepressant.

phenobarbital. Used to control or prevent seizures and convulsive disorders.

Provigil. Brain stimulant to improve attention and concentration.

Prozac. Used as an antidepressant.

Reglan. Used to increase peristalsis in gastrointestinal tract.

Ritalin. Used as a brain stem stimulant to help improve attention and concentration.

sleeping medications. A category of drugs used to assist in maintaining regular sleep/wake cycles; examples are Dalmane, Restoril, chloral hydrate, Ambien.

steroids. A category of drugs used to reduce brain swelling.

Symmetral. Used as a stimulant to the brain stem.

Tagamet. Used to help prevent stomach ulcers to which hospitalized patients are prone.

Tegretol. Antiseizure medication that also effects impulsive behaviors.

Tofranil. Used as an antidepressant.

Valium. Used to reduce anxiety, tension, and muscle activity.

Xanax. Antianxiety medication to help reduce tension and muscle activity.

Zanaflex. Antispasticity, treats muscle spasms.

Zoloft. Antidepressant.

APPENDIX C

Neurological Tests and Procedures

BEAM (brain electrical activity mapping). A computerized analysis of background EEG activity, more sensitive than conventional EEG, which is especially helpful in identifying abnormalities of early dementia or suspected brain damage from head injury.

BER (brainstem evoked responses). Brain stem response to a specific stimulus recorded electronically, used to examine the neurological integrity of certain sensory and motor pathways.

CT scan (Computerized Tomography). Computerized x-ray taken at different levels of the brain to yield a three-dimensional representation of the physical shape of the brain.

electrocardiogram (ECG or EKG). Electrical measure of heart activity and heartbeat that is produced on a chart recording.

electroencephalogram (EEG). An evaluation of electrical activity of the brain.

lumbar puncture. A tap into the spinal fluid to assess presence of toxic agents or infections that might be present in the brain.

MRI scan (Magnetic Resonance Imaging). An instrument that develops images from biochemical operations of the brain by using a magnetic field.

neurological examination. An assessment of gross nerve functioning via reflexes and reactions; performed by a neurologist or neurosurgeon.

PET scan (Positron Emission Tomography). An instrument that records chemical activity in specific regions of the brain

Appendix D

Common Neuropsychological Terms

abstract reasoning. Process of generalizing from concrete examples and experiences to larger, broader principles.

acalculia. Dysfunction or inability to perform mathematical operations, recognize numbers, or count.

acuity. Keenness of sensation.

agnosia. Loss of ability to recognize familiar people, places, and objects. Agnosia can occur in the tactile, visual, or auditory modalities.

agraphia. Loss of ability to express thoughts in writing.

alexia. Loss of ability to read or recognize words, or comprehend written language.

amnesia. General term referring to loss of memory.

anomia. Dysfunction or inability to name objects or recall individual names.

anosmia. Loss of ability to smell.

anosognosia. Unawareness or denial of impairment. Even though an individual may recognize an impairment, he or she denies that the impairment is real.

anoxia. Absence of oxygen in the brain.

anterograde amnesia. Loss of memory for events and periods of time following an injury or traumatic event.

apathy. Decrease in motivation, initiation, interest in life and growth; indifference.

aphasia. Loss in ability to speak coherent ideas or understand spoken language.

apraxia. Loss of ability to carry out voluntary movement or use objects. The individual may claim to understand how to perform some action but be virtually unable to execute the action.

astereognosis. Inability to recognize objects or shapes by feeling them.

asymmetry. Discrepancy in function or appearance between sides of organs.

ataxia. Dysfunction in voluntary motor coordination and balance.

attention. Ability for sustaining focus on task for a period of time to allow for coding and storing of information in memory.

catastrophic reaction. An explosive outburst of emotion in response to stress with which the individual is unable to cope.

cognition. Processes of thinking, understanding, and reasoning.

concentration. Ability to remain attentive to a specific task for a sufficient time.

confabulation. Giving incorrect or made up information in response to questions asked of a person with amnesia. The individuals are unaware of the inaccuracy of what they are saying.

confusional state. Disruption of ability to attend and focus appropriately and the inability to regulate one's direction of attention.

denial. Inability to recognize that a particular state of affairs exists (see anosognosia).

diaschisis. The idea that a lesion in the brain can have effects on functions normally considered located in a different area of the brain, due to multiple functional system overlap of neural networks.

diplopia. Seeing two superimposed images of a single object; known as "double vision"

disinhibition. Loss of restraint or decrease in ability to stop oneself from saying or doing something that is typically undesirable.

disorientation. Disturbance in recognition of person, place, and/or time and day.

dysarthria. Disruption or dysfunction in speech articulation.

dyslexia. General term referring to acquired disorders in reading.

emotional lability. Intense fluctuations of emotions in response to experiences.

frustration tolerance. Amount and degree of frustration; encounter with obstacles one can live with before losing control over affect and thinking.

hypomania. An elevation in mood, increased activity, and sometimes grandiose thinking.

impulsivity. Tendency to act without thinking or concern for consequences.

inflexibility. Rigidity in thinking; over reliance on stereotypes; difficulty in recognizing alternative possibilities.

judgment. Ability for resolving dilemmas and approaching problems; includes values, morals, and interpretation with respect for interactions.

memory. Stored recollections about experiences, events, feelings, dates, etc., from the recent and distant past.

perception. The brain's ability to take in sensory stimulation and provide it with meaning.

perseveration. Overreliance on or repetition of a specific response or behavior to different tasks.

plasticity. A general term referring to neural repair, neural reorganization, collateral sprouting, compensation, and other mechanisms of brain repair.

posttraumatic amnesia. Loss in memory for events related to a traumatic event and the period immediately following the trauma.

problem-solving. Skills for employing reasoning, judgment, experience, and discernment in resolving problems.

retrograde amnesia. Loss of memory for events and periods of time before an injury or accident.

spasticity. A movement disorder associated with impaired muscle tone, with an exaggerated jerking movement.

stereotypy. Repeated actions or use of words over and over, often associated with subcortical brain damage.

unilateral neglect. Unawareness or inattention to one side of the body or the space or events occurring on one side of the body.

visual field deficit. Inability to perceive vision in an area of the visual field, such as the right or left field, known as hemianopia.

0-595-23716-9

Printed in the United States
23075LVS00001B/79-87